About the Author

Stephen C. LeSueur has worked as a historian for the Religious Studies Center at Brigham Young University and is currently a Graduate Teaching Fellow in the Department of Economics at the University of Utah.

The 1838 Mormon War in Missouri

The 1838 Mormon War
in Missouri

Stephen C. LeSueur

University of Missouri Press
Columbia, 1987

Library of Congress Cataloging-in-Publication Data

LeSueur, Stephen C.
The 1838 Mormon war in Missouri.

Bibliography: p.
Includes index.
1. Mormons–Missouri–History–19th century.
2. Missouri–History. I. Title.
F466.L47 1987 977.8'03 86-16090
ISBN 0-8262-0626-3 (alk. paper)

To Arthur Cobery and John Taylor LeSueur
History Teachers

Preface

My interest in the Mormon experience in Missouri began nearly ten years ago when I worked as a researcher for Professor LaMar C. Berrett at the Religious Studies Center at Brigham Young University. The friendship and scholarly example of Professor Berrett and others with whom I worked (including Max H. Parkin, Leland H. Gentry, Lyndon W. Cook, and Charles W. Allen) stimulated my own desire to write on the subject. Although much has been written about the Mormon War, a re-examination of these events was justified for several reasons. The recent discovery of new source materials, including journals, letters, petitions, and official documents, made available a wealth of new information. In addition, most histories have been written by Mormons and focus on their actions; a more detailed description of the Missourians' attitudes and activities was needed. Insufficient attention has been given to the non-Mormons who opposed the anti-Mormon vigilantes, and to their efforts to quell the disturbances. The new source materials offer interesting information and insights regarding the causes of conflict and the reasons why local authorities were unable to halt the violence.

The original version of this work was read by Professor Ernest Cassara at George Mason University in Fairfax, Virginia. The advice and criticism of Professors Cassara, Vernon G. Spence, and Josephine F. Pacheco improved immensely the work's content and style. In addition, my friends at the Religious Studies Center offered encouragement and often pointed me toward valuable sources. I especially benefited from discussions with Dr. Leland H. Gentry and Dr. Max H. Parkin, who have written extensively on the Mormons in Missouri. Although we disagree regarding the interpretation of many important issues, our discussions served to clarify my own thinking on these matters. Professor Parkin generously shared source materials collected for his own study of these events.

Many librarians and specialists in Utah, Missouri, and Washington, D. C., assisted me in my research. The archivists and librarians at the following institutions merit special thanks: The Historical Archives and Library of the Church of Jesus Christ of Latter-day Saints in Salt Lake City; The Manuscript and Special Collections Library at Brigham Young University in Provo, Utah; The Archives and Library of the Reorganized Church of Jesus Christ of Latter Day Saints in Independence, Missouri; and the State Historical Society of Missouri, Columbia. I benefited by the competent and professional service provided by the employees of these institutions.

The contributions of a number of people require mention. James L. Kimball, Jr., provided not only competent service but a kindly face at the LDS Archives. Bill Slaughter, also at the LDS Archives, was especially helpful in securing some of the photographs for the book. Madelon Brunson, Sara J. Hallier, and Shirley Crandall rendered prompt and friendly service at the RLDS Archives. Michael Jorgensen, a talented graphic designer, provided the artwork and design for the maps.

Among those who read various stages of the manuscript I would like to thank Craig Jolley (who suffered through a very rough first draft), Jack Censer, Max Parkin, Bill Russell, and Valeen Avery for their helpful advice. Another deserving my gratitude is my friend Jack Wertzberger, whose advice on previous articles and papers contributed to the writing of this work. Finally, I am indebted to Kathleen A. Reeder for her invaluable editorial assistance on numerous drafts of this manuscript. None of these readers, however, necessarily agreed with all aspects of this history; I alone take responsibility for its content.

Finally, a personal thanks to Sunny, for the inspiration to begin this work; and a special word of appreciation to Kathy, for the love and encouragement to complete it.

S. C. L.
Salt Lake City
September 1986

Contents

1
Introduction

Twenty-five hundred Missouri troops surrounded the Mormon town of Far West on the night of 31 October 1838. Nearly eight hundred Mormon defenders waited silently behind their makeshift barricade of wagons, house logs, and floor planks, which extended three-quarters of a mile across the southern edge of town. Gen. Samuel D. Lucas, commander of the militia, warned Mormon leaders that he would destroy the town if they refused to surrender and leave the state. The Mormons prepared for attack. "We knew their determination was to exterminate us & [we] made up our determination to defend the City until the last man should fall to the ground," wrote a sleepless Mormon soldier that night. ". . . we have the promise that but little blood will be shed at this time. But God only knows how we are to be delivered." [1]

The confrontations between the Mormons and their Missouri neighbors vividly illustrate the powerful cultural forces that have fostered a tradition of extralegal violence in America. Since colonial times, when impassioned citizens tarred and feathered tax collectors, dumped English tea into Boston harbor, and declared their independence from Great Britain, Americans have claimed the right to take the law into their own hands to enforce justice. Such violence has generally been conservative in purpose, and thus supported or tolerated by a large portion of the population. Vigilante organizations, often led by members of the local elite, acted to preserve established customs and practices against persons and groups that were perceived as a threat to society. "One is impressed that most American violence . . . has been initiated with a 'conservative' bias," writes historian Richard Hofstadter. "It has been unleashed

1. Albert P. Rockwood, "Journal October 6, 1838 to January 30, 1839," p. 12. Typescript, Historical Archives of the Church of Jesus Christ of Latter-day Saints, Salt Lake City, Utah (hereafter cited as LDS Archives); original in the Yale University Library, New Haven, Connecticut.

against abolitionists, Catholics, radicals, workers and labor organizers, Negroes, Orientals, and other ethnic or racial or ideological minorities, and has been used ostensibly to protect the American, the Southern, the white Protestant, or simply the established middle-class way of life and morals."[2] Another historian of American violence, Richard M. Brown, similarly concludes, "American opinion generally supported vigilantism; extralegal activity by a provoked populace was deemed to be the rightful action of good citizens."[3]

Rioting and violence became especially prevalent during the 1830s as angry, self-righteous mobs and vigilantes, imbued with the Jacksonian spirit of popular sovereignty, asserted their right—as the ultimate source of authority and law—to step outside that law to define, protect, and enforce community values. Historian David Grimsted argues that President Andrew Jackson fitted perfectly the popular American image of the man who, because of his personal rectitude, was not required to follow accepted procedures. "Jackson's popularity was rooted in his embodiment of the deepest American political myth: that man standing above the law was to be not a threat to society but its fulfillment," Grimsted concludes.[4]

Local authorities proved ineffectual in suppressing the extralegal violence. Nineteenth-century Americans, with their traditional distrust of strong governments and standing armies, refused to give their governments substantial police power, lest some tyrant use that power to oppress the people. Volunteer state-militia units, most often called upon during disturbances, had neither the training nor the desire to quell citizen uprisings. Civil authorities consequently lacked the force necessary to preserve order in times of rioting and widespread lawlessness. Moreover, the willingness of ordinary citizens to rely on vigilante organizations, whether to enforce laws, expel unwanted persons, or combat other vigilante organizations, further undermined the authority of local officials and often rendered

2. "Reflections on Violence in the United States," in *American Violence: A Documentary History*, ed. Richard Hofstadter and Michael Wallace (New York: Alfred A. Knopf, 1970), p. 11.

3. *Strain of Violence: Historical Studies of American Violence and Vigilantism* (New York: Oxford University Press, 1975), p. 130.

4. "Rioting in Its Jacksonian Setting," *American Historical Review* 77 (April 1972): 368.

them powerless in suppressing extralegal violence.

These attitudes and conditions nurtured the animosities in northwestern Missouri that erupted in the Mormon War of 1838. The disturbances were instigated by many of the same fears that caused previous conflicts between the Mormons and their neighbors. The Mormons (or Saints, as they called themselves)[5] migrated to Missouri in response to their prophet's command to build a New Jerusalem in the West, but their efforts met with resistance from the older settlers. The Missourians were suspicious of the Mormons' religious beliefs, including the Saints' claims that they were God's chosen people and that He had set aside western Missouri for their Zion, the Mormons' closed economic and religious community, and the Mormons' seemingly fanatic loyalty to their leaders and the Church. The Mormons, as northerners and Canadians, represented an alien and threatening subculture to the predominantly southern population of western Missouri. In addition, the Mormons posed a serious economic threat to local settlers. Non-Mormon land speculators could not hope to compete with the Mormons, who were purchasing large tracts of land with Church funds. And the new Mormon towns of Diahman and DeWitt threatened to displace older towns as the political and commercial centers for their counties. The Missouri settlers saw their status and security threatened by the burgeoning Mormon population. The rapid migration of the Saints into the state during the summer and fall of 1838, which brought the Mormon population to about ten thousand, increased these fears until the Missourians decided they must act before they were overrun.

The citizens of northwestern Missouri acted without compunction in their extralegal efforts to remove the Mormons from their communities. They regarded their actions as a supplement to, rather than a rebellion against, constituted law. The participants believed their activities were justified by the extraordinary circumstances connected with the Mormon problem. They held meetings, passed resolutions, published their intentions, and called upon local civil authorities to assist them. Their anti-Mormon activities, at least in the beginning, were

5. The official name for the church popularly known as the Mormon Church is the Church of Jesus Christ of Latter-day Saints; hence, its members often refer to themselves as Saints or Latter-day Saints.

not the spontaneous ravages of angry mobs but the deliberate proceedings of citizen committees acting rationally and with restraint.

The activities of the Mormons during this period often contributed to, rather than allayed, hostility toward their presence in Missouri. In Caldwell County, Mormon leaders dominated local politics, while the Danites, a secret Mormon vigilante organization, enforced religious orthodoxy, thus reinforcing the Missourians' perception of Mormonism as a fanatic and un-American religion. The Mormon army and the Danite band inspired a terrible fear among the non-Mormon settlers, who regarded the Mormon soldiers as ruthless cutthroats. Although Mormon military action was generally initiated in response to reports of violence, the Mormons tended to overreact and in some instances retaliated against innocent citizens. Their perception of themselves as the chosen people, their absolute confidence in their leaders, and their determination not to be driven out led Mormon soldiers to commit numerous crimes. The Mormons had many friends among the Missourians, but their military operations undercut their support in the non-Mormon community.

The degree of Joseph Smith's complicity in the Mormon military activities has long been debated by historians. Evidence now available, however, demonstrates that he directed much of the plundering and burning committed by Mormon soldiers in Daviess County. He viewed these actions as necessary for the defense of his people. In addition, Smith and other Mormon leaders knew and approved of the activities of the Danite organization, including the forcible expulsion of dissenters from the Mormon county of Caldwell. Mormon leaders justified the Danite actions with the claim that a republican people have the right to remove undesirable citizens from their communities— the same principle cited by Missourians to expel the Mormons.

Civil officials made numerous attempts to resolve peacefully the developing conflict. They brought to trial a number of Mormons and non-Mormons accused of committing crimes, and when these measures failed to dispel the unrest, they called upon the state militia to intervene. The Missouri troops prevented a clash between the Mormons and vigilantes during an early outbreak of hostilities, but continued pressure by the vigilantes finally wore down the militia's resolve. The Missouri troops lacked the training and disposition for combat in civil disturbances, and their sympathies rested with their neighbors in the vigilante army. Inclement weather and a rebellious, anti-Mormon spirit among the militiamen finally forced the generals to dismiss the troops, leaving the Mormons and vigilantes to fight it out themselves.

Perhaps the only person who had the prestige or power to quell the disturbances was Gov. Lilburn W. Boggs, but he failed to use his influence effectively. He ignored numerous requests by Mormons, Missourians, and militia officers to come to the scene of trouble. The governor's presence, as one of his generals remarked, would have had more effect in subduing the vigilantes than an entire regiment. Boggs might have been able to secure at least a temporary peace. By the time he intervened, however, the conflict had escalated beyond the control of local authorities.

The conflict was not finally resolved until the more lawful and responsible citizens, men like Gen. David R. Atchison, Gen. Alexander W. Doniphan, and State Sen. Josiah Morin, joined the vigilantes against the Saints. These men had steadfastly opposed the extralegal activities of the citizen committees, but the military operations of the Saints eventually convinced them that the Mormons represented a greater threat to their communities. When forced to choose, they sided with the vigilantes against the Saints. Their reports to Governor Boggs convinced him to call out state troops to expel the Mormons from the state. Although the governor's extermination order was of questionable legality, the Mormons agreed to surrender. On 1 November 1838, Joseph Smith instructed the Mormon soldiers to submit to the civil and military authorities of the state.

Perhaps more than anything else the conflict between the Mormons and Missourians reveals the many weaknesses of human nature. Most people in both groups tried to follow a peaceful and moderate course, but rumors, prejudice, fear, and a misconceived devotion to God carried the conflict beyond the control of its participants, leading normally law-abiding citizens to commit numerous crimes. In 1837 Abraham Lincoln, then a young and relatively unknown lawyer from Illinois, warned of vigilante violence:

> When men take it in their heads to-day to hang gamblers or burn
> murderers, they should recollect that in the confusion usually attending
> such transactions they will be as likely to hang or burn some one
> who is neither a gambler nor a murderer as one who is, and that,
> acting upon the example they set, the mob of to-morrow may, and
> probably will, hang or burn some of them by the very same mistake.
> And not only so; the innocent, those who have ever set their faces
> against violations of law in every shape, alike with the guilty fall
> victims to the ravages of mob law; and thus it goes up, step by
> step, till all the walls erected for the defense of the persons and
> property of individuals are trodden down and disregarded.[6]

The bitterness and suffering caused by the hostilities in Missouri
tragically confirmed Lincoln's warning.

The Mormon War can be best understood when it is viewed
as several related problems. At one level, the disturbances
represented a conflict between the Mormons and a portion of
their non-Mormon neighbors. Their differences eventually led
to bloodshed and destruction. At another level, the conflict
represented a struggle by civil authorities and responsible
citizens to maintain law and order. Many people opposed
the lawless activities of both the Mormons and the vigilantes,
and tried to prevent the outbreak of hostilities. Finally, the
disturbances represented an expression of attitudes and beliefs
that have fostered a tradition of extralegal violence in the
United States. The American people, believing they are the
ultimate source of civil law and authority, have employed the
principles of democracy and majority rule to justify taking the
law into their own hands to enforce their will and values. Both
the Mormons and Missourians recognized and used extralegal
violence as a legitimate means to protect their interests during
the 1838 Mormon War. The eventual outcome, the expulsion
of the Saints from Missouri, represented a triumph of popular
will over rule by law.

A Semantical Note

Historians of American violence distinguish between *vigilante*

6. Quoted in Richard M. Brown, ed., *American Violence* (Englewood
Cliffs, N.J.: Prentice-Hall, 1970), p. 10.

groups and *mobs*. *Vigilantism* represents an organized, semi-permanent, and extralegal movement that usurps the functions of government and law.[7] *Mobs* are generally less organized and more spontaneous and ephemeral in nature. Most anti-Mormon groups in Missouri were vigilantes; their published proceedings sometimes referred to their organizations as Committees of Vigilance. The more commonly used term to describe these groups, however, was *mobs*. Both Mormons and Missourians generally referred to the anti-Mormon organizations as *mobs* and to their members as *mobbers*. This monograph primarily uses the term *vigilante*, rather than *mob*, because it more accurately describes the anti-Mormon groups. The term *mob* is used only when it describes Mormon perceptions and statements regarding the vigilantes, or when it appropriately defines the group dynamics of the Missourians.

7. See Brown, *Strain of Violence*, p. 21.

2

Early Mormonism and Missouri

Mormonism began in upstate New York, where the revivals of the Second Great Awakening stirred religious fervor during the first quarter of the nineteenth century. The religious excitement seriously affected a young man from Palmyra (near Rochester) named Joseph Smith, who decided to take his questions about religious authority and personal salvation directly to God. Smith reported that, beginning in the year 1820, he received a series of revelations from God and other heavenly messengers who gave to him the authority to restore the ancient church of

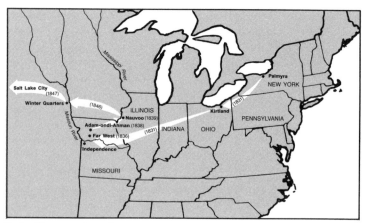

Early Mormon Locations.

Jesus Christ. This church would be organized with the same structure as the primitive church (apostles, prophets, bishops, etc.), it would possess the same gifts of the spirit (healing, speaking in tongues, miracles, etc.), and its teachings would

8

correspond to the gospel as originally taught by Jesus Christ. Smith also said that the heavenly messengers gave to him an ancient record, a religious history written by pre-Columbian Americans, which he translated into English as the Book of Mormon. In 1830, at the age of twenty-four, Joseph Smith officially organized the restored Church of Jesus Christ, later renamed the Church of Jesus Christ of Latter-day Saints. Smith served as its prophet-president. [1]

In some respects early Mormonism represented an amalgamation of the many religious and social movements that emerged during this period, but the new church also developed a spirit and character all its own. Mormonism claimed to be the restored gospel of Jesus Christ, containing the authority, spiritual gifts, and doctrine of the primitive church. It was the only true church of God; the rest were an abomination in His sight. Mormon adherents considered Joseph Smith to be a prophet of God, equal in greatness to Moses, Isaiah, and other biblical prophets, raised up by the Lord to lead His people in the latter days. As the prophet and leader of the Church, Smith organized a lay priesthood and published a book of revelations to guide the members in their lives. He said the Church was the literal Kingdom of God, restored to earth to usher in the millennium. The Mormon prophet told his people that the "signs of the times" showed that the Second Coming of the Lord was near. "Fifty-six years should wind up the scene," he prophesied concerning the subject in 1835. [2] In preparation for the Second Coming the Mormons "gathered" to Zion, identified by Smith as being located in western Missouri. He taught that this Zion would be the only place of safety for the Saints during the calamitous last days; so the Mormons began almost immediately to gather and build their New Jerusalem

1. For the background and general history of Mormonism, see Leonard J. Arrington and Davis Bitton, *The Mormon Experience: A History of the Latter-day Saints* (New York: Alfred A. Knopf, 1979); James B. Allen and Glen M. Leonard, *The Story of the Latter-day Saints* (Salt Lake City: Deseret Book Company, 1976); Richard L. Bushman, *Joseph Smith and the Beginnings of Mormonism* (Urbana and Chicago: University of Illinois Press, 1984); and Thomas F. O'Dea, *The Mormons* (Chicago: University of Chicago Press, 1957).

2. Joseph Smith, *History of the Church of Jesus Christ of Latter-Day Saints*, 7 vols. (Salt Lake City: Deseret Book Company, 1978), 2:182. (Hereafter cited as *HC*.)

in Missouri. As part of the restoration of the ancient church, many Saints adopted the practice of sharing all things in common and established several experimental communities. Early Mormonism thus made little distinction between secular and religious matters, and its leaders often exercised considerable control over both.

Mormonism gained its early notoriety from the Book of Mormon, an ancient scripture purportedly inscribed on gold plates and given to Joseph Smith by an angel. The nickname "Mormon" was given to Smith's followers because of their belief in the book. The Book of Mormon, written in the biblical style of the King James translation, describes the history of a band of Israelites led by God from Jerusalem to the American continent in 600 B.C. The religious concerns of these ancient Israelites paralleled those of nineteenth-century American Protestantism, and the Book of Mormon discusses many of the same theological issues (infant baptism, faith versus works, the nature of God) that preachers and revivalists frequently debated in upstate New York.

The book cannot be easily dismissed as the work of an imaginative youth. It maintains a complex narrative, presents consistent doctrinal themes, and answers questions not fully explained in the Bible. In addition, a number of Smith's friends and relatives signed statements that they examined the gold plates from which the Book of Mormon was translated; and three of them, Oliver Cowdery, David Whitmer, and Martin Harris, claimed they saw the angel who delivered the plates to Smith. Opponents of the new religion denounced the Book of Mormon as an elaborate hoax; believers regarded it as the word of God, a potent witness to Smith's prophetic calling.

The Mormons believed that the American Indians, allegedly the descendants of these Book-of-Mormon Israelites, would play an important role in helping to establish the Kingdom. The Saints rejoiced at the relocation of the Indians (by order of the federal government) just across the Missouri border and viewed this gathering as a wondrous sign of the times. Believing that their red brothers would join the Church in large numbers, the Mormons made great efforts to proselytize the Indians and introduce them to the Book of Mormon. Although Mormon missionaries succeeded in arousing the suspicions of white settlers regarding their motives and intentions, they failed to convince many Indians of their Old Testament heritage.

Joseph Smith's message, however, proved popular with many white Americans. Mormonism's enthusiastic missionary program, in which hundreds of new members volunteered to preach "without purse or script," brought thousands of converts to the Church during the 1830s.

A high percentage of the first Mormon converts came from New York, with most of the rest coming from New England and the mid-Atlantic states.[3] They generally came from rural backgrounds and were of average means and education. Among these converts were also men of exceptional talent and intelligence, including the brothers Parley P. and Orson Pratt, Campbellite minister Sidney Rigdon, and Joseph Smith's eventual successor, Brigham Young. Like the Puritans of old, the Mormons saw themselves as forming a special covenant society with God. Their distinctive beliefs and extraordinary sacrifices, along with the unrelenting persecution, created a strong in-group loyalty and feeling of uniqueness. The Mormons believed they were God's chosen people and saw His hand guiding them in all their activities. They trusted and followed the instructions of Joseph Smith and other Mormon leaders, who they believed spoke on behalf of God.

Early Mormon converts found much that was appealing in the practices and teachings of Mormonism, but perhaps most attractive was its charismatic prophet-leader, Joseph Smith, who inspired the love, respect, and faith of countless followers.[4] Born in Sharon, Vermont, on 23 December 1805, Smith grew up in Palmyra, New York, living and working most of his early years on his father's and neighbors' farms. He sprang from a family whose Christianity was steeped in folklore and

3. Arrington and Bitton, *Mormon Experience*, p. 2; and Laurence M. Yorgason, "Preview on a Study of the Social and Geographical Origins of Early Mormon Converts, 1830–1845," *BYU Studies* 10 (Spring 1970): 281–82.

4. The two most comprehensive biographies of Joseph Smith are Fawn M. Brodie, *No Man Knows My History: The Life of Joseph Smith, the Mormon Prophet* (New York: Alfred A. Knopf, 1971); and Donna Hill, *Joseph Smith: The First Mormon* (Garden City, N.Y.: Doubleday and Company, 1977). Linda King Newell and Valeen Tippetts Avery, *Mormon Enigma: Emma Hale Smith* (Garden City, N.Y.: Doubleday and Company, 1984), also provides insights into the life of the Mormon prophet.

magic, where supernatural dreams and visions were common experiences, seer stones and treasure lay buried in nearby hills, and Bible reading was a daily pursuit. His mother, Lucy,

Joseph Smith, Jr.: Prophet leader of the Mormons. Courtesy RLDS Historical Archives.

diligently recorded a number of her own dreams as well as visions of his father, Joseph Smith, Sr. Young Joseph's accounts of revelations and visitations from angels were readily believed not only by the immediate members of his family but also by many aunts, uncles, and cousins. Like many nineteenth-century Americans, they looked for a restoration of the true Christian religion. God's selection of Joseph Smith, Jr., as an instrument for His work fulfilled the prophecy of his grandfather, Asael Smith, who predicted that "one of my descendants will promulgate a work to revolutionize the world of religious faith." [5]

Smith grew to be a tall, handsome man, standing six feet in height and weighing about 190 pounds. He had blue eyes and thick, dark hair, but his Roman nose was the most prominent feature of his youthful-looking visage. Though he received little formal education (the equivalent of about three years), Smith was intelligent and inquisitive. He studied Hebrew, revised the Bible, developed plans for model communities, and lectured on politics, religion, and philosophy. A personable man, Smith gained the friendship of his followers with his outgoing personality and informal manner, and enjoyed their company as much as they did his. "From the first day I knew brother Joseph to the day of his death, a better man never lived upon the face of this earth," Brigham Young declared. "My first impressions were that he was an extraordinary man, a man of great penetration; [he] was different from any other man I ever saw," recalled Bathsheba W. Smith, wife of the Prophet's cousin, George A. Smith. The love and devotion Smith inspired in his followers resulted partly from his loyalty to them. "He was always Ready to Fight for the Rights & Liberties of his Friends and his heart was ever full of Sympathy & tears to Sorrow with those he Loved," wrote Benjamin F. Johnson, who served in the Mormon armies during the Missouri troubles. So great was their admiration that Smith's friends credited him with nearly every human virtue. "My first impression of the Prophet was that he was a meek, humble, sociable and very affable man, as a citizen, and one of the most intelligent of men, and a great prophet," Daniel Tyler wrote. "My subsequent acquaintance with him more than confirmed my most favorable impressions in every particular. He was a great statesman, philosopher and philanthropist, logician, and last, but not least, the greatest prophet, seer and revelator that ever lived, save Jesus Christ

---

5. Quoted in Ivan J. Barrett, *Joseph Smith and the Restoration* (Provo, Utah: Brigham Young University Press, 1973), p. 22. See also *HC* 2:443.

only." [6]

Joseph Smith devoted nearly all his energy toward building and expanding the Mormon kingdom. His detractors noted that his activities also expanded his own power and wealth—and the Prophet had many detractors. He suffered intense

Hyrum Smith: Joseph Smith's brother and counselor. Courtesy LDS Historical Department.

persecution because of his claims, yet it only spurred him on toward greater activity. Intensely loyal to his followers, Smith was also quick to condemn those he believed opposed him; and he generally viewed people as either for him—and God—or against him. He did not take criticism easily, even from close friends, but relatively few Mormons felt it necessary to criticize their beloved leader. Joseph Smith firmly believed in his prophetic calling and the special mission of the Church of Jesus Christ. He inspired a similar confidence among his followers.

6. These statements about Smith are found in Brigham Young, "Address July 11, 1852," in *Journal of Discourses*, 26 vols. (London: Latter-Day Saints' Book Depot, 1855–1886), 1:41; Hyrum L. and Helen Mae Andrus, *They Knew the Prophet* (Salt Lake City: Bookcraft, 1974), pp. 49, 122 (for the statements by Daniel Tyler and Bathsheba Smith); and Dean R. Zimmerman, *I Knew the Prophets: An Analysis of the Letter of Benjamin F. Johnson to George F. Gibbs* (Bountiful, Utah: Horizon Publishers, 1976), p. 63.

Although the first Mormon congregations were organized in New York, the future of the Church lay west. In late 1830 Sidney Rigdon and his congregation in Kirtland, Ohio, converted to Mormonism, soon followed by conversions in nearby farms and towns. Joseph Smith, continually harassed by persecution in the East, decided to move to Kirtland and instructed the New York Saints to join him. In July 1831 the Prophet identified Jackson County, Missouri, as the location for the Saints' Zion, and many of his followers migrated there as well, making Kirtland and Jackson County the gathering centers of Mormonism. Smith remained in Kirtland, where Sidney Rigdon became his chief aide and counselor.

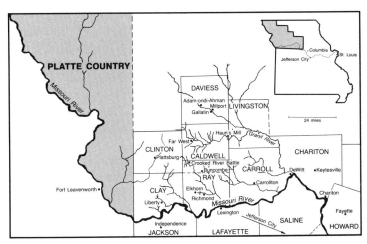

Northwestern Missouri 1838.

Kirtland served as headquarters for the Church from 1831 until Smith's departure in 1838. From the town he issued revelations on doctrine, secular issues, and church organization. At the top of the Mormon hierarchy were Smith and his counselors, the First Presidency, who represented the highest decisionmaking body in the Church. In late 1837 the First Presidency consisted of Joseph Smith as president and Sidney Rigdon and Joseph's brother Hyrum as counselors. The Mormon Prophet organized the Ohio congregations into a "Stake," headed by a Stake president and counselors, and governed by a twelve-member High Council. Smith later established similar Stake organizations in Missouri. Mormon leaders also selected twelve apostles, who functioned primarily as missionaries and mission leaders during this period. Mormonism flourished in Ohio, where its membership grew to about four thousand.

Problems with dissension, however, plagued the Church leadership. Economic difficulties within the Mormon community—a bank failure and increasing debts—brought open rebellion in 1837 as a faction of apostles and Mormon leaders sought to depose Joseph Smith and place David Whitmer in his stead. This group charged that the Prophet had accumulated too much power, especially in his control over the secular affairs of his people, and had led them astray with his meddling in economic affairs. While dissent grew, a number of non-Mormon creditors brought suit against Smith for debts incurred in an unsuccessful Mormon banking venture. Increasing turmoil, accented by threats of violence and imprisonment, finally forced Smith, Rigdon, and other loyal Mormon leaders to flee to Missouri, where they sought to reestablish their leadership.

Early Mormon Experiences in Missouri

Joseph Smith had designated Jackson County, Missouri, as the site for the Saints' Zion in 1831, and many of his followers began gathering there soon afterward. A small group of Mormons attempted to establish a communitarian society in Jackson County, but they came into conflict with their Missouri neighbors, who viewed suspiciously their strange beliefs and practices. In 1833 angry Jackson County vigilantes attacked Mormon leaders, destroyed their printing press, and drove the Saints from their homes. After several brief skirmishes, including one in which two Missourians and one Mormon were killed, the Mormons were driven from the county. In the spring of 1834 Joseph Smith raised an army of two hundred men in Ohio and marched to Missouri to restore the exiled Saints to their homes, but the project was abandoned when they did not receive the expected support from the governor. Following their expulsion from Jackson County, Mormon exiles fled to neighboring Clay County, where they were treated with kindness and respect. But Clay citizens offered their county only as a temporary refuge for the Saints. In 1836 some of Clay's settlers became agitated because the Mormons still remained in the county and additional Mormons were arriving from outside the state. When vigilantes began gathering in large numbers and a county war seemed imminent, Clay's leading citizens met with Mormon leaders and asked them to leave the county. [7]

A variety of motives and fears stimulated the Missourians' opposition to the Mormons. Although most of the older settlers were not particularly religious, they regarded the Mormons' beliefs as obnoxious. They resented the Saints' claims to being God's chosen people, and they considered the Mormons to be deluded fanatics, victims of the scheming designs of Joseph Smith and other Church leaders. Additionally, the Mormons were mainly northerners: their Yankee background and style contrasted sharply with the cruder backwoods manner of the predominantly southern population of western Missouri. The Missourians suspected that the Saints were tampering with their slaves and stirring up the Indians with their preaching. They also distrusted the Saints' communitarian economic system. In Jackson County, the Mormons bought land and started businesses with Church funds, presenting their neighbors with what seemed to be unfair business competition. Individual businessmen and land speculators felt threatened by the Mormons' peculiar, corporate-style religious organization. Finally, the Missourians feared that the Mormons would dominate local politics to the exclusion of all non-Mormons. Religious prejudice stimulated much of the opposition to the Mormons, but the Missourians' antipathy was also sustained by the social, economic, and political threat the Mormons posed to their communities. [8]

The Mormons were partly responsible for causing, or at

---

7. For a history of the Mormons in Jackson County, see Warren A. Jennings, "Zion Is Fled: The Expulsion of the Mormons from Jackson County, Missouri" (Ph.D. diss., University of Florida, 1962). Jennings's history, though dated, is still the most comprehensive for this period. For a history of the Mormons in Clay County, see Max H. Parkin, "A History of the Latter-Day Saints in Clay County, Missouri, from 1833 to 1837" (Ph.D. diss., Brigham Young University, 1976).

8. Arrington and Bitton, *Mormon Experience*, Chapter 3, "Early Persecutions," presents a brief discussion of Mormon conflicts with their neighbors. See also Bushman, "Mormon Persecutions in Missouri, 1833," *BYU Studies* 3 (Autumn 1960): 11–20.

least reinforcing, the suspicions and prejudice against them. Their claims about establishing the Kingdom of God in Jackson County, that they would "literally tread upon the ashes of the wicked after they are destroyed from off the face of the earth," excited fears that the Mormons intended to obtain their "inheritance" by force. [9]   According to Joseph Thorp, a Clay County resident, the Mormons told local settlers that "this country was theirs [the Mormons'] by the gift of the Lord, and it was folly for them [the Missourians] to improve their lands, they would not enjoy the fruits of their labor; that it would finally fall into the hands of the saints."[10] In July 1832, a Mormon journal in Independence published a Joseph Smith revelation in which the Lord declared that "I will consecrate the riches of the Gentiles [non-Mormons], unto my people which are of the house of Israel."[11] Similar claims regarding the role of the Indians in building the Kingdom and punishing God's enemies stimulated rumors that the Mormons were exhorting the Indians to drive the non-Mormon settlers from their land. And just as the Missourians disliked the Mormons, many Mormons regarded the Missourians as ignorant, backward, and wicked people. Whatever the faults of the Mormons, however, it was the Missourians who initiated the conflicts between the two groups. In Jackson and Clay counties the Mormons, on the whole, had been peaceable, industrious, and law-abiding citizens.

A number of Clay County leaders, including David R. Atchison, Alexander W. Doniphan, and Judge Elisha Cameron, sympathized with the Mormons, who they believed had been unjustly persecuted. These men volunteered to help them find a new

9. *Messenger and Advocate* 1 (January 1835): 58, quoted in Grant Underwood, "Seminal Versus Sesquicentennial Saints: A Look at Mormon Millennialism," *Dialogue: A Journal of Mormon Thought* 14 (Spring 1981): 41. See also William Swartzell, *Mormonism Exposed, Being A Journal Of A Residence In Missouri from the 28th of May to the 20th of August, 1838* (Pekin, Ohio: Published by the Author, 1840; Salt Lake City: Modern Microfilm, n.d.), pp. 25, 27–28.

10. *Early Days in the West: Along the Missouri One Hundred Years Ago* (Liberty, Mo.: Liberty Tribune, 1924), p. 79.

11. *The Evening and Morning Star* 1 (July 1832): 1. This revelation, issued by Joseph Smith in February 1831, was also published in *A Book Of Commandments, For The Government Of The Church of Christ, Organized According To Law, On The 6th of April, 1830* (Zion: Published by W. W. Phelps, 1833; rpt. Independence, Mo.: Herald House, 1972), 44:32.

place to settle. A committee of Mormon and Clay leaders scouted northern Ray County and located a relatively unsettled tract of land where the Saints could organize their own county. The Missourians hoped that by segregating the Mormons they could avoid the problems that had led to previous conflicts. Alexander Doniphan, representative to the state legislature from Clay, initiated legislation to create the new Mormon county, which was named Caldwell.

At that time, the proposed Mormon county contained isolated farms and settlements, none older than six years. Abner Blackburn, whose family moved to Caldwell in 1837, said that residents could travel a day or more without seeing another settler in that country. [12] Wild game, nuts, berries, and honey were plentiful in this heavily wooded region. Joseph H. McGee, another young settler in the region, said the Grand River country was well spoken of by all who visited the area. [13] McGee's father built a cabin on Marrowbone Creek, where a large community of Mormons also settled. The largest settlement lay in the north on Grand River, where Robert P. Peniston, Sr., settled with his family in 1831. With the help of Milford Donaho, a local blacksmith, Peniston built the only horse mill north of Richmond, Ray County. Settlers traveled up to forty miles to grind their wheat and corn, and sometimes stayed a week waiting their turn to hitch up their horses and get their grist. Consequently, a thriving community arose and in 1837 Millport, the name of the new town, boasted ten dwelling houses, a post office, six stores, and Donaho's blacksmith shop. Nearly all of the area's early settlers came from the South, mainly from Virginia, Tennessee, and Kentucky. "They were a rough, uneducated class, delighting in fighting and quarreling, but in the main hospitable," said Joseph McGee of his early neighbors. [14]

Many of the settlers lived a crude, simple life. They built cabins about fifteen feet square and owned enough utensils and furniture, generally homemade, to live comfortably. Dirt floors

12. Diary, p. 1. Typescript, Manuscript and Special Collections, Brigham Young University Library, Provo, Utah (hereafter cited as BYU Special Collections).
13. *Story Of The Grand River Country 1821–1905: Memoirs of Major Joseph H. McGee* (Gallatin, Mo.: The North Missourian Press, 1909), n.p.
14. "Some of the Waste Places of Zion as They Appear Today," *Deseret News* (Salt Lake City), 10 September 1904, p. 23.

were common. The slow, costly process of clearing land meant that often, for the first few years, they cultivated only enough land to feed their families. Corn dominated their tables and was used to make a variety of breads and meals, such as Johnny-cake, ash-cake, and corn dodgers. Because sugar was scarce, the women added honey and maple syrup to sweeten their food. Frontier settlers, who often lived isolated lives, gladly accepted invitations to house raisings, corn huskings, and bees of any kind, where they renewed friendships and exchanged local gossip. In addition, Missouri farmers welcomed strangers; travelers often remarked on their friendliness. "The back settlers are generally very honorable, and more hospitable than any people I ever saw, you are in most instances, welcome to the best they have," wrote W. W. Phelps, a Mormon elder, shortly after returning from an expedition to locate a county for his people. [15]   The northwestern Missouri population was not homogeneous: some of the people were surprisingly well educated, others were not; some would make the upper counties their permanent homes, others would move on. Election results revealed, however, that most of the voters counted themselves Jackson men. Many of these farmers and backwoodsmen were rough, independent, adventurous, quick-tempered, and emotional, but also generous and hospitable, as were many of Andrew Jackson's fervent supporters. [16]

The generosity of northern Missouri's settlers did not usually extend to the Indian tribes located just beyond the Missouri River. Most of these settlers shared the contemporary prejudices regarding the Indians' moral character and violent nature. Although they had relatively few conflicts with the American natives, the proximity of the many Indian tribes that had been forcibly relocated just beyond the Missouri caused uneasiness, for settlers feared that frustrated Indians would vent their anger upon the nearest white villages and settlements. In addition, many Missouri settlers had fought in Indian wars outside the region; in 1837, a Missouri regiment fighting in the Florida

15. *HC* 2:445, 2 June 1836, "Letter from W. W. Phelps to the Brethren in Kirtland."

16. County histories and articles from the *Missouri Historical Review* provided most of the background material on frontier Missouri life and culture. The most informative articles are listed in the Bibliographical Essay.

War was nearly wiped out by Seminole Indians at the battle of Okeechobee. Most county histories acknowledge that the small bands of Indians that continued to hunt and trap in the upper counties were generally peaceful and friendly, but their mere presence frightened local settlers.[17] Minor incidents of stealing by the Indians, which seemed to represent northern Missourians' major complaint, occurred often enough to keep alive suspicions regarding Indian activities.

Northern Missouri's Platte country, only recently annexed by the state, had previously served as a government relocation center for American Indians. In 1830 Congress assigned the Sacs, Foxes, Iowas, and a number of other tribes two million acres of choice land east of the Missouri River, bordering Missouri's northwestern boundaries. Local settlers complained loudly; not only did they object to having the Indians located so close to their borders, but they also coveted the country's fertile valleys and prairies, and they wanted the easy access to the Missouri River those lands would provide. In addition, Fort Leavenworth lay directly across the Missouri River, the garrison's six hundred soldiers and the numerous Indian tribes nearby providing an abundant market for Missouri produce and labor. The temptation proved too much for Missouri settlers, and by 1835 more than two hundred families had settled illegally on Indian lands. The endless complaints from Missouri's congressmen—Sen. Thomas H. Benton labeled the Indians a "useless and dangerous population"; Sen. Lewis F. Linn warned that the illegal white settlers could not be removed without violence—finally persuaded the federal government to move the Indians across the Missouri River.[18] Land-hungry settlers from Missouri's western counties immediately swarmed to the new area when it was officially attached to the state in 1837.

Part-time preachers served the religious needs of most northern Missouri settlers. An itinerant Methodist minister stopped regularly at Millport, which was known as the "Methodist Campground" before the town was laid out in 1836. Baptist

17. See, for example, *History of Hickory, Polk, Cedar, Dade, And Barton Counties, Missouri* (Chicago: Goodspeed Publishing Company, 1889), pp. 214, 273, 360, 440, and 504.
18. Perry McCandless, *A History of Missouri, Volume II: 1820 to 1860* (Columbia: University of Missouri Press, 1972), p. 54; and Howard I. McKee,

ministers also traveled the circuit in the upper counties
during this period; only the larger towns, such as Liberty,
Richmond, and Carrollton (in Carroll County) had established
churches. In Carrollton, for example, Sashel Woods preached
for the Cumberland Presbyterian Church. The Cumberland
Presbyterians were less orthodox than the regular Presbyterians,
not as ritualistic or dogmatic. The orthodox Presbyterians condemned the emotional camp meetings held by the Cumberland
Presbyterians, where people shouted, wept, and prostrated
themselves before God; but such meetings appealed to the
emotional nature of many frontier men and women and filled
a void left by the day-to-day drudgery of pioneer life. Because
Missouri's frontier ministers generally earned their living by
means other than preaching—many announced publicly that
they would not accept money—they lived and worked with
the people in their congregations, served in positions of local
leadership, and often exercised considerable influence in their
communities. A number of these ministers played prominent
roles in the Mormon War.

A part-time minister from Clinton County, Cornelius Gilliam,
typified the kind of settler with whom the Mormons would
come into contact—and conflict—as they settled the northern
counties. Born in Florida in 1798, Gilliam settled consecutively
in five western Missouri counties, always moving on to the
frontier's edge when civilization crept too close. Though not
particularly well-educated, he possessed considerable native
intelligence. As a teenager he gained prominence tracking
runaway slaves; later he became known for his skills as a hunter.
A local Missouri history reports that, after being awakened one
night by a bear scrounging among his hogs, Gilliam leaped
from his bed and chased the bear several miles, carrying only
an axe and wearing nothing but his homespun underwear, until
he finally caught and killed the animal.[19] Gilliam was ordained
a Baptist preacher sometime after moving to Missouri. "He was
one of the Old Testament style of preachers. He wasn't very
strong on turning the other cheek," Gilliam's daughter recalled.

"The Platte Purchase," *Missouri Historical Review* 32 (January 1938): 134.
    19. *History of Clay and Platte Counties, Missouri* (St. Louis: National
Historical Company, 1885), pp. 376–77.

"If a man hit him on one cheek he would think he was struck by an earthquake or a cyclone before he got time to hit father on the other cheek."[20] Gilliam described himself as "a Jackson man up to the hub," and when running for county sheriff he boasted, "I have killed more wolves and broke down more nettles than any man in Clay county."[21] Following his term as sheriff, Gilliam was elected to three terms in the Missouri state senate. He also served as an officer in two Indian wars and became known as an experienced and savage fighter of the American natives, whom he publicly denounced as a nuisance and threat to settlers.

A history of Oregon, where Gilliam later settled, described him as "impulsive, even headstrong, but brave and desirous of doing right."[22] The historian Hubert H. Bancroft said Gilliam was "an honest, patriotic, and popular man, whose chief fault as an officer was too much zeal and impetuosity in the performance of his duties . . . ."[23] Neil Gilliam possessed that volatile mixture of courage, intelligence, leadership, and chauvinism that enabled American pioneers to conquer and civilize the West—and to overrun individuals and groups that impeded the civilizing process.

The Mormons were such a group. In 1836, when Alexander Doniphan proposed that a Mormon county be created in Missouri's upper counties, few of the region's settlers had ever met a Mormon. They knew little about the religion. They knew, however, based on the Mormons' reputation in Jackson and Clay counties, that they did not want the Saints settling among them. Following reports that a large portion of Ray County would be included in the Mormon county, settlers in the northern and southern portions of the proposed county organized vigilante committees to prevent Mormon immigration into their region. The settlers argued that Mormon settlements would "retard the prosperity of the county, check future emigration of any other class except the Mormons and disturb the peace of

20. Fred Lockley, "Reminiscences of Mrs. Frank Collins, Nee Martha Elizabeth Gilliam," *Oregon Historical Quarterly* 17 (December 1916): 359.

21. *History of Clay and Platte Counties*, p. 121.

22. S. A. Clarke, *Pioneer Days Of Oregon History*, 2 vols. (Cleveland, Ohio: Arthur H. Clark Company, 1905), 2:554.

23. *The Works of Hubert Howe Bancroft: History of Oregon*, 2 vols. (San Francisco: The History Company, Publishers, 1886), 1:725.

our community." [24] As a result of this opposition the proposed boundaries for Caldwell County were reduced by more than half. The disputed territory to the south, a six-mile strip of land along Crooked River, remained attached to Ray County; the disputed land to the north, which included the town of Millport, was organized into a separate county, called Daviess, for the non-Mormons. Although disappointed that Caldwell had been so greatly reduced, the Mormons were still pleased to be given their own county where they could practice their religion without fear of violence. Most of the non-Mormon settlers in Caldwell, about twenty in number, sold their farms and moved out. The Mormons had the county almost entirely to themselves.

After the organization of Caldwell County (in December 1836) the prospects for peaceful coexistence, even friendly relations, between the Mormons and the citizens of northern Missouri stirred sanguine expectations in both groups. Despite initial misgivings, some of the Missourians reached out to assist their Mormon neighbors: merchants furnished Mormon individuals with large stocks of goods on credit; others lent the Saints money to purchase land; and the poorer Mormons found employment outside of Caldwell among non-Mormon friends. [25]   Cooperation and trust replaced the suspicions of the past as relations between the Mormons and Missourians improved remarkably during the next year. The *Elders' Journal*, a monthly periodical published by the Mormons in Caldwell County, reported in July 1838 that "the Saints here are at perfect peace with all the surrounding inhabitants, and persecution is not so much as once named among them . . . ." [26]   John Corrill, a Mormon resident of the new county, concurred, stating, "Friendship began to be restored between them [the Mormons] and their neighbors, the old prejudices were fast dying away, and they were doing well, until the summer of

24. *Far West* (Liberty, Mo.), 25 August 1836.
25. For friendly relations between the Mormons and Missourians at this time, see John Corrill, *A Brief History Of The Church Of Christ Of Latter Day Saints* (St. Louis: For the Author, 1839; Salt Lake City: Modern Microfilm, n.d.), p. 26; *Missouri Argus* (St. Louis), 27 September 1838; and Reed Peck, "The Reed Peck Manuscript" (Typescript, Salt Lake City: Modern Microfilm, n.d.), p. 4.
26. 1 (July 1838): 34.

1838." [27]

The friendly relations between the Mormons and their neighbors, especially the tolerant attitudes of formerly anti-Mormon settlers, rested primarily upon the Missourians' belief that the Mormons would confine themselves to Caldwell County. The organization of Caldwell carried with it the implicit understanding that the Mormons would settle exclusively in that county—or so thought the Missourians. Certainly that is why they created Caldwell: to segregate the Mormons from the non-Mormon population. Many believed the Mormons had verbally agreed to confine themselves there. Neil Gilliam, who served on the Clay County committee that helped the Saints locate in the new county, said the Mormons promised "they would never settle above or north of the line of [Caldwell] county." [28] Alexander Doniphan, the Clay representative who secured Caldwell County for the Mormons, recalled many years later that the Mormons began having problems when "they commenced forming a settlement in Davis county, which, under their agreement, they had no right to do." [29] Throughout the summer and fall of 1838, when vigilantes threatened to drive the Saints from their settlements and towns, they charged the Mormons with violating this agreement. [30]

The Mormons do not mention any agreement to confine themselves to Caldwell. They did, however, seek the permission of local settlers before they moved into that region. They also agreed *not* to settle in certain areas. When negotiating to obtain Caldwell, Mormon leaders met several times with the citizens of Ray County, in whose jurisdiction the proposed county was located. In order to placate Ray citizens, the Mormons pledged to abandon their settlements in Ray County and agreed to refrain from settling in the disputed six-mile strip of land directly south of Caldwell. [31] The Mormons' willingness to abandon their

27. *A Brief History*, p. 26.

28. *Missouri Argus*, 15 February 1839, speech by Cornelius Gilliam.

29. "Gen. Doniphan's Recollections of the Troubles of that Early Time," *The Saints' Herald* 28 (1 August 1881): 230. This article was reprinted from an interview with Doniphan in the *Kansas City Journal*, 12 June 1881.

30. See, e.g., *Missouri Argus*, 27 September 1838; *Missouri Republican* (St. Louis), 18 August 1838; and Arthur I. H. Bradford to Thomas G. Bradford, 13 August 1838. Thomas G. Bradford Correspondence, LDS Archives.

31. The Mormon proposal to the citizens of Ray County, and the minutes

settlements in Ray apparently led northern Missouri citizens to
believe that the Mormons had agreed to confine themselves to
their new county, or at least to seek permission from local
settlers, as they did in Ray, before establishing new settlements. [32] No evidence has been found in Mormon sources to
suggest that they had agreed to these restrictions. The Missourians
apparently assumed such an agreement had been made.

Despite this misunderstanding, no serious problems arose
during the year and a half after the creation of the new county.
Throughout 1837 the Mormons settled primarily in Caldwell
County, where they established numerous farms and small
communities. Haun's Mill, founded by Jacob Haun near the
county's eastern border, boasted a sawmill as well as a gristmill
and became the locus for Mormon settlements in that area.
Caldwell's county seat, Far West, developed into a prosperous
and fast-growing town. Using a pattern they later followed in
Illinois and Utah, the Mormons laid out Far West with large
blocks and wide streets in anticipation of a thriving community.
By the summer of 1838 the town contained one hundred fifty
log cabins (with perhaps an equal number under construction),
four dry-goods stores, three family groceries, six blacksmith
shops, two hotels, and a large school. Church leaders banned
saloons and the selling of spirituous liquors in the town. The
Mormons also owned a printing press, which they used to
publish the *Elders' Journal* and miscellaneous pamphlets. The
Far West population eventually reached nearly two thousand,
making it the second-largest town (after Liberty) in western
Missouri.

The Mormons also started a number of farms and small
settlements outside of Caldwell, and many of the Saints remained
on their farms in Ray County. They encountered no opposition

of a joint meeting between Mormon and Ray citizens, are found in the *Far
West*, 25 August 1836; and in the Journal History of the Church of Jesus
Christ of Latter-day Saints, 30 July 1836. LDS Archives. (Hereafter cited as
Journal History, this latter source is a day-by-day documentary record of
events, containing newspaper clippings, excerpts from letters and diaries, and
miscellaneous documents relating to Mormon history.)

    32. *History of Caldwell and Livingston Counties, Missouri* (St. Louis:
National Historical Company, 1886), p. 117, states that the Mormons agreed
not to settle in any other county without the prior consent of two-thirds of
the settlers already there.

to these settlements, except briefly in Daviess County, where during the summer of 1837 a group of about twenty men, including the Penistons from Millport, visited fifteen to twenty Mormon families and ordered them to leave the county. A large number of the Daviess settlers, however, actually welcomed, or at least did not oppose, the Mormon migration into their county. As in Caldwell, many Daviess citizens helped the Mormons settle into their new homes.[33] Some allowed the Mormons to use their horses to cultivate crops. Jacob Stollings, a Gallatin merchant, sold the Mormons goods on credit. Judge Josiah Morin supplied the Mormons with corn and other provisions for their farms, and Mormon leaders often stayed at Morin's home near Millport while they located lands for settlement in that part of the county. The enemies of the Saints could get no community support and consequently took no further action against them. The Mormons did not experience any problems in their other settlements outside of Caldwell, perhaps because their numbers were relatively small. As long as most Mormons settled in Caldwell County, which they did throughout 1837 and early 1838, the Missourians did not feel threatened. A friendly and cooperative spirit thus developed between the Mormons and non-Mormon settlers of northwestern Missouri.

33. *The History of Daviess County, Missouri* (Kansas City, Mo.: Birdsall & Dean, 1882), pp. 189–90; Ephraim Owen, Jr., "Memorial, December 20, 1838," *House of Representatives Executive Documents*, vol. 346, no. 42, 25th Congress, 3d Session (Washington: U.S. Government Printing Office, 1839), p. 1 of "Memorial"; John D. Lee, *Mormonism Unveiled; or The Life and Confessions of the Late Mormon Bishop, John D. Lee* (St. Louis: Bryan, Brand, & Co., 1877), p. 56; and James H. Hunt, *Mormonism: Embracing the Origin, Rise and Progress of the Sect, With an Examination of the Book of Mormon; Also, Their Troubles in Missouri, and Final Expulsion from the State* (St. Louis: Printed by Ustick and Davies, 1844), p. 186.

3

Rumblings of a Conflict

Three developments among the Mormons in the spring and summer of 1838 drastically altered their relations with their Missouri neighbors. First, the Mormons began to gather in Missouri in great numbers and established large settlements outside of Caldwell County. Second, some of the more faithful men formed a secret society to purge the Church of dissenters. Finally, the Mormons adopted a belligerent stance against their perceived enemies outside of the Church. Because of these changes, the developing good will between the Mormons and Missourians deteriorated and was replaced by former patterns of distrust and fear.

The Mormons Expand throughout
Northwestern Missouri

Although Missouri had long been designated as the place of gathering for the Saints, opposition from local citizens had prevented them from instituting a sustained migration into any one area. Additionally, as long as Joseph Smith and his counselors remained in Kirtland, that town served as the hub of the Church, making it the de facto focal point for gathering. When persecution and dissension drove the thirty-two-year-old Prophet and other Mormon leaders to Missouri, the headquarters for the Church shifted to Far West, the leading town in Caldwell County, and Missouri became the sole gathering center for the Saints.

Joseph Smith arrived in Far West on 14 March 1838. About a month later he issued a revelation instructing the Saints to migrate to Missouri:

And again, verily I [the Lord] say unto you, it is my will that the city of Far West should be built up speedily by the gathering of my saints;

And also that other places should be appointed for stakes [dioceses] in the regions round about, as they shall be manifested unto my servant Joseph, from time to time.[1]

Church publications reported favorably concerning the climate, economy, and prospects for establishing settlements and towns in northwestern Missouri, while missionaries throughout the United States encouraged converts to gather and help build the Kingdom of God in the West.[2]

When Joseph Smith arrived in Far West, the Mormon population in northwestern Missouri was probably between three and four thousand.[3] Most of the Saints lived in Caldwell County. From March through October 1838, over five thousand Mormons, including several wagon companies with more than two hundred people, migrated to the state. Thousands more were expected. With Caldwell rapidly filling with immigrants, Mormon leaders made plans to expand throughout the upper counties of Missouri.[4]

In May 1838 the Mormons laid out a town in Daviess County, which the Prophet named Adam-ondi-Ahman. Diahman, as the Saints began calling the new town, held important religious significance in the developing Mormon theology. Joseph Smith taught that the Garden of Eden was located in Jackson County, and that Adam and Eve fled to Adam-ondi-Ahman after their fall from grace. Adam-ondi-Ahman, said the Prophet, means "the place where Adam dwelt."[5] Smith reportedly identified

1. *The Doctrine and Covenants of the Church of Jesus Christ of Latter-Day Saints* (Salt Lake City: Published by the Church of Jesus Christ of Latter-day Saints, 1969), 115:17–18, "Revelation given through Joseph Smith the Prophet, at Far West, Missouri, April 26, 1838."

2. *Elders' Journal* 1 (July 1838): 33–34, 39; *Elders' Journal* 1 (August 1838): 52–54, 62; and Swartzell, *Mormonism Exposed*, p. 39.

3. There are no reliable statistics on the Mormon population in northwestern Missouri. The estimates stated above are based upon my own study of the primary and secondary source materials, including the election results in Caldwell and the surrounding counties. I believe that approximately ten thousand Mormons were living in Missouri when they were expelled.

4. Joseph Smith, anticipating a large gathering of Saints in northern Missouri, had made plans to expand outside of Caldwell in September 1837, but no action was taken until after he moved to Missouri in March 1838. See the *Elders' Journal* 1 (November 1837): 27–28.

5. Joseph Smith and Sidney Rigdon to Stephen Post, 17 September 1838. Photocopy, LDS Archives. See also Robert J. Matthews, "Adam-ondi-Ahman,"

an altar built by Adam near the town and prophesied that Adam would return to bless his posterity at Christ's Second

Lyman Wight's cabin at Adam-ondi-Ahman, ca. 1908. Courtesy LDS Historical Department.

Coming. The Mormons thus regarded the area as holy ground and viewed their settlement there as a marvelous fulfillment of God's millennial plan: the history of man would end where it all began. "And when we look upon this beautiful situation, with the transcendant landscape which surrounds it . . . ," wrote Alanson Ripley, the Mormon surveyor at Diahman, "we are ready to say truly this is like unto the land which the Lord our God promised to his saints in the last days." [6]

The new Mormon town became the focal point for gathering in Daviess County. Joseph Smith organized a Stake of Zion at Diahman in June, and by the end of the summer several hundred Saints had settled there, making it by far the largest town in the county. In July the Saints began colonizing DeWitt, in Carroll County, where they purchased half of the town lots. DeWitt was sparsely populated but contained an excellent landing site for steamships on the Missouri River; Mormon leaders expected a large and prosperous community to grow there. Diahman and

BYU Studies 13 (Autumn 1972): 29–31; and Leland H. Gentry, "Adam-ondi-Ahman: A Brief Historical Survey," *BYU Studies* 14 (Summer 1973): 564–76.

6. *Elders' Journal* 1 (August 1838): 52.

DeWitt represented their most ambitious settlements outside of Caldwell, but the Mormons planned for many more. Mormon immigrants settled farms in Clinton, Chariton, Ray, Livingston, and all the surrounding counties.

Mormon kingdom building resembled in many ways the "town booming" and "boosterism" of frontier America. The builders of western towns, whether primarily speculators or home seekers, needed to attract other settlers and buyers to insure their own financial success. Speculators hoped to turn a profit by reselling their land at high prices, while permanent residents, such as the merchants, lawyers, shopkeepers, and farmers, depended on their town's rapid growth to bring business and prosperity. These people boosted their town by advertising heavily in newspapers and by publishing broadsides, pamphlets, and official "fact finding" reports that extolled the virtues of their town's location, climate, and potential for future development. Local governments, generally controlled by the dominant landowners, financed schools, roads, and bridges, encouraged business and commerce, secured public grants and services— did everything possible to give their town the appearance of prosperity. Competition between contending towns for public and private services, especially for the county seat, provoked election brawls, litigation, and even gunfights. A town that attracted permanent home seekers provided speculators with quick profits. But if the town failed to grow into the anticipated prosperous community, the new owners, who often gambled their entire savings on the high-priced land, were left with worthless property and no future prospects. [7]

Although the Saints gathered to Missouri primarily for religious reasons, they encountered the same economic opportunities and risks as the frontier town boomers. Mormon leaders sent out reports of prosperous settlements to induce their people to gather in Missouri. Immigrants were instructed to settle in

7. See Paul W. Gates, *Landlords and Tenants on the Prairie Frontier* (Ithaca, N.Y.: Cornell University Press, 1973), Chapter 2, "The Role of the Land Speculator in Western Development"; Leslie E. Decker, "The Great Speculation: An Interpretation of Midcontinent Pioneering," in *The Frontier in American Development*, ed. David M. Ellis (Ithaca, N.Y.: Cornell University Press, 1969); and Daniel J. Boorstin, *The Americans: The National Experience* (New York: Random House, 1965), pp. 113–68.

the new Mormon towns "according to the order of God," and those who sought out their own locations, contrary to counsel, received severe reprimands and threats of excommunication from their leaders. [8] "Never do another day's work to build up a Gentile city," Smith instructed his people, "never lay out another dollar while you live, to advance the world in its present state."[9] The Mormons who owned land on the principal settlements anticipated great wealth from their holdings. Lyman Wight reported that his property rights at Diahman were "worth to me at least ten thousand dollars."[10] Although some disputes arose concerning the disposition of land—leading Joseph Smith to chastise those who sold land at a profit to their fellow Saints—most Mormons expressed satisfaction with their new homes and their prospects for material success.[11] The fertile yet unsettled land in northern Missouri presented the Saints with the opportunity to finally realize their dream of establishing God's kingdom on earth.

Central to that dream was their vision of a cooperative society. In Jackson County and in Ohio the Saints had initiated United Orders, as the communal organizations later became known, in which they consecrated (that is, gave) all their property to the Church, after which they received back the land, tools, goods, food, and other property necessary for their needs and responsibilities. The system proved unworkable— due largely, it was said, to the selfishness and disobedience of the Saints—and so in July 1838 Smith issued the Law of Consecration and Tithing for the Saints to practice in Missouri. Under this law the Saints initially gave all of their surplus property to the Church and thereafter paid one-tenth of their increase as a tithing to the Lord. This new program worked much like the previous communal experiments except that

8. George W. Robinson, "The Scriptory Book of Joseph Smith Jr. President of the Church of Jesus Christ of Latterday Saints in All the World," p. 65. LDS Archives (hereafter cited as "Scriptory Book"); and Swartzell, *Mormonism Exposed*, p. 15.

9. Brigham Young, "Sermon, February 3, 1867," in *Journal of Discourses*, 11:294–95.

10. Quoted in Rollin J. Britton, "Early Days on Grand River and the Mormon War," *Missouri Historical Review* 13 (January 1919): 115.

11. David Osborne, "Recollections of the Prophet Joseph Smith," *Juvenile Instructor* 27 (March 1892): 173.

the Saints themselves, rather than their bishop, decided how much of their property was "surplus." Smith's revelation on this principle warned the Mormons that those who did not obey the law "shall not be found worthy to abide among you." [12]

The Saints at Far West also organized three United Firms, large cooperative agricultural organizations to which Mormon farmers leased their property, both real estate and personal property. Members of the firms generally retained ownership of their homes in Far West, but the land, tools, and other production goods were held in common by the firm. According to this arrangement, the Saints would live in the city and then cultivate lands in the vicinity. The members selected their own managers, and those not chosen to manage were expected to work as laborers. The firms paid each laborer one dollar for a day's work. The firms' profits were paid as dividends to the member-stockholders, but such dividends were allocated according to the members' needs rather than to the amount of property they invested in the firm. In addition to the agricultural firms, the Saints also planned to organize mechanics, shopkeepers, and laborers into similar corporations. "All kinds of necessary articles will be manufactured by these firms, that [there will] be no necessity of purchasing of our enemies . . . ," Albert Rockwood wrote enthusiastically. "Arrangements will soon be made that a person can get every necessary to eat, drink and live on and to wear at the store house of the firms." [13]

The Saints' stay in northern Missouri was so short that they had little time to fully implement either the Law of Consecration and Tithing or their plans for the United Firms. Some Mormons, such as Brigham Young, said that the Saints were generally unwilling to give their surplus to the Church. Yet, the favorable references to these programs in the Saints' journals and reminiscences, especially by those who consecrated their property and joined

---

12. *Doctrine and Covenants*, 119:5, "Revelation given through Joseph Smith the Prophet, at Far West, Missouri, July 8, 1838."

13. "Journal," 6 October 1838, pp. 4–5. For more information on the Law of Consecration and Tithing, see Leonard J. Arrington, Feramorz Y. Fox, and Dean L. May, *Building the City of God: Community and Cooperation Among the Mormons* (Salt Lake City: Deseret Book Company, 1976), Chapter 2, "Communitarianism under Joseph Smith: The Law of Consecration and Stewardship."

the firms, and the constant preaching of the new tithing law following its inception, indicate that the Saints believed these programs were inspired by God and destined to bring about a heaven on earth. Lyman Wight, speaking to the Saints at the public square in Diahman, highlighted the virtues of the Law of Consecration:

. . . by this law all [are] as one[,] a band of brethren all "free & equal," all of us "free agents" for ourselves, all of us stewards over our own property, & all of us ought to be faithful stewards, as unto the Lord. In short, bound together by common consent, a bundle of truth & righteousness tied with cords of love & disinterestedness, seeking the good of all & bringing all to one common [good]; every mountain made low, every valley exalted, none poor among us. [14]

Samuel D. Tyler, who had just arrived at Diahman following a three-month journey from Kirtland, Ohio, remarked concerning Wight's exposition of this principle: "Now this I say looks to me like the Wonder of Man, the Height of Republicanism, Independence itself, the Zenith of Wisdom, One of the Masterpieces of the Lord our God." [15] Thousands of Saints gathered in Missouri during the summer and fall of 1838 to participate in this new order.

The rapid influx of Mormons alarmed the older settlers, especially those who had purchased land or town lots in areas they hoped to develop into prosperous communities. John Corrill reported that the Mormon settlement at Diahman "stirred up the people of Davies in some degree, [because] they saw that if this town was built up rapidly it would injure Gallatin, their county seat . . . ." [16] In addition, once the Saints moved into a neighborhood, property values would decline because non-Mormons refused to settle there. Anderson Wilson, a Clay County resident, claimed that after the Mormons got a foothold in a neighborhood by buying out one settler, "they would harang the rest away & get theirs at their own price." [17]

14. Reported in Samuel D. Tyler, "A Daily Journal of the Travelling of the Camp of Latter Day Saints Which Went Out From Kirtland for Zion July 6th 1838," p. 76. LDS Archives.

15. Ibid.

16. *A Brief History*, p. 28.

17. Letter, 4 July 1836, published in Durwood T. Stokes, "The Wilson Letters, 1835–1849," *Missouri Historical Review* 60 (July 1966): 504. See also *Far West*, 25 August 1836; Joseph Smith and Sidney Rigdon to Stephen Post, 17 September 1838; and Rockwood, "Journal," p. 2.

The developing Mormon enterprises also threatened to displace established merchants and businesses, especially in their trade with Fort Leavenworth. The garrison, located just thirty miles west of Caldwell County, purchased supplies not only for itself, but also for the numerous Indian tribes whose reservations surrounded the fort. Local settlers considered the fort's presence a godsend because of the great wealth it brought to the region.[18] Leavenworth's vast market also caught the notice of Mormon leaders, who published enthusiastic reports of the large quantities of goods and grains purchased—and the high prices paid—at the fort. By early October the Mormons' newly organized cooperative firms began bidding for government contracts.[19] The increased competition was not welcomed by the non-Mormon citizens. Consequently, while some merchants viewed the burgeoning Mormon population as an opportunity for increased business, others feared their investments in their farms and towns would be wiped out by the new Mormon communities.

The Mormon population in Missouri, which eventually reached 10,000, represented only a fraction of the state's 1838 population of 325,000. But the majority of Missouri's inhabitants lived in the eastern counties, while the Mormons migrated to the sparsely settled counties in the northwestern portion of the state. Chariton County numbered about 3,400, Carroll 1,800, Clinton 2,200, and Ray 4,500.[20] The Saints could have easily dominated any of these smaller counties, each of which had plenty of available land for Mormon settlements. When Vinson

18. Thorp, *Early Days in the West*, p. 64.

19. See W. W. Phelps, "Letter No. 1, October 20, 1834," *Messenger and Advocate* 1 (November 1834): 23; Phelps, "Letter No. 3, November 13, 1834," *Messenger and Advocate* 1 (January 1835): 50; *Elders' Journal* 1 (July 1838): 34; and Joseph Holbrook, "The Life of Joseph Holbrook," p. 22. Typescript, LDS Archives. Alphonso Wetmore, a non-Mormon, suggested in 1837 that one of the reasons why the Mormons settled in Independence was to take advantage of Leavenworth's profitable market (*Gazetteer of the State of Missouri* [St. Louis: Published by C. Keemle, 1837], p. 93). I am indebted to Michael Riggs for pointing out the importance of Fort Leavenworth's trade for both Mormons and Missourians, and the potential for conflict it engendered.

20. These population statistics are estimates based upon voting statistics of 1838 compared with voting and census records of 1840. See also Wetmore, *Gazetteer of the State of Missouri*, p. 267, for population estimates for each of the counties.

Knight moved to Daviess in May 1838, he estimated that about 120 Mormon families and 140 Missouri families lived in the county. [21] By November the Mormon population in Daviess exceeded 2,000, outnumbering the non-Mormon population by at least two to one. The Mormons in Caldwell numbered about 5,000, which means another 2,500 settled in Carroll, Ray, Chariton, and the surrounding counties. [22] In addition, the Saints anticipated a return to Jackson County, where, in expectation of Zion's imminent redemption, they retained the deeds to their former homes.

The citizens of two of the larger counties in western Missouri, Jackson and Clay, had driven the Saints from their boundaries when the Mormon population was much smaller and less threatening. And citizens in Ray and Daviess had already announced, prior to 1838, that they did not want Mormons settling in their counties. The fact that many of the Mormon immigrants came from Canada reinforced the Missourians' perception of Mormonism as an alien, un-American religion. [23] Mormon leaders understood that many Missourians objected to their presence, but saw this as working to their advantage. "Urge all the saints to gather immediately if they possibly can . . . ," Joseph Smith and Sidney Rigdon advised a Mormon elder in Pennsylvania. "Land is very cheap the old settlers will sell for half price yes, for quarter price they are determined to get away." [24] Much to the dismay of settlers throughout the region, a continuous stream of Mormons

21. Vinson Knight to William Cooper, 3 February 1839. Typescript, LDS Archives.

22. For example, land records and Mormon petitions and reminiscences show that at least twenty-five to thirty Mormon families lived in northern Ray County. About four hundred Mormons settled in DeWitt, Carroll County. According to the *History of Caldwell and Livingston Counties, Missouri*, p. 118, fifty Mormon families lived in Clinton County in 1838.

23. As the disturbances progressed, many of the settlers complained to Governor Boggs that they were being overrun by "Canadians and refugees." See *Document Containing The Correspondence, Orders, &c. In Relation To The Disturbances With The Mormons; And The Evidence Given Before The Hon. Austin A. King* (Fayette, Mo.: Office of the Boon's Lick Democrat, 1841), pp. 19, 41, 44, Citizens of Daviess and Livingston counties to the Governor, 12 September 1838; Captain Bogart to the Governor, 13 October 1838; and Colonel Peniston to the Governor, 21 October 1838. (Hereafter cited as *Document.*)

24. Letter to Stephen Post, 17 September 1838.

followed their prophet to Zion.

The Mormon Vigilante Organization: The Danites

Relations between the Mormons and Missourians were also strained as a result of dissension in the Mormon Church. The methods adopted by the Saints to purge dissenters from the Church fostered a militant and intolerant spirit among the Mormons and aroused the suspicion of Missouri settlers.

Dissension plagued Mormonism in its early years. Much of the opposition to the new religion was instigated by apostates: dissenters in Kirtland, for example, helped to drive Joseph Smith, Sidney Rigdon, and other Mormon leaders from that town in early 1838. Dissenters proved most troublesome, however, not because they stirred up hatred from without, but because they generated contentions, doubting, and disobedience within. Internal strife, Smith said, had led to the Saints' expulsion from Jackson County. Attempts to redeem Zion similarly failed due to "the transgressions of my people." [25] In 1834 the Mormon prophet issued a revelation in which the Lord warned:

And Zion cannot be built up unless it is by the principles of the law of the celestial kingdom; otherwise I cannot receive her unto myself.

And my people must needs be chastened until they learn obedience, if it must needs be, by the things which they suffer. [26]

The Far West Saints, not wishing to repeat the experiences of Jackson and Clay counties, sought to create a righteous community—one pleasing unto God—by strictly enforcing God's commandments given through His prophet. Shortly after Smith arrived in Far West, local church leaders brought Oliver Cowdery, David Whitmer, and a number of other known dissenters before a High Council court. Mormon leaders variously charged these men with selling their land in Jackson County contrary to Smith's revelations, violating the Word of Wisdom,[27] and undermining the Prophet's authority by falsely accusing him of adultery. Cowdery

---

25. *Doctrine and Covenants*, 105:2, "Revelation given through Joseph Smith the Prophet, on Fishing River, Missouri, June 22, 1834." See also 101:1–8.

26. Ibid., 105:5–6.

27. The Word of Wisdom is a Mormon health code forbidding the consumption of alcohol, tobacco, coffee, or tea.

believed this court action would lead to "the subversion of the liberties of the whole church" because ecclesiastical leaders were intruding upon the secular affairs of their people.[28] The Mormons, however, saw little distinction between spiritual and secular matters—for God is ruler over both—and Cowdery and the others were excommunicated in April 1838. Rather than leaving Far West, however, the dissenters continued to oppose Smith and soon aroused suspicions that they were plotting to destroy the Church. Consequently, in June, the Mormons determined to remove the troublemakers from their community.

A group of Mormons met secretly in Far West to discuss how to get rid of the dissenters. The group adopted the name Daughters of Zion, which they later changed to Sons of Dan, or Danites.[29] Some of the Mormons proposed killing the dissenters, but these and other radical plans were successfully opposed by Thomas Marsh, president of the Twelve Apostles, and John Corrill. The Danites took no action against the dissenters until Sunday, 17 June, when Sidney Rigdon preached what later became known as the Salt Sermon.[30] Rigdon denounced Mormon apostates, comparing them to the salt that Jesus spoke of in the Gospel of St. Matthew. If the salt has lost its savor, Rigdon said, it must be cast out and trodden under the feet of men. Rigdon accused the dissenters in Far West of seeking to overthrow the Church and committing various crimes. Although he mentioned no names, the Mormons knew of whom he spoke. The next day the Danites sent a letter to the chief dissenters, warning them that the citizens of Caldwell County would no longer tolerate their abusive conduct. The letter, reportedly written by Sidney

28. Oliver Cowdery to Warren and Lyman Cowdery, 4 February 1838. Photocopy, LDS Archives (Originals located at the Huntington Library, San Marino, California).

29. John Corrill believed the name "Daughters of Zion" was taken from Micah 4:13 (*A Brief History*, p. 32). Albert P. Rockwood stated that the Mormon Armies of Israel were called Dan "because [the] Prophet Daniel has said the Saints shall take the Kingdom and possess it forever" ("Journal," p. 8).

30. For information on the Salt Sermon and the subsequent expulsion of the dissenters, see Robinson, "Scriptory Book," p. 47; Peck, "Manuscript," pp. 6–7; Corrill, *A Brief History*, p. 30; Ebenezer Robinson, "Items of Personal History," *The Return* 1 (October 1889): 146–47; John Whitmer, "The Book of John Whitmer" (Typescript, Salt Lake City: Modern Microfilm, n.d.), p. 22; and *Document*, pp. 103–7, 110, 120, 139, testimonies of Sampson Avard,

Rigdon, was signed by eighty-three Mormons, including Joseph's brother and counselor, Hyrum Smith, several Far West high councilmen, and George W. Pitkin, the Caldwell County sheriff. After describing the many offenses allegedly committed by the dissenters, the letter announced that the Mormons intended to drive them from the county. "There are no threats from you—no fear of losing our lives by you, or by any thing you can say or do, will restrain us," the Mormons warned, "for out of the county you shall go, and no power shall save you." [31]

The threat of violence created the desired effect. On 19 June the dissenters fled with their families to Richmond, Ray County. "These men took warning, and soon they were seen bounding over the praire like the scape Goat to carry of[f] their own sins," wrote George W. Robinson, one of the Danite leaders, regarding the dissenters' flight; "we hav not seen them since, their influence is gone, and they are in a miserable condition, so also it [is] with all who turn from the truth . . . ." [32] The Mormons seized their property in Far West and held it for debts allegedly owed to the Church. The dissenters, claiming the Mormons stole the property, initiated a series of lawsuits for its recovery.

The expulsion of these men from Far West reflected a growing militant spirit among the Mormons, revealed a rigid intolerance for those who opposed their practices and teachings, and demonstrated their willingness to circumvent the law to protect their interests. Some Mormons objected to this lawless spirit, claiming that it violated the principles of republican government, but Sidney Rigdon defended the Saints' treatment of the dissenters:

. . . when a county, or body of people have individuals among them with whom they do not wish to associate and a public expression is taken against their remaining among them and such individuals do not remove it is the principle of republicanism itself that gives

John Corrill, Reed Peck, and John Whitmer.

31. *Document*, p. 103, testimony of Sampson Avard; and Robinson, "Items of Personal History," p. 146.

32. "Scriptory Book," p. 47. For the dissenters' expulsion, see also Corrill, *A Brief History*, p. 30; Peck, "Manuscript," p. 7; and Whitmer, "Book," p. 22.

that community a right to expel them forcibly and no law will prevent it.[33]

The action against the dissenters proved especially disturbing to John Corrill. A member of the Church since January 1831, the forty-three-year-old Corrill had passed through the persecutions in Jackson and Clay counties. Like many of his fellow Saints, he had risked his life to defend Mormon rights in Independence, where he was briefly imprisoned during the disturbances there. He held numerous positions of leadership in the Church, serving as counselor to Bishop Partridge for six years, and was intimately involved in nearly every phase of Mormon history in Missouri. Corrill's ability to negotiate and settle disputes between the Mormons and their neighbors gained him the respect of non-Mormons and the trust of Mormon leaders. His election in 1838 as representative to the state legislature from Caldwell County evidenced that trust. Notwithstanding his own loyalty to the Church, which he believed "to be much nearer the religion of the Bible than any other I could find," he opposed the action against the Missouri dissenters.[34] He spoke out against the initial attempt to remove David Whitmer, John Whitmer, and W. W. Phelps from their positions of leadership in Far West; at the first Danite meeting he opposed proposals to expel these men from the county; and, finding his efforts to counter those proposals unsuccessful, he secretly warned the dissenters of the Danite plans. "This scene I looked upon with horror, and considered it as proceeding from a mob spirit," Corrill said regarding the dissenters' expulsion.[35] His dissatisfaction would continue to grow.

The Danite organization likewise continued to grow throughout the summer and fall of 1838. About three to four hundred Mormons, including some of Joseph Smith's most loyal followers, joined the band. The men organized into militia units and openly marched and drilled, as if they were preparing for war.[36] Under the skillful leadership of Dr. Sampson Avard, the Danites developed into an effective regulatory force among

33. Peck, "Manuscript," p. 8. Rigdon compared their action to the hanging of gamblers in Vicksburg by a vigilante committee (ibid., p. 7).

34. *A Brief History*, p. 16.

35. Ibid., p. 30.

36. Hosea Stout, a member of the Danite band, reported that the Nauvoo

the Saints, pressuring, encouraging, and even threatening fellow Mormons to obey the commandments. The Danites bound themselves with secret oaths and signs and pledged to support each other and the leaders of the Church—whether right or wrong—in all conflicts with their enemies.[37] They prohibited excessive criticism of the First Presidency, demanded adherence to the communitarian practices of the Church, and served as an arm of the Church leadership in controlling local politics. The Danites sought by these activities to purge the Church of evil and to help build a righteous city of Zion.

Dr. Sampson Avard, leader of this Mormon vigilante organization, deserves further mention. Little is known about Avard prior to his connection with Mormonism. A former Campbellite preacher, he joined the Mormons sometime in 1835, served on a mission, and was a member of the Far West High Council in early 1838. Although he never held the top position as captain-general in the Danite organization, nearly every source agrees that Avard was the "teacher and active agent" of the society.[38] Most of these sources also assert that he was a first-class scoundrel who used the Danites to further his own ambitions within the Mormon power structure. John Corrill said Avard "was as grand a villian as his wit and ability would admit of."[39] Lorenzo D. Young considered him "a dishonest, hypocritical man."[40] Mormon Judge

Legion later performed "Danite evolutions of horsemanship as practised in the War in Davis County Missouri in the fall of 1838." He also stated that the Nauvoo troops practiced "the old Missouri Danite drill." See *On the Mormon Frontier: The Diary of Hosea Stout: 1844–1861*, 2 vols., edited by Juanita Brooks (Salt Lake City: University of Utah Press, 1964), 1:141, 197. Brooks states that the Danite evolutions of horsemanship were used in southern Utah as part of parades and celebrations as late as the 1860s (1:141, n. 17).

37. This Danite oath, and the willingness of many Danites to break the law in order to protect the Church, are described in several loyal Mormon sources: Morris Phelps, "Reminiscences," pp. 4–5. Typescript, LDS Archives; David Lewis, "Excerpt From The Journal Of David Lewis," p. 5. Typescript, LDS Archives; and Abner Blackburn, "Diary," p. 2. See also Corrill, *A Brief History*, pp. 30–32; Peck, "Manuscript," pp. 6–11; Swartzell, *Mormonism Exposed*, p. 22; and *Document*, p. 58, Thomas B. Marsh, affidavit, 24 October 1838.

38. *Document*, p. 114, testimony of John Cleminson.

39. *A Brief History*, p. 31.

40. Quoted in James Amasa Little, "Biography of Lorenzo Dow Young," *Utah Historical Quarterly* 14 (January-October 1946): 52.

Elias Higbee, who served as captain-general and Avard's superior in the Danites, described Avard as "a man whose character was the worst I ever knew in all my associations or intercourse with mankind . . . ."[41]   Higbee, as well as most Mormons, however, had little critical to say about Avard until after the doctor's disaffection with Mormonism. Only John Corrill, Thomas Marsh, and a few others who later were viewed as dissenters opposed Avard's schemes from the beginning. Peter Burnett, editor of the *Liberty Far West*, said Avard was "a very eccentric genius, fluent, imaginative, sarcastic . . . ."[42]   The crafty doctor used these talents to organize and direct the Danites and to gain the support of Mormon leaders for his policies.

A company of Danites was also organized at Adam-ondi-Ahman, where the fiery Lyman Wight assumed command of the group. Here too the Danite members bound themselves with oaths and promised to support each other. William Swartzell, who was initiated into the organization in mid-July, reports that Wight instructed the new recruits:

. . . if any brother should have stolen a horse, or committed any other offence, and is arraigned before a justice of the peace for trial, you must, at the risk of your lives, rescue him, and not permit him to be tried by the Gentile law; but bring him before our tribunal, (or court of justice,) and let him be tried by our own High Council.[43]

Wight's instructions corresponded with those given in Far West by Sampson Avard, who similarly advised his men not to submit to the civil authorities. "As the Lord liveth I would swear a lie to clear away any of you," Avard said. [44]   Reports of these

41. *HC* 4:82–83, "Elias Higbee's Letter to the Prophet, February 20, 1840."

42. *Recollections and Opinions of An Old Pioneer* (New York: D. Appleton and Company, 1880), p. 63.

43. *Mormonism Exposed*, p. 22. Historian John E. Thompson has found evidence to suggest that the Danites met every Saturday at Diahman from 14 July to 1 September ("A Chronology of Danite Meetings in Adam-ondi-Ahman, Missouri, July to September 1838," *Restoration* 4 [January 1985]: 11–14). Although the Danites apparently met less regularly after this period—due to the developing conflict—they continued to meet and add new members until the end of the disturbances. See Oliver B. Huntington, "History of the Life of Oliver B. Huntington," p. 36. Typescript, Library of the Utah State Historical Society, Salt Lake City, Utah (hereafter cited as Utah State Historical Society Library).

44. Phelps, "Reminiscences," p. 4.

Danite oaths alarmed Missouri settlers and contributed to the deteriorating relations during the next several months.

Joseph Smith and the Role of the
Danites among the Mormons in 1838

The existence of the Danite organization has long been known to Mormon historians, but less certain has been the degree of influence the group wielded among the Mormons and the extent to which Joseph Smith and other Mormon leaders knew about its activities. Many historians have discounted evidence linking Smith with the Danites because that evidence came from Mormon dissenters. More importantly, the Prophet's journal account for this period states that he knew little about the Danites or their activities. However, evidence from this period—even from loyal Mormon sources—demonstrates that Joseph Smith did indeed know about and approve of the Danite organization, and that the Danites were a highly influential group in the Mormon community. The controversial nature of these assertions requires a brief discussion of the evidence contained in the journals and accounts of loyal Mormons.

Mormon historians have cited Joseph Smith's condemnation of the Danites in the *History of the Church* as evidence that the Prophet did not know about and did not approve of the organization's activities and teachings.[45] Smith's statement credits Sampson Avard with responsibility for organizing and directing the Danite band. The statement implies that the group had little influence among the Mormons and asserts that Avard's schemes were "manfully rejected" by the Danite officers. "When a knowledge of Avard's rascality came to the Presidency of the Church, he was cut off from the Church, and every means proper used to destroy his influence," states the passage attributed to the Mormon prophet.[46] Because Smith's denial of complicity with the Danites is so explicit, assertions that he knew about the Danite activities have been regarded as tantamount to calling him a liar.

Joseph Smith, however, did not write this passage. The

45. *HC* 3:178–81; cf. Phelps, "Reminiscences," pp. 3–5.
46. *HC* 3:181.

statement was actually written by Morris Phelps, a Mormon resident of Caldwell County, but was edited and inserted in the *History of the Church* as if written by Smith. Neither Joseph Smith, Sidney Rigdon, nor any of the prominent Mormon leaders in Missouri criticized or condemned the Danites in their writings or recorded statements. After the Mormon War, Smith denounced the "false and pernicious" teachings of Sampson Avard, the leader of the Danites, and recommended against reorganizing the band in Illinois—but he did not criticize the Danites.[47] Thus, Smith's own statements regarding the Danites do not contradict the evidence linking him with the group.

The contemporary Mormon accounts of this period indicate that the Danites operated freely and openly in Far West and Diahman. John Smith, the Prophet's uncle and the Stake president at Adam-ondi-Ahman, recorded five different instances in which the Danites met:

Saturday August 4. This day the Danites met the third time in Adamondiahman since the 22 July. Nothing uncommon has taken place more than the common business of the Church. Last Sabbath Presidents Smith & Rigdon held meeting in this city.
Saturday, Aug 18. The Danites met.
Saturday, September 1. George [Smith] has gone to Far West. The Daughters of Zion meet today. Had a lecture on the consecration by President [Lyman] Wight.[48]

George W. Robinson, the Church recorder, described the role of the Danites in a 27 July entry in his journal:

They have come up hither Thus far, according to the order of the Danites, we have a company of Danites in these times, to put to right_____ that which is not right, and to cleanse the Church of

47. *HC* 3:231, The Prophet's Letter to the Church, 16 December 1838; and *HC* 3:303, The Prophet's Epistle to the Church, 25 March 1839. In his only other known statement regarding the Danites, Smith claimed that Avard's testimony (at the Richmond hearing) linking the First Presidency with the Danite constitution was false, but the Prophet did not deny any of the other accusations made by Avard and other witnesses concerning his association with the organization. See "Appeals to Supreme Court of Missouri," *Journal of History* 9 (April 1916): 209, affidavit, 15 March 1839, signed by Joseph Smith, Jr., Alanson Ripley, Heber C. Kimball, William Huntington, and Joseph B. Noble.

48. Diary, n.p., 4 August, 18 August, and 1 September 1838. Typescript, LDS Archives.

every great evil which has hitherto existed among us . . . .[49]

Robinson's account served as the basis for Joseph Smith's *History of the Church* for this period, but this reference to the Danites was not included. The role of the Danites as protectors of the Saints was also mentioned by Albert P. Rockwood, who wrote that "the Mob disperse by hundreds on the approach of the Danites." [50]

The journals kept by Robinson, Rockwood, and Smith were contemporary accounts of these events, written before the Danite activities became a scandal and source of embarrassment to the Church. The surprisingly casual, matter-of-fact references to the Danites by these Mormons indicate the group was well known among the Saints in Missouri. The favorable references by Robinson and Rockwood leave no doubt as to how the group was viewed by loyal Mormons.

These and other Mormon sources also show that the Danites played key roles in several important events in which Joseph Smith and the First Presidency participated. George W. Robinson's journal describes Sidney Rigdon's Salt Sermon and the subsequent expulsion of dissenters from Caldwell County. The expulsion, as detailed in other sources, was carried out by the Danites. Robinson also reports that, during the Mormon Fourth of July celebration in Far West, he commanded the Danite regiment that marched in the festivities. According to the *Elders' Journal*, an official publication of the Church, Danite leaders were publicly honored with positions of prominence at the Fourth of July ceremonies. In August, Danite leaders organized the posse that Joseph Smith led to Diahman to quell reported anti-Mormon violence. The First Presidency not only knew of the Danites' teachings and goals, but they also used the organization as an extralegal vigilante force to protect the interests of the Church. [51]

49. "Scriptory Book," pp. 60–61.
50. "Journal," p. 8.
51. On the Salt Sermon and the expulsion of the dissenters, see Robinson, "Scriptory Book," p. 47. On the Fourth of July celebration, see ibid., p. 46, and *Elders' Journal* 1 (August 1838): 60. On the incident at Diahman, see Robinson, "Scriptory Book," pp. 66–67. In addition, two Danite generals, Jared Carter and Sampson Avard, were present with a select group of Mormon leaders when Joseph Smith received a series of revelations in Far West in July 1838. Although Carter and Avard were probably not functioning in any official capacity as Danite officers, their presence on this occasion

Important and influential Mormons belonged to the Danite band. Elias Higbee, a Caldwell County judge, served as captain-general and leading officer in the Danites; George W. Robinson was a colonel; Reynolds Cahoon, a counselor in the Stake Presidency at Adam-ondi-Ahman, was a captain. Other prominent members of the Danite organization included Dimick Huntington, Anson B. Call, Allen J. Stout, Hosea Stout, Moses Clawson, John L. Butler, and Luman Shurtliff. [52] Anson Call states that all members of the Mormon militia belonged to the Danites, while Albert P. Rockwood claims that the Mormon militia, the Army of Israel, was the Danites. [53]

In the past, Mormon historians have been reluctant to link Joseph Smith with the Danites because they perceived the secret organization as emanating from a spirit contrary to Mormonism. As will become apparent, however, the activities of the Danites reflected a growing spirit of militancy within the Church, as evidenced by the militant speeches of Joseph Smith, Sidney Rigdon, and Lyman Wight. Similarly, some of the aggressive activities encouraged by the First Presidency paralleled the teachings and activities of the Danite band. For example, Joseph Smith's proposal to confiscate the property of all Mormons who refused to take up arms against the Missourians was as radical as the measures advocated by the Danites. [54] The Danite organization was the product of, not an aberration from, Mormon attitudes and teachings. The Danites represented mainstream Mormonism.

One other point deserves mention. Beginning in early September, the Missourians wrote letters to Governor Boggs

---

represents further evidence of their growing influence within the Mormon hierarchy ("Scriptory Book," p. 54).

52. See Robinson, "Scriptory Book," p. 66, cf. Peck, "Manuscript," pp. 11–12; Allen Joseph Stout, "Journal," pp. 8–9. Typescript, LDS Archives; Hosea Stout, *On the Mormon Frontier*, 1:141, 197; Dimick B. Huntington, "Journal From 1808 to Salt Lake City," n.p. LDS Archives; Anson Call, "Statement, December 30, 1885," p. 2. LDS Archives; Moses Clawson, "Reminiscences," p. 9. Photocopy, BYU Special Collections; Journal History, 6 August 1838, John L. Butler, account of the Gallatin election battle; and Luman A. Shurtliff, "History of Luman Andros Shurtliff," pp. 120, 125. Photocopy, LDS Archives.

53. Call, "Statement, December 30, 1885," p. 2; and Rockwood, "Journal," pp. 7–8.

54. Warren Foote, "Autobiography of Warren Foote," pp. 29–30. Photocopy, LDS Archives.

and printed articles in local newspapers describing the militant nature of the Danite band. [55] The existence of the Danites became so well known that non-Mormon settlers asked Mormons questions about the secret society. [56] It is difficult to believe that Joseph Smith and other Mormon leaders knew little about the Danites when the group's teachings and activities were common knowledge—and a chief source of anxiety—among the citizens of northwestern Missouri.

Information about the Danites from loyal Mormon sources thus corroborates and confirms the statements of Mormon dissenters, who described the Danites in more detail. The dissenters do not claim that Joseph Smith or his counselors actively directed the Danites, but they do contend that Smith and the others approved of and encouraged the Danites' activities. "The first presidency did not seem to have much to do with it at first," John Corrill said regarding their involvement with the Danites. "They would, however, go into their meetings occasionally, and sanction their doings." [57] John Cleminson also said that Joseph Smith attended at least one meeting and gave his support to the Danites, stating that "it was the will of God these things should be so." [58]

Joseph Smith had good reason to praise the secret organization: the Danites, by purging the Church of dissenters, by encouraging obedience to the Prophet's policies, and by their own willingness to conform, exerted a positive influence upon the Mormon community. Only enemies of the Church needed to fear these loyal followers of the Mormon prophet.

The Growing Militant Spirit among the Mormons: Sidney Rigdon's Fourth of July Oration

Mormon vigilance extended to enemies outside the Church

55. See *Document*, pp. 15–16, D. Ashby and others to the Governor, 1 September 1838; ibid., p. 17, The Clerk of the Circuit Court to the Governor, 6 September 1838; ibid., p. 50, T. C. Burch to the Governor, 23 October 1838; *Commercial Advertiser* (Hannibal, Mo.), 18 September 1838; Lee, *Mormonism Unveiled*, p. 67; and *Missouri Argus*, 8 November 1838, letter to the editor, 20 October 1838.

56. George A. Smith, "History of George Albert Smith," n.p. LDS Archives.

57. *A Brief History*, p. 31.

58. *Document*, p. 114, testimony of John Cleminson.

as well as to those within. Always willing to stand against persecution, the Mormons had formed defensive organizations during earlier skirmishes with vigilantes in Jackson and Clay counties. Their prayers often beseeched God to curse their enemies, and the Prophet's revelations assured the Saints that God would indeed wreak havoc upon their persecutors. In March 1836 Joseph Smith resolved with his people "that if any more of our brethren are slain or driven from their lands in Missouri, by the mob, we will give ourselves no rest, until we are avenged of our enemies to the uttermost." [59] Moreover, the Mormons believed that, because they were fulfilling God's purposes in Missouri, He would literally fight on their side. Smith told his people that angels accompanied Mormon soldiers during the Zion's Camp march to Jackson County; and in January 1836, the Prophet saw in a vision "the armies of heaven protecting the Saints in their return to Zion." [60] The failure of past military ventures had not persuaded Smith of the inefficacy of force; rather, each failure served to convince

Sidney Rigdon, 1873: Joseph Smith's chief counselor. Courtesy LDS Historical Department.

him that greater military force was needed to protect the Saints. The persecution that drove Smith from Kirtland in 1838 strengthened that conviction.

59. *HC* 2:432.
60. *HC* 2:73, 381.

Shortly after Joseph Smith arrived in Missouri, he and a number of other Mormon leaders issued the "Political Motto of the Church of Latter-day Saints," which proclaimed their loyalty to the United States Constitution and their opposition to tyrants, toryism, and mobs.[61] The Motto also condemned all who initiated "unrighteous and vexatious lawsuits," a reference to recent troubles in Kirtland. A few months later, at their Fourth of July celebration in Far West, the Mormons staged an ostentatious display of their military force and announced their intention to resist all persecution and mob violence. Several thousand people attended the festivities. Smith presided over the events of the day, which included a parade of the Danite militia, a review of the military band by the Danite generals, the laying of the cornerstone of the Far West temple, and an oration by Sidney Rigdon. Rigdon's speech represented the highlight of their celebration.

A short, portly, middle-aged man, Sidney Rigdon was second only to Joseph Smith in authority and influence among the Mormons.[62] He had abandoned a successful career as a Campbellite minister to join the Church in 1830 and quickly rose to prominence. Serving as Smith's chief aide and collaborator, he participated in nearly every major endeavor of Mormonism and helped to shape many of its distinctive practices and teachings during the 1830s. Like Smith, Rigdon suffered intense persecution because of his activities in the Church. A reformer and fiery crusader, he also had a dour, intemperate disposition, and he exhibited at times a violent intolerance for suspected enemies of the Church. After seeing the Church nearly destroyed by apostates in Kirtland, Rigdon had come to Missouri with a fierce determination to eradicate all dissent. Perhaps Mormonism's finest orator, he could stir great excitement with his impassioned speeches. His Salt Sermon in June had spurred the Danites to expel the dissenters from Caldwell County. Now, on the Fourth of July, Sidney Rigdon prepared

61. *HC* 3:9.
62. The most comprehensive biography of Sidney Rigdon is F. Mark McKiernan, *The Voice of One Crying in the Wilderness: Sidney Rigdon, Religious Reformer, 1793–1876* (Lawrence, Kans.: Coronado Press, 1971). For additional information about Rigdon and his role in early Mormonism, see the general histories of Mormonism and the biographies of Joseph Smith cited above in Chapter 2, notes 1 and 4.

to announce the Mormons' "declaration of independence from mobs."

During his speech Rigdon made the usual references to patriotism, the Founding Fathers, and liberty. He also declared his belief in the separation of church and state. Rigdon then issued a provocative warning to the enemies of the Church. After describing at length the persecution endured by the Saints over the years, he declared that they would endure it no more:

We take God and all the holy angels to witness this day, that we warn all men in the name of Jesus Christ, to come on us no more forever, for from this hour, we will bear it no more, our rights shall no more be trampled on with impunity. The man or the set of men, who attempts it, does it at the expense of their lives. And that mob that comes on us to disturb us; *it shall be between us and them a war of extermination*, for we will follow them, till the last drop of their blood is spilled, or else they will have to exterminate us; for we will carry the seat of war to their own houses, and their own families, and one party or the other shall be utterly destroyed— Remember it then all Men.

We will never be the agressors, we will infringe on the rights of no people; but shall stand for our own until death. We claim our own rights, and are willing that all others shall enjoy theirs.

No man shall be at liberty to come into our streets, to threaten us with mobs, for if he does, he shall attone for it before he leaves the place, neither shall he be at liberty, to vilify and slander any of us, for suffer it we will not in this place.

We therefore, take all men to record this day, that we proclaim our liberty on this day, as did our fathers. And we pledge this day to one another, our fortunes, our lives, and our sacred honors, to be delivered from the persecutions which we have had to endure, for the last nine years, or nearly that. Neither will we indulge any man, or set of men, in instituting vexatious law suits against us, to cheat us out of our just rights, if they attempt it we say wo be unto them.

We this day then proclaim ourselves free, with a purpose and a determination, that never can be broken, "no never! no never!! NO NEVER"! ! ![63]

At the conclusion the Mormon people waved their hats high

___

63. Peter Crawley, "Two Rare Missouri Documents," *BYU Studies* 14 (Summer 1974): 527 (italics mine). This article reprints an 1838 pamphlet of Rigdon's speech.

above their heads and shouted, "Hosanna! Hosanna! Hosanna to God and the Lamb!"[64]

The Saints' spontaneous, enthusiastic response to Rigdon's speech pleased their leaders. Joseph Smith and his counselors had carefully prepared the speech and afterward had it published and distributed to their people. Smith recommended that all Church members buy a copy. "We are absolutely determined no longer to bear [persecution], come life or come death," the Prophet wrote in the August issue of the *Elders' Journal*, "for to be mobed any more without taking vengeance, we will not."[65] Smith and Rigdon believed that mobs continued to threaten the Church, and they wanted their enemies to know that the Saints intended to defend their rights.

The evidence suggests, however, that the Mormon leaders' fear of violence was exaggerated, even unfounded, at that time. The journals and reminiscences of the Saints do not mention any trouble with non-Mormons prior to the Fourth of July oration. W. W. Phelps testified that throughout the summer and fall he received assurances from the citizens of Ray and Clay counties that no mobs were being raised against the Saints in that quarter.[66] William Swartzell, a Mormon resident of Diahman, recorded that the Mormons were the only ones talking about mobs at this time—he had heard nothing from the Missourians.[67] In later years, Mormon leaders such as Brigham Young, Wilford Woodruff, Orson Hyde, and Jedediah M. Grant condemned Rigdon's speech as a foolish and overly aggressive statement of Mormon rights that unnecessarily provoked anti-Mormon violence. "Elder Rigdon was the prime cause of our troubles in Missouri, by his fourth of July oration," Young said.[68]

64. Robinson, "Items of Personal History," p. 149; and Parley P. Pratt, *Autobiography of Parley P. Pratt* (Salt Lake City: Deseret Book Company, 1976 [1874]), p. 173.

65. See p. 54 of that issue. See also Robinson, "Items of Personal History," *The Return* 1 (November 1889): 170–71.

66. *Document*, p. 122, testimony of W. W. Phelps.

67. *Mormonism Exposed*, p. 29. During the months of July and August, Swartzell noted with dismay the growing militant spirit of the Mormons. He subsequently left the Church and published this somewhat biased diary account of his experiences among the Mormons in northwestern Missouri.

68. "Elder Rigdon's Trial," *Times and Seasons* 5 (1 October 1844): 667. See also *Times and Seasons* 5 (1 November 1844): 698; John Jaques, "The Life and Labors of Sidney Rigdon," *Improvement Era* 3 (June 1900): 583;

Nevertheless, at that time, the Saints overwhelmingly supported this declaration that warned Missourians not to molest the Mormon people.

Most Missourians were not aware of any unusual strain in their relations with the Mormons. Many believed that interaction between the two groups had become remarkably friendly. Rigdon's warnings therefore surprised and alarmed Missouri settlers, who interpreted the speech as an open, defiant declaration of Mormon intentions to set themselves outside the law. The *Liberty Western Star* reported:

Until the 4th of July we heard of no threats being made against them, in any quarter. The people had all become reconciled to let them remain where they are, and indeed were disposed to lend them a helping hand, but one Sidney Rigdon, in order to show himself off as a great man, collected them all together in the town of Far West, on the 4th of July, and there delivered a speech containing the essence of, if not treason itself. This speech was not only published in the newspapers, but handbills were struck for distribution in Caldwell and Daviess counties. We have not the speech now before us, but we recollect amongst other threats, that this author said: "We will not suffer any vexatious lawsuits against our people; nor will we suffer any person to come into our streets and abuse them." Now, if this is not a manifestation of a disposition to prevent the force of law, we do not know what is.[69]

Reports of Rigdon's speech spread through the upper counties, increasing suspicions of and reviving old prejudices against the Saints. Mormon leaders had issued the statement as a defensive measure, prompted by their history of persecution. Although they wanted to frighten anyone who might threaten them, they did not intend to begin a conflict with their non-Mormon neighbors. The Missourians, believing the Mormons had no

and Jedediah M. Grant, *A Collection of Facts Relative to the Course Taken By Elder Sidney Rigdon* (Philadelphia: Brown, Bicking & Guilbert, Printers, 1844), p.11. It is worth noting that many of these criticisms of Rigdon's speech were made while Brigham Young and Sidney Rigdon contested for leadership of the Church after Joseph Smith's death. Thus, Young and his supporters may have been tempted to ignore Smith's involvement in the oration and to exaggerate its consequent effect.

69. This 14 September article was reprinted in the *Missouri Argus* of 27 September 1838.

reason to fear persecution from them, interpreted Rigdon's vigorous warnings as a threat against the citizens and law in northwestern Missouri.

4

Trouble Begins

Trouble between the Mormons and Missourians began in Carroll County, not as an immediate result of the excitement caused by Sidney Rigdon's Fourth of July oration, but because Carroll settlers objected to the Mormons' settlement at DeWitt. When David Thomas and Henry Root, both Carroll residents, invited the Saints to settle there, they informed Joseph Smith that they had been "consulted on this business by others."[1] Carroll citizens, however, claimed they did not discover that the lots had been sold to Mormons until after the sale. The citizens of this sparsely settled county, who numbered about eighteen hundred, immediately protested when John Murdock and George M. Hinkle, Mormon leaders from Far West, moved with their families to DeWitt in early July.

Disturbances in Carroll County

Originally named Eldersport, DeWitt was located on a bluff overlooking the Missouri River near its confluence with the Grand River, which flowed through several northern Missouri counties. Eli Guthrie laid out the town and then sold his interest to Henry Root in January 1837. Despite DeWitt's excellent location as a landing for two rivers, only seven individuals purchased lots during the year and a half after Root's purchase. Root and other local citizens probably recognized, however, that the growing Mormon community at Diahman, located to the north on the Grand River, would send much of its traffic through DeWitt if a sizable Mormon community settled there. It was undoubtedly the half-dozen residents of DeWitt with whom Root and Thomas conferred when they invited the Mormons to settle there, because a thriving Mormon community would

1. G. W. Robinson, "Scriptory Book," p. 28.

enhance the value of everyone's property in that town.

Soon after Murdock and Hinkle arrived, handbills were circulated throughout the county, notifying the people to meet at the county clerk's office in Carrollton on Saturday, 14 July 1838. Dr. W. W. Austin was appointed chairman at this meeting, which perhaps fifty people attended. More than a dozen county leaders, including Judge John Standly and several ministers, spoke to their fellow citizens about the unexpected arrival of the Saints. The citizens decided that the Mormons must not be allowed to settle in their county; but after discussing the danger of attempting to drive them forcibly from DeWitt, the citizens decided to meet again before taking any action. [2]

Carroll citizens packed the next meeting, held the following Saturday, overflowing the clerk's small office. Many of the spectators watched through the windows and doors. A. C. Blackwell, secretary for the citizens' meeting, reported that "great enthusiasm prevailed" and popular opinion favored immediate action against the Saints. [3] Joseph Thorp recalled that "some of the hot-headed citizens were in favor of marching right on them and driving them out forthwith." [4]   After a lengthy discussion, passions cooled and the citizens decided to ask nearby counties for assistance to expel the Mormons. They also resolved to place the question on the ballot in the approaching August election: Carroll citizens could either vote for or against allowing the Mormons to remain in the county. The meeting adjourned without any decision as to when or how the Mormons should be expelled. The settlers presumably planned to wait until they knew the results of their local referendum and received responses from the other counties.

Agitation against the Mormons continued throughout the summer. Carroll settlers voted overwhelmingly at the August

2. Most of the information on the early disturbances in Carroll County is taken from "History of Carroll County, Missouri," in *An Illustrated Historical Atlas of Carroll County, Missouri* (n.p.: Brink, McDonough, & Co., 1876), p. 13 (A. C. Blackwell, a Carroll resident who actively participated in the anti-Mormon activities, provided the information for this history); John Murdock, Journal, pp. 95–96. Photocopy, LDS Archives; Murdock, "Affidavit, January 10, 1840." Petitions, U.S. Archives; *The History of Carroll County, Missouri* (St. Louis: Missouri Historical Company, 1881), pp. 247–62; *Missouri Republican*, 18 August 1838; and *Southern Advocate* (Jackson, Mo.), 1 September 1838.

3. "History of Carroll County," p. 13.

4. *Early Days in the West*, p. 84.

election for the Mormons to leave the county, after which several citizen committees visited DeWitt and requested, then demanded, that the Saints move back to Caldwell. Shortly after, a local sheriff arrested George Hinkle on a complaint from the Rev. Sashel Woods, who claimed that Hinkle threatened him when his committee visited DeWitt. Hinkle was released when Woods failed to appear against him. On another occasion, a company of about one hundred men, including Woods, rode into DeWitt and shot up the town, taking prisoners and threatening the Mormon inhabitants. The Saints rallied under the leadership of George Hinkle, who held the rank of colonel in the state militia. An early convert to Mormonism, Hinkle had served in a number of successful proselytizing missions for the Church, and recently had sat on the High Council at Far West, where he was also one of the town's leading merchants. He informed the vigilantes in Carroll County that the Mormons would fight rather than abandon their homes. A steady stream of Mormon emigrants from the East moved into DeWitt during the summer months, inciting even greater animosity toward them. Carroll citizens feared that the Mormons would become so well entrenched in DeWitt that they could not be removed.

During the series of meetings held in Carrollton, the settlers sent reports of their proceedings to various Missouri newspapers to publicize their reasons for driving the Mormons from the county. Several newspapers subsequently published accounts of their meetings. Although the Carroll citizens in their minutes and resolutions linked the Mormons with "abolitionists and other disorderly persons," they never directly accused the Saints of committing any crimes. Their actions rested primarily upon the assertion that the "Mormons have broken the covenant so by them made, and are now settling in Carroll county contrary to the express wishes of the citizens thereof."[5] They regarded the Mormons as religious fanatics, undesirable citizens who must be removed from the county.

Carroll citizens never questioned their right to expel the Mormons. They proceeded with order, restraint, and propriety, as if they were following a specified code for driving people from their homes. They held public meetings and took popular votes;

5. *Missouri Republican*, 18 August 1838.

many of the county's leading citizens participated; and they published the minutes of their meetings so that all Missourians would know that they were acting justly and properly in the affair. Although the majority at several meetings favored a direct march to DeWitt, Carroll citizens refrained from using violence or terror until after they officially notified the Mormons of their resolutions and demands. Their repeated warnings to the Saints created an impression of forbearance, making it appear as if the Mormons, by refusing to leave, were bringing the violence upon themselves. These attitudes and actions seemed to legitimize their proceedings, allowing the Carroll citizens to rationalize and carry out their lawless task. When one of the citizen committees visited DeWitt and ordered the Mormons to leave, the Mormons asked Abbott Hancock, a local minister and spokesman for the committee, by what authority the settlers made such a demand. "By the authority of Carroll County," Hancock replied.[6] The vigilantes operated under the assumption that their extralegal organization carried the same legitimate force as their official county government.

Although Carroll settlers made numerous threats against the Saints, they did not attempt forcibly to expel the Mormons during the first months of the conflict. Some of the settlers were perhaps reluctant to use violence against the Mormons, who, after all, had broken no laws. At this time public opinion outside Carroll County did not generally support their actions against the Mormons. The *Missouri Republican*, published in St. Louis, reported the disturbances in Carroll and then condemned the proceedings of the vigilantes:

We look upon it as an infraction of all law and right, as a stain on the American character, and as deserving the reprehension of the press every where. If they [the Mormons] have infracted the law, let its severeties be inflicted to the utmost, but that one set of men should drive out another, on account of their religious, or rather bigoted, heresies, ought not to be tolerated in any land, much less in a land boasting of its freedom.[7]

The *Jackson Southern Advocate* supported these views, asserting that the Mormons held the same rights as other Missouri

---

6. Murdock, "Affidavit, January 10, 1840." Petitions, U.S. Archives.
7. 18 August 1838.

citizens and therefore should be dealt with according to the law. Neither of these newspaper articles was sympathetic toward the Mormons, whom they described as a "contemptible and degraded class of beings" and "the deluded followers of Jo Smith." [8] But the articles expressed the views of many citizens: they disliked the Mormons, but they also abhorred the threatened violence. Carroll settlers knew they needed both public support and active assistance from nearby counties before they could drive the Mormons from DeWitt.

Carroll citizens hoped they would not have to use force. But as the summer progressed, and the Mormons continued to pour into DeWitt and all the upper counties, the settlers expected conflict. I. H. Arnold, a resident of Carrollton, described local sentiment:

We are getting into trouble with the Mormons our neighbors. they now occupy mostly two counties adjoining us + are coming into the country in droves + attempting [to] settle in the adjoining counties much to the dissatisfaction of the inhabitants + they [the inhabitants] are calling meetings + appointing committees inviting them to leave + saying if they refuse to do so peaceably other measures will be resorted to, in short implying they will be driven out as they were from Jackson County . . . . I have been frequently to their new Jerusalem + am acquainted with several of them who will fight on their own sail till they die. some of their leaders have threatened to carry the war into the enemy camp + a war of extermination shall follow. I think for myself it will all end in smoke. [9]

The Mormons too expected trouble. After being informed of the threats against DeWitt, Joseph Smith alerted Mormon soldiers and ordered them to stand ready to ride to Carroll. Meanwhile, a political dispute between the Mormons and Missourians led to violence in Daviess County.

Disturbances in Daviess County: The Gallatin Election Battle

Daviess County was a sparsely settled, heavily wooded region. In 1838, eight years after pioneers began farming in Daviess,

8. *Southern Advocate*, 1 September 1838; and *Missouri Republican*, 18 August 1838.

9. I. H. Arnold to Isaac Arnold, 12 August 1838. Typescript, Library-Archives of the Reorganized Church of Jesus Christ of Latter Day Saints, Independence, Missouri (hereafter cited as RLDS Archives).

fewer than one hundred fifty non-Mormon families had moved into the county. Nearly all of these early settlers came from the South. Peter H. Burnett stated that many of these settlers were "rude and ungovernable" backwoodsmen. [10]   Lyman Wight, the Mormon leader at Diahman, claimed the older citizens of Daviess "were an ignorant set, and not very far advanced before the aborigines of the country in civilization or cultivated minds." [11]   The Daviess settlers had protested against being included in the Mormon county (Caldwell) in 1836, so Daviess was organized as a separate county. A number of Saints settled farms in that county anyway. They met with brief resistance from some of the older settlers, but on the whole the Mormons' relations with their neighbors in Daviess were friendly until they laid out Diahman and moved into the county in large numbers in the spring and summer of 1838.

The Mormons quickly became the dominant political force in the county. By August they numbered about one-half of the two thousand county residents and represented at least one-third of the voting population. Most of the Mormons belonged to the Democratic party, but they would vote for any candidate who they believed would protect their rights. They also tended to vote as a bloc and therefore held the balance of power in the Daviess election.

The state and county elections, scheduled for 6 August, stirred considerable excitement among the Daviess settlers because it would be their first opportunity to elect their own county officers. Few Mormons ran for office, so the candidates visited Diahman frequently, making promises and soliciting votes. The candidates focused their attention on Lyman Wight, who was considered the most influential Mormon at Diahman. One of the candidates who spoke with Wight was Col. William Peniston, son of Robert Peniston, the founder of Millport. "Peniston was a rough, quarrelsome fellow, but he had more influence in Daviess county in 1838 than any other man," recalled Joseph McGee, who ran a clothing store in Gallatin. [12]   Peniston had previously objected to the Saints' immigration into Daviess, but

10. *Recollections*, p. 57.
11. *HC* 3:441, Lyman Wight, affidavit, 1 July 1843.
12. "Some Waste Places Of Zion As They Appear Today," *Deseret News*, 10 September 1904, p. 23.

when Wight questioned him regarding his opposition, Peniston replied that "he never designed to drive them out of the County [and] that if he could not scare them so as to cause them to leave, he intended to let them alone."[13]   Another non-Mormon resident, perhaps sent by a local candidate, went out among the Saints to find out whom they supported for the county offices.[14]   The older settlers realized that whoever received the Mormon vote would win the election.

Tensions increased throughout the campaign. Personal threats were made against Wight as local citizens expressed their resentment of the Mormon influence in their county. Judge Josiah Morin, a candidate for state senator and an avowed friend of the Saints, told Sterling Price that he would have to leave his Millport home if he lost the election.[15]   As election day approached, many Daviess citizens began to assert that the Mormons should not be allowed to vote. Judge Morin, hearing rumors of planned violence, informed the Mormons that there would probably be trouble at the polls. According to Morin, the Daviess Whigs planned to vote early at the outside precincts and then rush to Gallatin to prevent the Mormons from voting there. The Mormons, believing that Judge Morin was merely electioneering for the Democrats, paid little attention to his warning.

A small, quiet town with only eight to ten cabins, Gallatin was filled with enthusiasm and excitement on 6 August. More than one hundred settlers, including about thirty Mormons, had come to Gallatin to cast their ballots. Summer days in western Missouri are hot and muggy; most of the men probably stopped at George Worthington's dram shop for a swig of whiskey or whatever other spirits were available. Many of the local candidates were present and mingled freely with the people, hoping by their friendliness—and by their generosity at the saloons—to win a few additional votes.[16]   The election gave the settlers from around the county a chance to meet with distant

13. Col. [Sterling] Price, Letter, 8 September 1838. Petitions, U.S. Archives.

14. John L. Butler, "A Short History of the Biography of John L. Butler," p. 15. Typescript, LDS Archives.

15. Col. Price, Letter, 8 September 1838.

16. A Mormon candidate from Diahman, John Lemmons, was later reprimanded by his brethren for treating the settlers to wine (Swartzell, *Mormonism Exposed*, pp. 31–32).

neighbors and discuss business as well as politics; but since this was Daviess County's first election, conversation undoubtedly centered on the various candidates for local office. Prior to the voting, William Peniston mounted a barrel and began speaking to the crowd. [17]

Peniston, a Whig candidate for the state legislature, had seen that his attempts to gain the Mormon vote had not succeeded. He now sought to eliminate their influence. He denounced the Mormons as horse thieves, liars, counterfeiters, and dupes, and boasted to the crowd that he had previously led a company of men that ordered the Saints to leave the county. In what was perhaps a reference to Danite teachings, Peniston also claimed that the Mormons would swear to false oaths. "If we suffer such men as those to vote," he concluded, "you will soon lose your suffrage." [18]

The Mormons, about thirty in number, watched cautiously as Peniston stepped from the barrel and good-naturedly called on everyone to have a drink. While the Missourians passed around the whiskey, Dick Weldon, a longtime resident of Daviess County, informed the crowd that in Clay County the Mormons had not been allowed to vote "no more than the negroes." Weldon, who was reportedly drunk, accosted a small Mormon shoemaker, Samuel Brown.

"Are you a Mormon preacher, sir?" he asked Brown.

"Yes, sir, I am."

"Do you Mormons believe in healing the sick by laying on

17. Accounts by Mormon witnesses and participants in the Gallatin election battle include Butler, "History," pp. 15–18; Journal History, 6 August 1838, Butler account, and Lee and Stewart account; Lee, *Mormonism Unveiled*, pp. 56–60; and Sidney Rigdon, *An Appeal To The American People: Being An Account Of The Persecutions Of The Church of Jesus Christ of Latter Day Saints; And Of The Barbarities Inflicted On Them By The Inhabitants Of The State Of Missouri* (Cincinnati: Printed By Shepard & Stearns, 1840), pp. 15–18. One non-Mormon witness left an account: Joseph H. McGee, *Story of the Grand River Country*, n.p. Others who describe this incident include Burnett, *Recollections*, 57; Corrill, *A Brief History*, p. 33; Owen, "Memorial," pp. 1–2; Peck, "Manuscript," p. 15; Col. Price, Letter, 8 September 1838. Petitions, U.S. Archives; Robinson, "Scriptory Book," pp. 66–67; and Swartzell, *Mormonism Exposed*, p. 28. Reed C. Durham, Jr., "The Election Day Battle at Gallatin," *BYU Studies* 13 (Autumn 1972): 36–61, brings together many of these sources in an excellent description of the election-day violence at Gallatin.

18. John D. Lee and Levi Stewart account, Journal History, 6 August 1838.

of hands, speaking in tongues, and casting out devils?"

"We do," said Brown.

"Fight At Gallatin, Missouri, Between Mormons And 'Gentiles.' " From John D. Lee, *Mormonism Unveiled* (St. Louis: Bryan, Brand & Co., 1877).

"You are a damned liar. Joseph Smith is a damned imposter," Weldon replied. [19]

Weldon then began striking Brown. When other Mormons attempted to restrain Weldon, five or six Missourians jumped into the fray. John L. Butler, a large and powerful Mormon, rankled at the abuse heaped upon his people. "The first thing that came to my mind was the covenants entered into by the Danites to the effect that they were to protect each other, etc.," Butler recalled, "and I hollowed out to the top of my voice saying 'O yes, you Danites, here is a job for us.' " [20] When Butler gave the Danite signal of distress, about ten more Latter-day Saints ran to the defense of their brethren. Seeing this, forty or fifty Missourians stepped in to battle the Mormons.

"I had witnessed many knock-downs in my time, but none on so grand a scale," wrote Joseph McGee, a non-Mormon

19. Lee, *Mormonism Unveiled*, p. 58.
20. Journal History, 6 August 1838, Butler account.

observer of the fight. [21]   The participants used no guns, but struck at one another with whips, clubs, rocks, and knives. The Mormons rallied behind Butler, who wielded a large wooden club he found in a nearby pile of wood. "When I called out for the Danites a power rested upon me such as one as I never felt before," Butler later wrote. ". . . I never struck a man the second time, and while knocking them down, I really felt that they would soon embrace the gospel." [22]   Another Mormon, Harvey Olmstead, used as a weapon a handkerchief filled with newly purchased earthen bowls, tea cups, and saucers, which he cracked over the heads of his opponents. By the end of the fray his earthenware was in pieces, not one piece larger than a dollar, and his handkerchief looked as if it had been chewed by a cow. The Mormons knocked dozens of men to the ground, and several Missourians, foreheads and faces bleeding, were carried off by their comrades. William Peniston escaped injury by running up the hill to a grocery, but Dick Weldon was felled by a blow that tore three to four inches off the side of his head. On the opposite side, a Mormon retreated with a knife between his shoulders. The conflict raged briefly but intensely. No one from either side sustained fatal injury, but many suffered gashes, cuts, and bruises. Despite their inferior numbers, the Mormons held their ground and finally drove the Missourians from the field.

Conflicting evidence makes it impossible to determine whether many of the Mormons voted. [23]   Although they won the scuffle, they were still surrounded by a large and hostile crowd. When some of the settlers ran to get their guns, the Mormons retreated to their homes for safety. After the Mormons left, enraged settlers gathered around the stores, swearing and threatening to take vengeance against the Saints. Chapman Duncan, a Mormon resident of Daviess County, said that a group of ruffians returning from Gallatin shot up the door of

21. *Story of the Grand River Country*, n.p.

22. Journal History, 6 August 1838, Butler account.

23. Several of the participants gave contradictory accounts regarding this point. For example, John D. Lee reported in *Mormonism Unveiled*, p. 60, that "the Mormons all voted"; but in his account coauthored with Levi Stewart in the Journal History, 6 August 1838, he reported that "very few of the 'Mormons' voted that day." John L. Butler stated that he "declined voting" when the scuffle ended (Journal History, 6 August 1838). Although

his cabin. [24] The rumor quickly spread that the settlers were organizing a mob. Josiah Morin, while traveling through Far West the next day, informed the Mormons that he had been told—he was not present at the fight—that two Mormons had been killed in Gallatin and the Missourians would not allow them to be buried. Morin also reported that he heard anti-Mormon vigilantes were gathering to drive the Saints from Daviess County.

The Mormons in Far West, already on the alert because of the threats against DeWitt, reacted swiftly to the news. Volunteers collected, and soon almost one hundred fifty men, mostly Danites, were riding for Diahman. Joseph Smith and his counselors, Sidney Rigdon and Hyrum Smith, also joined the expedition. The men organized under their Danite leaders: Col. George W. Robinson assumed command of the regiment, while Gen. Sampson Avard and Gen. Elias Higbee served as his superior officers. Although Smith was not a Danite, he held overall responsibility and directed the movements of the men. [25]

The Mormon vigilantes arrived that evening, 7 August, at Diahman, where they found their people extremely frightened. They learned that no Mormons had been killed or seriously injured at Gallatin, but the Daviess Saints feared local settlers would retaliate. Many of the Mormon men who participated in the election brawl had fled with their families to Diahman to escape the anticipated violence. John L. Butler reported that a group of about thirty Missourians had gathered suspiciously around his home. [26] After the arrival of the troops from Far West, the Mormons butchered a few cattle and cooked up a large supply of corn meal in preparation for a siege. No armed bands, however, came against them.

Mormon tradition suggests that the Mormons voted, this author found many accounts reporting that few or none of the Mormons voted. See, e.g., Rigdon, *Appeal*, p. 17; Vinson Knight to William Cooper, 3 February 1839; *HC* 3:58, 441; Eliphas Marsh, "Affidavit, January 10, 1840," Petitions, U.S. Archives; and James H. Rollins, "Affidavit, January 13, 1840," Petitions, U.S. Archives.

24. Chapman Duncan, "Biography of Chapman Duncan, 1812–1900," p. 36. Typescript, BYU Special Collections.

25. Rockwood, "Journal," p. 2; Robinson, "Scriptory Book," p. 66; and Peck, "Manuscript," p. 15.

26. "History," p. 18.

The Adam Black Incident

Mormon leaders did not believe the trouble had ended. The next morning, after the Mormons realized there would be no attack on Diahman, they decided to visit prominent Daviess citizens to see whether they supported the anti-Mormon violence. The Mormons first visited Judge Adam Black, who lived less than a mile from Diahman. Judge Black, one of the county's earliest settlers, had sold a farm to Lyman Wight about eighteen months previously, but afterward he reportedly headed a mob requesting Wight and other Mormons to leave the county. The Mormons now heard that he intended to lead another mob gathering at Millport. Joseph Smith sent a committee of three Danite leaders, Lyman Wight, Sampson Avard, and Cornelius P. Lott, and several election-battle participants to call upon Black. [27]

The Mormons made two visits to Black's home. At their first meeting they confronted the judge with the reports of his anti-Mormon sympathies and requested that he sign a prepared statement disavowing his alleged connections with the vigilantes. Black indignantly refused, claiming the Mormons had no right to require a civil officer to sign such a document. A heated argument ensued, but repeated efforts by the Danite leaders failed to persuade Black to sign their statement.

The Mormons left, but returned about a half-hour later with a hundred armed men, including Joseph Smith, and surrounded Black's home. "We have come to be plain with you," threatened Avard, "the only alternative is for you to sign this obligation." [28] When Black again refused, Wight invited him to discuss the matter

27. There are many descriptions of the incident at Black's home in court testimony, affidavits, reminiscences, and newspaper articles. The Mormons contend that their visits to Judge Black were cordial, while Mormon dissenters and Missourians (including Black) contend that the Mormons threatened the judge. Although Black and others exaggerated their claims regarding the incident, the fact that the Mormons made two visits to his home (sending one hundred armed men on the second visit), and then called on other citizens as well, supports the contention that the Mormons threatened the Missourians. The most detailed accounts of this incident are found in Robinson, "Scriptory Book," p. 67; Swartzell, *Mormonism Exposed*, pp. 29–30; *HC* 3:70–72, Joseph Smith, affidavit, 5 September 1838; and *Document*, pp. 159–63, testimony of Adam Black, 18 September 1838.

28. *Document*, p. 161, testimony of Adam Black, 18 September 1838.

with Joseph Smith, who was waiting outside near a spring. Judge Black asked the Mormon Prophet whether he shared Avard's "savage disposition," to which Smith replied, "No." Black then protested the Mormons' action, claiming they had no right to force him to sign their document. The Prophet insisted that they would not compel Black to act against his will, but asked that he sign to allay the excitement among local Mormons, who feared anti-Mormon violence. Black, however, was more persuaded by the large number of soldiers, who continued urging him to sign. Finally, fearing for the safety of his family, Black agreed to write a statement of his own:

I, Adam Black, a Justice of the Peace of Daviess county, do hereby Sertify to the people, coled Mormin, that he is bound to suport the Constitution of this State, and of the United State, and he is not attached to any mob, nor will not attach himself to any such people, and so long as they will not molest me, I will not molest them. This the 8th day of August, 1838.

Adam Black, J.P. [29]

Black's statement proved satisfactory. Sampson Avard later testified, "if Black had not signed the paper he did, it was the common understanding and belief that he would have shared the fate of the dissenters." [30]

The Mormons visited several other leading Daviess citizens, including Sheriff William Morgan, and compelled some of them to sign statements similar to the one written by Judge Black. [31] There are no detailed accounts of these incidents, nor is it known how many people the Mormons visited, but the other citizens, like Black, apparently signed the statements against their will.

The Mormons did not consider their actions to be overly aggressive or illegal; their intent was to enforce the law, not break

29. *HC* 3:59–60.

30. Avard was referring to the Mormon dissenters who were driven from their homes in Far West. *Document*, p. 98, testimony of Sampson Avard. See also Swartzell, *Mormonism Exposed*, p. 30, for Mormon threats against Black. Swartzell refers to Avard as Brigadier-General Eberly.

31. Evidence and descriptions of these visits are found in Corrill, *A Brief History*, p. 34; Peck, "Manuscript," p. 15; Swartzell, *Mormonism Exposed*, p. 30; *HC* 3:59; *Missouri Republican*, 25 August 1838; *Missouri Argus*, 6 September 1838; *Missouri Argus*, 15 February 1839, speech by Cornelius Gilliam; and Willard Snow, "Statement," n.d. Petitions, U.S. Archives.

it. Daviess citizens, however, regarded the Mormons' activities with suspicion and alarm. The invasion of their county by the Mormon vigilantes violated Missouri law, which prohibited bodies of armed men from crossing into another county without proper authorization.[32] And the threats against local officials seemed to confirm previous allegations of the aggressive and fanatical nature of Mormonism. Although Mormon leaders protested that their intentions were peaceful, the Missourians assumed otherwise— why else would they send one hundred armed men to back up their threats? On the night of 8 August a group of frightened Daviess citizens visited Diahman to "sue for peace" and to learn the intentions of the Mormon troops.[33]

Daviess County and Mormon leaders met the following afternoon at the home of Lyman Wight. Josiah Morin, state senator elect, John Williams, state representative elect (having defeated William Peniston), and several other leading citizens represented the Daviess settlers. The ecclesiastical leaders at Diahman, Lyman Wight, John Smith, Reynolds Cahoon, and Vinson Knight, represented their fellow Mormons. Both sides pledged to preserve the peace. They agreed that they would not protect any persons who had broken the law, but would deliver up all offenders to the proper authorities. The Mormon and Missouri leaders parted on friendly terms, both groups apparently convinced of the peaceful intentions of the other. Joseph Smith and the Danite army returned to Far West that evening.

The Excitement Spreads to Neighboring Counties

Trouble in Daviess County was just beginning. While Mormon and Missouri leaders met at Diahman, a number of angry and frightened Daviess settlers, including Judge Black, Colonel Peniston, and former sheriff William Bowman, rode to Richmond and gave exaggerated reports of the Mormons' activities. These men signed affidavits that claimed the Mormons, with more than five hundred men under arms, were threatening the lives of

---

32. Such authorization usually came from either the circuit court judge or the commanding general in that district. See *HC* 3:454–56, Sidney Rigdon, affidavit, 1 July 1843.

33. Robinson, "Scriptory Book," p. 67.

Daviess citizens. Peniston stated that he believed the Mormons intended to "intimidate and drive from the county all the old citizens, and possess themselves of their lands, or to force such as do not leave, to come into their measures and submit to their dictation." [34]   In response to these charges, local judges issued writs for the arrest of Joseph Smith, Lyman Wight, and other Mormons allegedly involved in the incident at Black's home.

Alarmed citizens from Richmond, Ray County, where Adam Black and others filed their affidavits, appointed a committee to investigate the allegations against the Mormons. On the way to Daviess County, the Ray committee stopped in Far West and met publicly with Mormons there. Later, the committee stopped at Millport, where Judge Charles Morehead told William Swartzell that Mormon lawlessness would not be tolerated. "Every Mormon would be killed, unless they complied with the laws of the State," Morehead warned. [35]   At Diahman, the Ray County committee conferred with Mormon leaders, informing them that they wished to settle the controversy peacefully, but they also insisted that the Mormons obey the law. According to Swartzell's journal account, Lyman Wight replied:

That he owed nothing to the laws—the laws had not protected him—he had been on the rack, and persecution had followed him these seven years—he had suffered enough—God did not require him to endure more—and that he would not yield to the laws of Missouri—he would sooner die and be buried. [36]

Other Mormons expressed similar sentiments. John L. Butler, when earlier informed that he must stand trial for assault, told the Missourians, "I was a law abiding man, but I did not intend to be tried by a mob." [37]

---

34. *HC* 3:61, William Peniston, affidavit, 10 August 1838. See also Corrill, *A Brief History*, p. 34; *Southern Advocate*, 8 September 1838; and *Document*, p. 15, Adam Black, affidavit, 28 August 1838.

35. Swartzell, *Mormonism Exposed*, p. 31.

36. Ibid., p. 32. Swartzell's account is supported by the report of the Daviess sheriff, who claimed he was told by Wight "that he would not be taken alive—that the law had never protected him, and he owed them no obedience—that the whole state of Missouri, could not take him . . . " (*Missouri Republican*, 3 September 1838).

37. Journal History, 6 August 1838.

No arrests were made at Diahman. Non-Mormon accounts report that the Daviess sheriff, intimidated by Wight's threats, dared not serve the writs against the alleged Mormon offenders. Mormon accounts state that Daviess officials issued the writs primarily to stir up anti-Mormon excitement, and so made no serious attempt to deliver them. Upon returning to Richmond, the Ray County committee reported that Wight had threatened local officials and refused to be tried. [38]

To allay the increasing excitement, Josiah Morin accompanied the Daviess sheriff to Far West to issue the writ against Joseph Smith. The Prophet informed them he was willing to be tried, but not by Daviess County citizens—and herein lay the reason why Smith and Wight refused to be taken by Daviess officials. Sterling Price and Edgar Flory, Chariton residents who investigated the controversy, reported:

> Messrs. Smith and Wight say that they have at all times been willing to give themselves up to an officer, to administer law, but not willing to be taken by a mob who were threatening their lives daily, and who were endeavoring to drive them from the county . . . .[39]

Smith and Wight refused to be tried in Daviess County because they believed they would receive little justice from a "mob court." Although the Prophet agreed to trial in Caldwell County, this concession proved unsatisfactory to Missourians, who believed that no Mormon judge or jury would convict him. Daviess officials, however, did not have the authority to arrest Smith in Caldwell and bring him to Daviess for trial. This momentary stand-off between Smith and Daviess officials prompted the *Western Star* to call for the state legislature to repeal the law organizing Caldwell County so that the Mormons could be brought under effective civil control. [40]

38. The report of the Ray committee was published in the *Southern Advocate*, 8 September 1838; and the *Missouri Republican*, 3 September 1838. For evidence from Mormon dissenters that the Mormons resisted the law, see Corrill, *A Brief History*, p. 34; Swartzell, *Mormonism Exposed*, p. 32; *Document*, p. 123, testimony of W. W. Phelps. For claims that the Mormons did not resist the law, see Robinson, "Scriptory Book," pp. 70–71; Vinson Knight to William Cooper, 3 February 1839; and George Albert Smith, "History," n.p.

39. *Niles' National Register* (Baltimore), 13 October 1838, Sterling Price and Edgar Flory, Letter to the citizens of Chariton, 10 September 1838.

40. As reprinted in the *Southern Advocate*, 8 September 1838.

The Mormons, believing that Smith and Wight had done nothing wrong, viewed these efforts to arrest their leaders as persecution. If the Missourians were so intent upon enforcing the law, the Mormons reasoned, why did they not suppress the armed bands that were then threatening the Saints at DeWitt? To some extent the legal action against the Mormon leaders was apparently carried out to hinder their efforts to establish settlements in Daviess County. Some of those pressing hardest for prosecution also wanted the Saints to leave the county, and their reports often contained highly exaggerated claims regarding the Mormons' activities and intentions.[41] Mormon resistance to arrest played into their hands. The Saints' belligerence and seeming disregard for the law increased fear and suspicion among the moderate Daviess settlers, who then joined in the appeals to the citizens of neighboring counties to help bring the Mormon offenders to justice.

The continual reports of Mormon lawlessness and the pleas for assistance from the citizens of both Carroll and Daviess counties finally stimulated action in the neighboring counties. In mid-August 1838 about two hundred men reportedly gathered in Livingston County and threatened to march on Diahman. At a meeting on 21 August in Saline County the citizens resolved to assist the Carroll settlers in expelling the Mormons from DeWitt. Near the end of the month citizens in Howard County also decided to send aid. Jackson, Chariton, Ray, and other nearby counties held, or would soon hold, similar meetings, though some resolved to investigate the disturbances before sending aid. As in Carroll County, the settlers from these other counties organized committees of vigilance, published the proceedings of their meetings, and acted with the propriety and restraint that seemed to legitimize their extralegal activities. A report circulated that a reward of three thousand dollars was offered for the head of Joseph Smith. The excitement continued

41. For example, a letter from Hiram Comstock, written 12 August and sent to the citizens of Carroll County, reported that the Mormons had overrun Daviess County, destroyed crops, threatened the lives of prominent citizens, threatened to attack Jackson County, and were "fortifying for a siege" in Far West. Comstock also reported that the citizens of Daviess County had sent representatives to Clay, Ray, Jackson, and Lafayette counties, but it was "seriously believed" that the Mormons had captured and killed the men (*Missouri Argus*, 6 September 1838).

throughout August and into September as rumors of violence abounded. [42]

At this time, suspicious Indian activities along the border further disquieted the Missourians, who received reports that a number of tribes were meeting secretly in preparation for war. Additionally, in early September two Mormon dissenters, Nathan Marsh and John Sapp, signed statements claiming that Mormon leaders were stirring up the Indians. "I have heard Sidney Rigdon and Lyman Wight say, they had twelve men of their church among the Indians," wrote Sapp, "and that their object was to induce the Indians to join them (the said Mormons) in making war upon the Missourians." [43]   Marsh affirmed this claim, adding, "It was a very common source of rejoicing among all classes [of Mormons] . . . that the time had arrived when all the wicked should be destroyed from the face of the earth, and that the Indians should be the principal means by which this object should be accomplished." [44]   Although it was true that some Mormons believed the Indians would serve as God's agents in destroying their enemies in Missouri, no evidence exists to support the claims by Marsh and Sapp that Mormon leaders actively sought a military alliance with local Indian tribes. [45]

The Missourians expected a battle with both Mormons and Indians. E. A. Lampkin, writing on 8 September from Carrollton, where Sapp signed his affidavit, described the predominant outlook of Carroll settlers:

There is still a good deal of excitement with the people of Carrol & Davis Counties, and the Mormons of Caldwell Cty. there are strong aprehensions also of hostilities by the Indians from the cherokees having built a large council house and inviting all the other tribes,

---

42. *Southern Advocate,* 8 and 29 September 1838; *Missouri Republican,* 6 September 1838; *Missouri Argus,* 6 and 13 September 1838; Robinson, "Scriptory Book," pp. 80–81; and Swartzell, *Mormonism Exposed,* p. 36.

43. *Document,* p. 17, John Sapp, affidavit, 4 September 1838.

44. Ibid., p. 16, Daniel Ashby, James Keyte, and Sterling Price to Governor Boggs, 1 September 1838, contains the statement by Nathan Marsh.

45. For descriptions of and references to Mormon beliefs concerning the role of the Indians in destroying the wicked, see Elizabeth Barlow, Letter, 24 February 1839. Typescript, LDS Archives; Blackburn, "Diary," p. 2: Roberts, "Introduction," *HC* 3:xliii; and *Doctrine and Covenants,* 87:5, "Revelation and Prophesy on War, given through Joseph Smith the Prophet, December 25, 1832."

and holding secret consultations, it is generally thought that we shall have war with the Mormons & Indians both, meetings have been held in adopting measures upon the Mormon subject.[46]

Troops were put on the alert throughout the state. Writing from Franklin County in eastern Missouri, Eli Haigler informed his family:

These superstitious people called Mormons have become a terror in the Counties of Davis, Ralls [Ray] and Caldwell. They are about 1,500 strong and daily increasing. They have fortified themselves and are prepared for battle. It is expected that one or two tribes of Indians are about to join them and so measures are adopted to surpress them.[47]

Although the Indian hostilities never occurred, the fear persisted throughout the disturbances that the Mormons and Indians would unite in a war upon Missouri settlers.

The Marsh and Sapp statements evidenced a small but growing dissatisfaction among the Saints with the militant course of the Church. Many Mormons believed that their brethren were overreacting to the rumors of anti-Mormon violence. Some tried, unsuccessfully, to convince their leaders that the Missourians did not intend to organize mobs against them. They believed that the Mormons, by their strident and defiant rhetoric, by their aggressive invasion of Daviess County after the election battle, and by their refusal to submit to legal process, had provoked much of the anti-Mormon hostility. William Swartzell, a recent convert living at Diahman, decided to leave the Church when he perceived that the Mormons' activities would eventually bring them into conflict with the entire state of Missouri. "I concluded that I had been fed on such stuff long enough," Swartzell wrote in his diary, "the idea of such a band attacking a State which could call to its aid twenty-five other free and independent sovereignties, more densely populated than itself, was preposterous. God (thought I) can have no dealings with this people, who have been led away by imposters; and I, for

46. E. A. Lampkin to Maj. Thomas G. Bradford, 8 September 1838. Bradford Correspondence.
47. Eli Haigler to Parents, Sister, and Brothers, 19 September 1838. Published in the *Franklin County Tribune*, 24 March 1922.

one, will leave them to their fate."[48] Because of the oppressive influence of the Danites, many of those who objected either kept quiet or left the Church.

One who did not keep quiet was John Corrill. For many years he had played a leading role in Mormon affairs in Missouri, but he now found it difficult to sanction many of his church's policies. Mormon leaders noted his dissatisfaction. George W. Robinson, a Danite colonel and Joseph Smith's personal secretary, recorded in his journal on 31 August that "Br. Corrils conduct for some time past, has been verry unbecoming indeed especially [for] a man in whoom so much confidence has been placed."[49] Sidney Rigdon reportedly told Burr Riggs he "strongly suspected" that Corrill and others "were using their influence against the presidency of the church."[50] Corrill had earlier opposed the Danites' forcible expulsion of dissenters from Far West, and he now opposed their efforts to enforce orthodoxy among the Saints, especially in the practice of the new communitarian policies.

Joseph Smith's recent revelation on the Law of Consecration stated that God required faithful adherence to that law in order for the the Saints to establish a Zion in Missouri. Those who failed to observe the law, the revelation stated, "shall not be found worthy to abide among you."[51] The Danites sought to carry out God's word. According to Reed Peck, Sidney Rigdon told the Saints that all those who did not comply with the new law would be turned over to the Danites.[52] The journal account of George W. Robinson affirms that the Danite attempts to "cleanse the Church of every great evil" were linked with obedience to the Law of Consecration.[53] Corrill said the Danites centered most of their efforts on promoting the United Firms:

Shortly after the Danites became organized, they set out to enforce the law of consecration; but this did not amount to much. Then they undertook another plan, in which Doctor [Avard] was very officious and forward, viz.: to constitute large firms, so that every male member of the Church could become a member of the firm.[54]

48. *Mormonism Exposed*, p. 33.
49. "Scriptory Book," p. 74.
50. *Document*, p. 134, testimony of Burr Riggs.
51. *Doctrine and Covenants*, 119:5.
52. "Manuscript," p. 8.
53. "Scriptory Book," p. 61.
54. *A Brief History*, p. 46. Avard's role in promoting Mormon communitarian

There is no evidence that any Mormons were punished for refusing to join the United Firms; most Saints willingly participated in what they believed were divinely inspired programs to eliminate poverty and promote equality. Corrill reported that Smith said each person could decide for himself whether to join. But those who did not participate objected to the "great exertions" used by Avard and others to persuade them to join, which, despite the Prophet's assurances, they found oppressive.

George A. Smith, ca. 1853: along with his father, John Smith, George helped build the Mormon town of Diahman. Courtesy LDS Historical Department.

In late August John Corrill told some Mormons who had newly arrived in Far West that he did not think the Mormons were duty bound to join the United Firms and "he had no confidence in the revelation that required it." [55] Smith and Rigdon, upon hearing of this remark, reprimanded Corrill for making such expressions in the presence of brethren "who might perhaps be weak in the faith." [56] "If you tell about the streets again that you do not believe this or that revelation I will walk on your neck Sir," the Prophet told Corrill as he

practices also received brief mention in "Elder John Brush, By Two Friends," *Autumn Leaves* (March 1891): 129, which states that in 1838 "Dr. Avard came among the Saints, preaching the 'common stock' theory . . . ."

55. Peck, "Manuscript," p. 13. An account of this incident is also found in Robinson, "Scriptory Book," pp. 74–75. Except where noted, these quotes are taken from Peck's account.

56. Robinson, "Scriptory Book," p. 74.

smacked his fists together to illustrate his point. Corrill replied that he would not yield his judgment to anything proposed by the Church, or by individuals in the Church, or by Joseph Smith, even when Smith purported to be speaking for God. Corrill said he was a republican; consequently, he would do, say, act, and believe what he pleased.

"If you do not act differently and show yourself approved you shall never be admitted into the Kingdom of Heaven," Smith responded. "I will stand at the entrance and oppose you myself and will keep you out if I have to take a fisty cuff in doing it."

"I may possibly get there first," Corrill replied.

While Corrill remained in Far West and tried to work out his differences with Mormon leaders, others who were similarly dissatisfied left the Mormon communities and informed their neighbors of the growing militant spirit among the Mormons. On 21 August, Swartzell spoke at a large anti-Mormon meeting in Richmond, where he revealed the practices and teachings of the Danite band.[57] In early September, Nathan Marsh and John Sapp signed statements, cited previously, detailing their objections to Mormonism. They both described the hostile nature of the Danites and reported that a growing intolerance among the Mormons made it difficult, even dangerous, for Mormons to criticize Joseph Smith and other Church leaders.

Much of what Sapp and Marsh said was exaggerated, such as their claims that the Mormons were planning to seize land from the Missourians and that they were building blockhouses and stirring up the Indians in preparation for war against their non-Mormon neighbors. Especially alarming were the dissenters' reports that the Danites had sworn allegiance to Joseph Smith and the Church above the laws of the state. As the disturbances progressed the Missourians came to believe, based upon the activities of the Mormons and upon the corroborative reports from Mormon dissenters, that the Danites would lie, steal, murder, or commit any crime necessary to advance the cause of the Church. Many of the dissenters' reports were published in local newspapers. Anxious citizens sent both Marsh's and Sapp's statements to Gov. Lilburn W. Boggs with

57. Swartzell, *Mormonism Exposed,* p. 36. Swartzell was a member of the Danite organization at Diahman.

pleas for immediate assistance.

Relations in Daviess County meanwhile remained tense. When George A. Smith and James Corbett went to Millport to grind corn, Robert Peniston told them he was no friend of the Mormons and he would not grind their corn. Following Peniston's short speech, the half-dozen men present at the mill stepped forward to enforce the threat. "We did not come for friendship, we came to mill," replied Smith. "Our horses go on to that wheel in their turn, [and] it makes no difference who says they shan't." [58]   Seeing that Smith intended to stand, the Missourians retired to a nearby grocery, where they continued to threaten Smith and Corbett.

The Mormons needed their grist, yet every trip to Millport risked a renewal of hostilities. William Swartzell reported that, after the Gallatin election battle, fellow Mormons warned him not to go to Millport "lest I should be killed." [59]   Most Mormons stayed away. Josiah Morin, playing the peacemaker, eventually sold a gristmill to Mormon friends at Diahman. [60]   The warring parties would no longer have to fight over turns at the mill wheel.

58. G. A. Smith, "History," n.p.

59. *Mormonism Exposed,* p. 31.

60. William Huntington, "Diaries of William Huntington," p. 5. Typescript, LDS Archives.

5
The Mormons Accused

The anti-Mormon sentiment then prevailing in upper Missouri alarmed Mormon leaders, who feared it would lead to a resumption of the persecution that drove the Saints from Jackson and Clay counties. They received reports in early September that vigilantes were collecting in eleven counties, allegedly to arrest

Gen. David R. Atchison: militia officer, representative to the state legislature, and lawyer for the Saints. Courtesy State Historical Society of Missouri, Columbia, Missouri.

Gen. Alexander W. Doniphan: lawyer and friend of the Saints. Courtesy State Historical Society of Missouri, Columbia, Missouri.

Joseph Smith and Lyman Wight. Despite the previous militant statements by Mormon leaders, their intentions were peaceful, and they now tried to avoid a conflict with Missouri settlers. On 2 September, Smith wrote to Circuit Court Judge Austin

A. King in Richmond, Ray County, and petitioned the judge
to prevent the outbreak of violence. The Prophet also asked
David R. Atchison and Alexander W. Doniphan to come to
Far West and serve as his lawyers, to advise him what to do
about the writs that had been issued against him. Atchison and
Doniphan, both longtime friends of the Saints, agreed to take
the case. [1]

David R. Atchison first became involved with the Mormons
during their troubles in Jackson County. Born in Kentucky in
1807, Atchison moved to Missouri in 1830 and was practicing
law in Liberty, Clay County, in 1833 when Mormon leaders
asked him to represent them. [2]   Despite threats from anti-
Mormons, Atchison agreed to take the Mormons' case and press
for their reinstatement in Jackson County. When the efforts
to secure redress through the courts failed, Atchison, as the
state representative from Clay, presented Mormon petitions to
the state legislature and spoke on their behalf. In 1836, when
the Mormon presence in Clay County threatened to provoke
a civil war, Atchison served on the committee that asked the
Mormons to leave the county. The Saints' reply, describing their
suffering and poverty, moved Atchison to tears, after which he
led the efforts of Clay citizens to secure Caldwell County for
the Mormons. [3]   About this time Atchison was elected major-
general of the Third Division in the state militia, making him
commander of all the troops in northwestern Missouri. William
F. Switzler, a contemporary of Atchison's, said that the general,
who was six feet two inches tall, was a man of imposing
presence. "He was a Democrat by nature and education with
profound sympathies for what Lincoln called 'The common
people,' " Switzler recalled. [4]

Alexander W. Doniphan also offered his services and friendship

1. G. W. Robinson, "Scriptory Book," pp. 77–78.

2. For biographical information about Atchison's early life, see William
E. Parrish, *David Rice Atchison of Missouri: Border Politician* (Columbia:
University of Missouri Press, 1961), pp. 1–15.

3. Thomas Baldwin Marsh, "History of Thomas Baldwin Marsh By Himself,"
Millennial Star 26 (18 June 1864): 391; *Times and Seasons* 1 (February
1840): 51; Peck, "Manuscript," p. 3; *HC* 1:424–25, Letter from David Atchison,
Alexander W. Doniphan, Amos Rees, and William Wood, 30 October 1833;
and *HC* 2:448–52, Minutes of a Public Meeting in Liberty, Missouri.

4. Quoted in Parrish, *Atchison*, p. 37.

to the Mormons. Born in Kentucky in 1808, Doniphan moved to Liberty in 1833 and opened a law office in the same building where Atchison worked.[5] Doniphan served with Atchison as one of the lawyers for the Mormons in 1833, and at a Clay meeting in 1834 he spoke out against the anti-Mormon vigilantes. Joseph Thorp, who was present at the meeting, reported that Doniphan defended "the right of citizen and individual liberty . . . and was opposed to Judge Lynch and mob violence; [and] was in favor of law and order . . . ."[6] Though he sympathized with the Mormons, Doniphan joined Atchison and other Clay citizens in asking the Mormons to leave their county to avoid civil strife. He also helped the Mormons find a new place to settle. After replacing Atchison in the state legislature in 1836, Doniphan introduced and guided through the House a bill organizing Caldwell County for the Saints. [7]   Doniphan also served as a brigadier-general in the state militia, commanding the First Brigade in General Atchison's Third Division. General Doniphan's character and talents matched his impressive six-foot-four-inch frame; since coming to western Missouri he had gained a reputation as one of the area's finest lawyers and leading citizens.

Before riding to Far West, General Atchison wrote to Joseph Smith, informing him that he had already spoken with Judge Black. The judge claimed the Mormons had threatened to drive the old settlers from Daviess County if they refused to sign a document pledging not to molest the Mormons. "Black states that he signed a obligation to that effect only because he feared a real danger to his family[;] he states that Dr. Avard is a mean man," Atchison wrote. "I will be in your society in two or three days at which time we may safely discuss this matter."[8]

An Appearance in Court

On 4 September, Joseph Smith met with Atchison and Doniphan and retained them as his legal counselors. The generals

5. Gregory Maynard, "Alexander William Doniphan: Man of Justice," *BYU Studies* 13 (Summer 1973): 462–63.

6. *Early Days in the West*, p. 80. See also *HC* 2:98.

7. Doniphan belonged to the Whig party; Atchison was a Democrat.

8. D. R. Atchison to Mr. Joseph Smith, 1 September 1838. Photocopy, LDS Archives.

believed the anti-Mormon sentiment could be assuaged if the Prophet and Lyman Wight (who was also present at this meeting) would volunteer to appear at a preliminary hearing in Daviess County for their alleged crimes. They informed the Mormon leaders that Circuit Judge Austin King had agreed to try the case, thus eliminating the possibility that Smith and Wight would be unfairly treated by a Daviess County judge. Smith agreed to the proposal but, because of the many threats against his life, wanted his troops to accompany him to the hearing. Atchison advised against this, but pledged to Smith that it would be "my life for yours" if trouble occurred.[9]

The hearing was held on 7 September in a grove of trees on John Raglin's farm, a half-mile from the Caldwell County line. A dozen Mormons, together with Atchison and Doniphan, accompanied Smith and Wight to the hearing. Despite Atchison's assurances, the Prophet still feared for his safety. He stationed a company of armed men just inside the Caldwell border, with orders to ride swiftly to the rescue if violence occurred. The Far West militia also stood ready to give assistance, and, as one further precaution, Joseph and Hyrum Smith hid their weapons nearby in the woods.

Attending the hearing was the Daviess County sheriff, William Morgan, who held writs for the arrest of other Mormons who had participated in the visit to Adam Black's home. George A. Smith, hoping to dispel rumors that the Mormons would not submit to local authorities, attempted to force the issue. "I went and shook hands with him and sat down at his feet on the ground[,] leaning against him for half an hour, giving him all possible chance to arrest me that could be desired," wrote the Prophet's cousin.[10] George, who was a large, stocky youth, could hardly be ignored; yet Sheriff Morgan made no attempt to serve his writ.

As the time neared for the hearing to begin, a large and unfriendly crowd of Daviess settlers gathered at Raglin's farm, cursing and threatening the Mormon defendants. Before trouble could begin, David Atchison stepped forward and, fingering

9. Philo Dibble, "Philo Dibble's Narrative," *Early Scenes in Church History: Eighth Book of the Faith-Promoting Series* (Salt Lake City: Juvenile Instructor Office, 1882), p. 88.

10. "History," n.p.

his gun, warned the men, "Hold on, boys, if you fire the first

Judge Austin A. King: presided over preliminary hearing of the alleged Mormon criminals in November 1838. From William Rufus Jackson, *Missouri Democracy: A History Of The Party And Its Representative Members—Past And Present*, 2 vols. (Chicago, St. Louis, and Indianapolis: S. J. Clarke Publishing Co., 1935).

gun there will not be one of you left." [11]   Atchison's threat reportedly checked the hostile crowd, and the trial proceeded without incident.

Circuit Court Judge Austin A. King presided at the hearing. The thirty-five-year-old King, though relatively young, was well known throughout western Missouri. He had served two terms as the representative to the state legislature from Boone County and became the circuit court judge shortly after moving to Ray County in 1836. [12]   Peter H. Burnett, a local attorney, described King as a very serious, religious man, not generally given to joviality, but respected for his legal knowledge and conduct of the court. [13]   Judge King was fully aware of the

11. Dibble, "Narrative," p. 89.

12. Floyd C. Shoemaker, *Missouri Day by Day*, 2 vols. (Jefferson City, Mo.: Mid-State Printing Co., 1943), 2:191.

13. *Recollections*, pp. 79–80.

history of Mormon problems in Missouri: his brother-in-law had been killed five years previously in a skirmish with the Mormons in Jackson County. How this affected King's view of the Mormons and his judgment at the hearing cannot be determined. Though he may not have liked the Mormons, it is doubtful that this sober-minded judge sympathized with the settlers who were then threatening the decorum of his court.

Col. Sterling Price: member of a Chariton County committee that investigated the disturbances and published favorable reports of the Mormons. From *Harper's Weekly*, 12 October 1861.

William P. Peniston, the man who had incited the Gallatin election riot, prosecuted the case for the state. Adam Black appeared as Peniston's only witness. Black's testimony emphasized what he perceived as the threatening tone and nature of the Mormons' visit to his home. He had refused to sign the document pledging to obey the law because he believed his oath as a county judge and the laws of the country to be sufficiently binding on him. Black admitted that Smith said the Mormons would not force him to sign the document; but the overwhelming number of Mormon soldiers, their expressions of hostility toward him and other local citizens, and Avard's threats persuaded him that his life was in danger. He had, in effect, been forced to sign a statement to satisfy the Mormons.[14]

Three Danite leaders, Dimick B. Huntington, Gideon Carter, and George W. Robinson, and one non-Mormon resident of Far West, Adam Lightner, testified for the defense. They argued that the Mormon visits to Black's home had been more cordial and less threatening than Black's depiction of the incident. They claimed that Smith clearly stated that Black would not be forced to sign the statement and that Smith requested it as a favor in order to show his people that the law would be enforced in Daviess County, thereby allaying the excitement caused by the recent election battle in Gallatin.

The Mormon testimony was convincing. The *Liberty Western Star* reported that the evidence proved that the affidavits signed by Black and other citizens, which described the Mormons' alleged lawless intentions, were completely false.[15] Judge King, however, concluded that sufficient evidence existed to warrant further investigation, and ordered the defendants to stand trial for a misdemeanor at the next examination of the grand jury.[16] George Robinson claimed that insufficient evidence was presented to incriminate the men, but King bound them over "to pacify as much as possible the feelings of the mo[b]bers."[17] Smith and Wight submitted to the verdict without protest, but they believed, as did most Mormons, that they were being unjustly persecuted for defending their rights in Daviess County. They regarded King's decision as evidence that they would not receive justice from local government officials.

Continued Unrest

Although dissatisfied with the hearing's result, Mormon

14. No record of the court testimony exists, but Adam Black's testimony at a later hearing, held 18 September 1838, was probably much the same as the testimony he gave at the 7 September hearing. See *Document*, pp. 159–63.

15. Reprinted in the *Missouri Republican*, 22 September 1838; and the *Missouri Argus*, 27 September 1838.

16. *Document*, p. 158. There is no record of the specific charge against the defendants. Joseph Smith, Lyman Wight, and a number of others were later indicted for riot as a consequence of their visit to Black's home.

17. "Scriptory Book," p. 80. Robinson asserted that Black "contrived to swear to a great ma[n]y things that never had an exist[ence]." Robinson also said that he was one of the defendants at the hearing, but there is no mention of this in the court records.

leaders hoped they had demonstrated their willingness to obey the law. At least two counties had sent representatives to investigate the disturbances. Col. Sterling Price and Edgar Flory, from Chariton, attended the 7 September hearing in Daviess and then went with the Mormons to Far West, where they met with the First Presidency and General Atchison. As a result of their investigation, Price and Flory wrote a lengthy letter to the citizens of Chariton, informing them that the activities and intentions of the Mormons had been misrepresented. Their letter implied that Daviess citizens had instigated the legal action against Mormon leaders in order to stir up excitement against them. "There were great fears manifested by the citizens of Daviess, that if the Mormons gave themselves up to be tried by the law it would allay the difficulty," they wrote.[18] Their letter, which was subsequently published in the *Columbia Patriot*, included an affidavit signed by Smith and Rigdon:

> We hereby certify that we have learned that a Mr. Nathan Marsh has certified that the people some time called Mormons have ingratiated themselves with the Indians, for the purpose of getting the Indians to commit depredations upon the people of this state, which certificate of Marsh (as represented to us) is utterly false. We have never had any communication with the Indians on any subject; and we, and all the Mormon church, as we believe, entertain the same feelings and fears towards the Indians that are entertained by other citizens of this state. We are friendly to the constitution and laws of this state and of the United States, and wish to see them enforced.[19]

Colonel Price, apparently convinced that he had been misinformed regarding Mormon intentions, also sought to dispel rumors linking the Mormons with abolitionists, a charge that had followed the Saints from Jackson and Clay counties. In

---

18. As published in the *Niles' National Register*, 13 October 1838. Robinson, "Scriptory Book," pp. 80–81, also contains a description of the visit to Far West by Price and Flory.

19. *Niles' National Register*, 13 October 1838, Joseph Smith and Sidney Rigdon, affidavit, 8 September 1838. It is interesting to note that Price had originally helped to publicize Nathan Marsh's statement—it was published in the *Booneslick Democrat* and then reprinted in the *Commercial Advertiser* on 18 September 1838—and sent a copy of the statement to the governor. *Document*, pp. 15–16, Daniel Ashby, James Keyte, and Sterling Price to Governor Boggs, 1 September 1838.

a private letter he informed a friend that the Gallatin disturbances resulted solely from a political dispute between Mormon
and non-Mormon settlers: ". . . there was nothing thought
about raising the Indians, about enlisting the Negroes or about
abolitionism." [20]

Citizens from Howard County, who received pleas for assistance from both Carroll and Daviess counties, also sent a
delegation to investigate the conflict. A member of the committee, P. M. Jackson, reported upon return "that things do not
present a scene so very alarming as has been represented by
various reports from that quarter. Some of the leading Mormons
have intimated their willingness to submit themselves to the
legal authorities . . . ." [21]

These favorable reports failed to dispel the unrest. Vigilantes
from several counties had already resolved to act against the
Saints. Immediately following the hearing, Daviess citizens sent
out petitions reporting that the Mormons were in a state of open
rebellion. Newspapers reported that the Mormons had from
fifteen hundred to two thousand men under arms and were
expecting reinforcements from Canada. And Sheriff William
Morgan and his deputies claimed the Mormons at Diahman
continued to resist arrest for their alleged participation in the
visit to Judge Black's home. Acting upon these reports, vigilante
committees from nearby counties voted to aid their friends
against the "set of Fanatics called Mormons." [22]

Within one or two days after the trial, vigilantes operating
in Daviess, Clinton, and Livingston counties began to harass
Mormon settlers, demanding their arms, taking prisoners, and
ordering the Saints from their homes. In one instance, a gang
of fifteen men drove Asahel Lathrop from his home and took
possession of his farm, where they held Lathrop's wife and
children virtual prisoners for over a week. [23] Some of the

20. Col. Price, Letter, 8 September 1838. Petitions, U.S. Archives.
21. *Missouri Argus*, 13 September 1838.
22. *Southern Advocate*, 29 September 1838, Resolution of Jackson County
Citizens, 4 September 1838; *Missouri Republican*, 19 September 1838;
Document, pp. 18–19, Citizens of Daviess and Livingston counties to the
Governor, 12 September 1838; *Document*, pp. 21–22, Statement of William
Dryden, 15 September 1838; and *Western Emigrant* (Boonville, Mo.), 13
September 1838.
23. Lathrop, "Affidavit, 8 May 1839," and "Affidavit, 17 March 1840," LDS
Archives; and Rigdon, *Appeal*, p. 27. One of Lathrop's children died and

vigilantes apparently attempted to arrest Mormons suspected of having participated in the visit to Black's home, but the Mormons refused to submit to extralegal tactics. Many of the vigilantes wanted to drive the Saints from the county; rumors spread that they planned to attack Diahman. The non-Mormon settlers in Daviess, fearing they would be caught in the middle of a bitter conflict, began moving their families from the county. Most of the Daviess Saints fled to Diahman, where they gathered for protection under the leadership of Lyman Wight.

Impetuous, bold, and fiercely loyal to Joseph Smith, Wight personified the growing militant spirit in Mormonism. He had no love for the Missouri people, who had driven him from his homes in Jackson and Clay counties, and he regularly denounced them from the pulpit. William Swartzell reported that Wight, in a sermon, referred to his Missouri neighbors as "hypocrites, long-faced dupes, devils, infernal hob-goblins, and ghosts . . . [who] ought to be damned, and sent to hell, where they properly belonged."[24] Throughout the summer he boasted of what the Mormons would do if their enemies would not let them alone, almost inviting an attack. Now that vigilantes were threatening the Saints, he wanted to fight. David Osborn, a Mormon settler from the southern portion of Daviess County, reports that when the men arrived at Diahman, "Lyman [Wight] received us gladly, & made a short speech to us—told us not to be excited nor afraid—we know our cause is good—we are called on to defend our wives & children & our homes . . . eat drink & be merry for tomorrow we fight."[25] Wight, who held the rank of colonel in the state militia, rode a large brown horse with a bear skin on the saddle. He wore a red scarf, tied around his head Indian-style, had his shirt open and sleeves rolled up, and carried a large cutlass and guns by his side,

---

was buried by the Missourians while they occupied his home. His wife and other two children, who were also sick at that time, died shortly after their rescue by a company of Mormons.

24. *Mormonism Exposed*, p. 13. Benjamin F. Johnson, a young Mormon convert from Diahman, reported that after the hostilities began, Wight taught the Mormon soldiers "to pray for our enemies that God would damn them and give us power to kill them" (Zimmerman, *I Knew the Prophets*, p. 27; Johnson's statement edited for clarity). See p. 59 above for Wight's own statement regarding the citizens of Daviess County.

25. "Autobiography," p. 31. Photocopy, LDS Archives.

his rough demeanor and cool leadership infusing his troops with confidence. "His manner of address struck terror to his enemies," wrote John D. Lee, "while it charged his brethren with enthusiastic zeal and forced them to believe they were invincible and bullet proof."[26] The Mormons organized a makeshift militia, sent out spies and picket guards, and set up a communication network with Far West in preparation for a siege at Diahman.

While the Mormons and Missourians prepared for battle in Daviess County, Ray County citizens contrived to send public arms and ammunition to the anti-Mormons in Daviess. On 9 September, William McHaney and Allan Miller, of Daviess, and John B. Comer, from Ray, secured forty-five rifles from the public arsenal in Richmond—apparently with the approval of the captain of the local militia—and attempted to transport the guns unobserved through Caldwell into Daviess County. The Mormons received word of their plan, intercepted the men, and took them to Far West, where a local judge ordered them to stand trial for running guns to the vigilantes. The Mormons confiscated the rifles and distributed them among their own troops. Meanwhile, a company of Mormons rode to Diahman to help defend the Saints.

The capture of the three Missourians increased suspicions on both sides. Many Missourians did not know that Comer and the others had been carrying weapons; they believed the Mormons had seized and imprisoned three innocent men. Others knew that the men were transporting guns and ammunition, but they believed the arms were being sent so that the citizens of Daviess County could defend themselves against Mormon aggressors. Missourians thus viewed the capture of these men and weapons, whatever the circumstances, as an outrageous violation of the law—further evidence of the Mormons' lawless intentions. The Mormons contended that their actions were legal, just, and necessary for their own protection. The abortive attempt to send arms to the vigilantes in Daviess County reinforced their belief that they were surrounded by enemies.

26. *Mormonism Unveiled*, p. 68. For other descriptions of Wight, see Corrill, *A Brief History*, p. 28; Levi Graybill, "Testimony of Levi Graybill," *Journal of History* 4 (January 1911): 106; Edward Stevenson, "The Life and History of Edward Stevenson," p. 32. Typescript, LDS Archives; and Lyman O. Littlefield, *Reminiscences of Latter-Day Saints* (Logan, Utah: The Journal Company, Printers, 1888), p. 65.

During these disturbances in Daviess and Caldwell counties, the settlers in Carroll continued to threaten the Mormons at DeWitt. On Wednesday, 12 September, a company of about sixty heavily armed men rode into DeWitt and ordered Mormon residents to leave. Vigilante leaders also advised their non-Mormon friends in the town to evacuate before they attacked. "We are determined that not one Mormon shall live in this county, be the issue what it may, and when we come to DeWitt, we want our friends out of it," they wrote. [27] Before the Missourians attacked, however, they received pleas for assistance from Daviess County, and so they decided to postpone their assault and assist their non-Mormon neighbors. Over one hundred fifty men, led by Dr. W. W. Austin, marched for Daviess County.

Circuit Court Judge Austin King was deluged with reports of disturbances and pleas for military intervention in Daviess County—from both Mormons and Missourians.[28] The Mormons claimed they were being harassed by unruly mobs; the Missourians contended that the Mormons refused to submit to local authority. Some Missourians did not take sides in the conflict, but merely requested that King intervene to prevent the outbreak of hostilities. Smith and Rigdon also wrote to King and informed him of the capture of the three Missourians and the weapons. On 10 September, Judge King wrote to Mormon leaders and advised them to release the prisoners. King then directed General Atchison to call out the state militia. Believing that citizens on both sides required protection, the judge ordered Atchison to:

Dispel the forces in Daviess, and all the assembled armed forces in Caldwell, and while there, cause those Mormons who refuse to give up, to surrender and be recognized, for it will not do to compromise the law with them. [29]

King's letter indicates that he believed lawlessness prevailed

27. Journal History, 10 September 1838, Citizens of Carroll to Mrs. Smith.
28. *Document*, pp. 28–29, Hon. A. A. King to General Atchison, 10 September 1838. See also ibid., p. 29, Citizens of Ray County to General Atchison; and *HC* 3:75–76.
29. *Document*, p. 28, Hon. A. A. King to General Atchison, 10 September 1838.

among both parties, but he considered the refusal of certain Mormons to obey local authorities to be the major cause of trouble. General Atchison promptly called out four hundred troops to march to Daviess County to restore order.

6
The Militia Intervenes

The Militia Act of 1792 required each state to maintain a militia to "execute the laws of the Union, suppress insurrections and repel invasions."[1] Despite the federal government's confidence in the quality of the state militias, these civilian military outfits proved to be poor substitutes for professionally trained soldiers. Historian Robert Reinders asserts that the state militias in nineteenth-century America represented "a staggeringly inept force."[2] The American tradition against large standing armies, and a democratic sense that the government should not use strong physical force against the people, limited Americans' trust in and dependence upon the military. Support for the militias was particularly weak in the western states, where settlers lacked the interest, money, or military tradition needed to maintain an effective militia. The general incompetence of the state militias contributed to the frequent occurrence of rioting and extralegal violence during the Jacksonian period, for there was no reliable peacekeeping force.[3]

The Missouri state troops, like their counterparts throughout the country, were poorly trained. Missouri laws required all able-bodied white males between the ages of eighteen and forty-five to enlist in the militia. The troops generally supplied their own arms and equipment, wore no uniforms or special clothing, and drilled four times a year, with drills (musters) lasting one or two days. The officers had little military experience and their men even less. Only a few of the higher officers had any real grasp of military tactics. The infrequent musters and frequent

1. Quoted in Robert Reinders, "Militia and Public Order in Nineteenth-Century America," *Journal of American Studies* 11 (April 1977): 84.
2. Ibid., p. 82.
3. See ibid., pp. 81–91; Grimsted, "Rioting in Its Jacksonian Setting," 394–96; and John C. Schneider, "Mob Violence and Public Disorder in the American City, 1830–1865" (Ph.D. diss., University of Minnesota, 1971), pp. 46–47.

changes in personnel made it difficult for the officers to impart their limited knowledge to their men, most of whom resented the compulsory militia training. Joseph Thorp, a member of General Doniphan's brigade from Clay County, reported that when the officers attempted to compete with each other in performing drills and maneuvers, their troops would often become tangled up.[4] The little training the troops did receive was mainly in anticipation of Indian uprisings. They were ill prepared to intervene in civil disturbances, and especially lacked the discipline required to handle the complex situations that would arise when they confronted their fellow citizens under arms.[5]

The Militia Intervenes

General Atchison called out two hundred troops from Clay County and another two hundred from Ray County to quell the disturbances in Daviess. Alexander W. Doniphan commanded the troops from Clay; Brig.-Gen. Hiram G. Parks led the troops from Ray. Atchison sent Doniphan to Caldwell County to release the three prisoners and to collect the captured weapons, while he rode to Ray to help Parks raise his troops. From Ray, Atchison and Parks planned to march directly to Daviess County, where they would meet Doniphan's brigade. The *Western Star* reported on 14 September that the citizens of northwestern Missouri "rely greatly upon the standing and influence of Generals Atchison and Doniphan, as well as other gentlemen who have gone out, to bring this matter to a peaceable termination."[6]

Doniphan marched to the Caldwell County line with his troops, but he continued to Far West accompanied only by his aide because he heard that the Mormons had fortified the town and would not allow the militia to enter. Doniphan encountered no resistance from the Mormons, who were eager for the Missouri troops to march to Daviess County to protect their fellow Saints from the vigilantes. Warren Foote reported

4. *Early Days in the West*, p. 65.
5. John G. Westover, "The Evolution of the Missouri Militia, 1804–1919" (Ph.D. diss., University of Missouri, 1948), provides general information on the Missouri state militia.
6. Reprinted in *Missouri Argus*, 27 September 1838.

that Doniphan "had a friendly chat with Joseph Smith and the leading men, and appeared to be very friendly to the 'mormons.' " [7]   Caldwell County officials released their non-Mormon prisoners into Doniphan's custody and gathered up the weapons, which had been distributed among the Mormon troops. Doniphan's men arrived in Far West the next day, after which he sent the weapons and John Comer, the prisoner from Ray, back to Ray County. The Clay troops, accompanied by the remaining prisoners, left early the next morning for Daviess County. Before leaving, Doniphan sent ahead Atchison's order requiring all unofficial troops to disperse.

The Carroll County vigilantes, led by Dr. W. W. Austin, arrived in Daviess County a day or two before the state militia. Strengthened by reinforcements from Livingston, Saline, and other nearby counties, Austin's forces swelled to almost three hundred. Neil Gilliam later rode in with a company of volunteers from the western counties. The vigilantes camped near Millport, about five miles south of Diahman, where they posted guards and prepared for battle. Many Daviess settlers who had not moved out of the county fled to Austin's camp for safety. The Mormons fortified and prepared for a siege at Diahman, where their forces, increased by reinforcements from Caldwell, numbered three or four hundred. Both groups sent out scouting parties and detained suspicious-looking travelers. The Missourians also killed and butchered Mormon cattle, and took one prisoner. Nearly the entire county east of the Grand River, except for Diahman and the vigilantes' camp, was deserted. [8]

After an all-day march of thirty-seven miles, General Doniphan's troops arrived at Austin's camp in the late afternoon of 14 September. Doniphan reported that the Missourians' professions were pacific but their actions were hostile. Although Atchison's order was read to Austin's troops, they refused to disband. Doniphan secured the release of the Mormon prisoner

7. "Autobiography," p. 29. Foote, a non-Mormon resident of Caldwell County, erroneously identified Doniphan as Atchison.

8. *Document*, pp. 24–26, General Doniphan to General Atchison, 15 September 1838; General Atchison to the Governor, 17 September 1838; and Rigdon, *Appeal*, p. 23. Reed Peck stated that, during the September disturbances, Mormon soldiers also killed the Missourians' livestock for their use ("Manuscript," p. 16). There is insufficient evidence, however, to substantiate this charge.

and then marched with two of his aides to Diahman.

Doniphan and his aides conferred with Lyman Wight, who, the general said, "professed entire willingness to disband and surrender up to me every one of the Mormons accused of crime."[9] Wight demanded, in return, that the troops commanded by Austin also disperse. Doniphan returned to his brigade and camped between the hostile forces.

Atchison arrived with the Ray County troops the next day, 15 September, and assumed command of the state militia, now numbering four hundred. The additional troops and Atchison's prestige prevented a clash between the two opposing forces. The Missourians, assured by Atchison that he would enforce the law in Daviess County, began slowly to disperse. Many of them refused to disband, however, until the alleged Mormon criminals were brought to trial. On 18 September a group of Mormons accused, of participating in the Black incident appeared at a preliminary hearing at Netherton Springs in Daviess County. [10]   Over one hundred Missourians, including many of the vigilantes, attended the hearing. Two local judges presided. According to George A. Smith, one of the defendants, the Missourians threatened the Mormons throughout the trial. "And had it not been for the stern vigilance of Generals Aitchison and Donophan," Smith wrote, "probably none of us would have left the ground alive . . . ."[11] Adam Black again testified for the state, after which a dozen Mormons were ordered, on a charge of riot, to appear at the next term of the circuit court. The hearing proved satisfactory to the Missourians, and General Atchison reported on 20 September that all hostile forces from outside Daviess County had returned to their homes. [12]

Following the hearing a Missourian named Riggs taunted George A. Smith and challenged him to reveal the Danite secrets. Smith, insulted by the taunts, agreed to do so if Riggs

9. *Document*, p. 25, General Doniphan to General Atchison, 15 September 1838.

10. Accounts of this hearing are given in George A. Smith, "History," n.p.; "History of Lyman Wight," *Millennial Star* 27 (22 July 1865): 456–57; and *Document*, pp. 159–63, which contains the minutes of the hearing and the testimony of Adam Black. Black was apparently the only person who testified.

11. G. A. Smith, "History," n.p.

12. *Document*, p. 27, General Atchison to the Governor, 20 September 1838; cf. Rigdon, *Appeal*, p. 26.

would first go through the Danite "passes and ceremonies." The Missourian eagerly consented. Smith related:

I then split a stick and put it upon his nose and told him to get upon his knees and I would put him through the signs. He did so to the great merriment of his comrades, but before I had time to fully confer the degrees upon him, one of his friends said, "You are a damned fool to let that God-damned Mormon impose on you in that way." [13]

Riggs turned around and discovered his comrades laughing at him. "The mob afterwards called him a Danite," Smith said.

General Atchison discharged the militia on 20 September, but he left behind one hundred men (two companies) under Brigadier-General Parks to insure that the peace was observed. Atchison, who reported regularly to Governor Boggs, explained:

I consider the insurrection for the present, at least, to be at an end, but from the state of feeling in the county of Daviess and the adjoining counties, it is very much to be feared it will break out again, and if so, without the interposition of the Commander-in-Chief [Boggs], the consequences will be awful. [14]

The general reported that the Mormons were acting on the defensive, but he believed if the Missourians attacked the Mormons in Daviess County, Mormon troops from nearby counties, estimated to number more than one thousand, would rush to the assistance of their brethren. A full-scale war would certainly erupt. Atchison described Lyman Wight, the Mormon commander at Diahman, as "a bold, brave, skillful, and . . . desperate man," adding:

I will further inform your Excellency, that the Mormons are well armed, most of them being equiped with a good rifle or musket, a brace of large belt pistols, and a broad sword, so that from their position, and their fanaticism, and their unalterable determination not to be driven, much blood will be spilt, and much suffering endured, if a blow is once struck, without the interposition of your Excellency. [15]

13. "History," n.p.
14. *Document*, p. 27, General Atchison to the Governor, 20 September 1838.
15. Ibid., pp. 27–28.

Atchison believed peace could not be maintained unless Boggs intervened.

Governor Boggs and the Mormon Disturbances

Boggs had been involved in conflicts with the Mormons on several previous occasions. Born in Lexington, Kentucky, in 1792, Boggs moved to Missouri shortly after the War of 1812 and resided in Independence, Jackson County, when the Mormons first settled there in 1831.[16]   A prominent merchant, Boggs served in the state senate from 1826 until 1832, when he became lieutenant-governor, and was elected governor of the state in 1836. The Mormons claimed that Boggs took an active part in the persecution that drove them from Jackson, an accusation he vehemently denied.[17]   The extent to which he participated in anti-Mormon activities is uncertain, but Boggs clearly shared the predominant prejudices against the Mormons. He openly referred to them as deluded people and his son, William Boggs, said that his father "could not endure the obnoxious doctrines promulgated by the Mormon leaders."[18]   Boggs speculated in large tracts of land in western Missouri, which brought him into conflict with the Mormons, who were also buying a considerable amount of land. When Alexander Doniphan initiated legislation in 1836 to organize Caldwell and Daviess counties for the Mormons, Boggs opposed the measure.[19]   He was not a friend of the Saints.

As governor of the state, Boggs did not seek confrontations with the Saints, nor did he attempt to disrupt their settlements in northwestern Missouri. Nevertheless, he was predisposed to believe the worst about this "deluded sect." Most of the early reports to the governor stated that the recent disturbances were

16. Joseph F. Gordon, "The Public Career of Lilburn W. Boggs" (Master's thesis, University of Missouri, 1949), pp. 2–31, on the early years of Governor Boggs.

17. Ibid., p. 93; and William M. Boggs, "A Short Biographical Sketch of Lilburn W. Boggs, By His Son," *Missouri Historical Review* 4 (January 1910): 107.

18. William M. Boggs, "Reminiscences of W. M. Boggs," p. 8, quoted in L. Dean Marriott, "Lilburn W. Boggs: Interaction with Mormons Following Their Expulsion from Missouri" (Ph.D. diss., Brigham Young University, 1979), p. 15.

19. Journal History, 8 January 1837, Alexander W. Doniphan to W. W. Phelps.

instigated by the Mormons. On 30 August 1838, after receiving reports of possible trouble with the Mormons and Indians in western Missouri, Boggs ordered twenty-eight hundred state troops to stand ready to quell the anticipated conflict.

Gov. Lilburn W. Boggs: issued his famous Extermination Order in October 1838 after receiving reports of Mormon lawlessness. From William Rufus Jackson, *Missouri Democracy: A History Of The Party And Its Representative Members—Past And Present*, 2 vols. (Chicago, St. Louis, and Indianapolis: S. J. Clarke Publishing Co., 1935).

When the disturbances broke out in Daviess County in early September, Judge King and General Atchison sent numerous reports of the growing feud to Governor Boggs, but because of the long distance to Jefferson City he did not receive their reports until several days after they were sent. After receiving letters from Atchison and King on 18 September, Boggs decided to mobilize several divisions of troops and march to the scene of trouble.[20] Atchison meanwhile dispersed the hostile Mormon and vigilante forces and brought the conflict to an apparent end. On 24 September, after riding to Boonville in preparation for the march to Daviess County, Governor Boggs received Atchison's letter of 20 September reporting that civil order had been restored. Upon receiving this letter Boggs directed that the troops called out by his 18 September order be discharged.[21] Much confusion had attended the governor's attempt to organize the militia—which the local press reported with considerable amusement—and in the end, the hasty mobilization of troops in Boonville proved costly and unnecessary.[22] Despite Atchison's request that he intervene in the conflict, Boggs returned to Jefferson City.

Unsettled Peace

Civil order had been restored in Daviess County: the Mormons agreed to obey local authorities, and Dr. Austin's troops disbanded and returned home. Yet neither the Mormons nor Daviess citizens were satisfied with the settlement. Mormon leaders complained that the militia arrived "after much delay" and then "made no attempt to disperse the mob."[23] Sidney Rigdon asserted that the Missouri generals should have arrested "this band of plunderers and murderers" and brought them to justice.[24] Mormon defendants claimed they were falsely accused and unfairly charged at the 18 September "mob court."[25]

20. Ibid., pp. 23–24, the Governor to General Atchison, 15 September 1838; the Governor to Captain Childs, 18 September 1838; and the Governor to General Lucas, 18 September 1838. See also the *Missouri Republican*, 24 and 25 September 1838, for Boggs's planned march to western Missouri.

21. *Document*, p. 31, the Governor to General Clark, 24 September 1838.

22. The *Missouri Republican*, 1 October 1838, reported that the state expended fifty to sixty thousand dollars to resolve the crisis in Daviess County. The newspaper also reported that there was "no scarcity of Generals [or] field and staff officers" at Boonville, and that Atchison's messenger was intercepted and detained as a Mormon spy before he was allowed to deliver the general's report (that the disturbances were at an end) to Governor Boggs.

23. *HC* 4:31, Joseph Smith, Sidney Rigdon, and Elias Higbee, The Saint's [*sic*] Petition to Congress, November 1839.

24. *Appeal*, p. 24.

25. George A. Smith, "History," n.p.; and "History of Lyman Wight," pp. 456–57.

Moreover, the Mormons asked for writs against the Missourians who had abused them, but the Daviess justices either refused their requests or released the accused after only superficial investigation. Mormon leaders also criticized General Doniphan and Judge King for releasing the three Missourians who had attempted to take guns to the vigilantes in Daviess. Rigdon stated that King's order releasing these men "put at defiance" the laws of the land.[26] Additionally, the rumor spread among the Mormons that Governor Boggs had raised three thousand troops and marched them to within sixty miles of Far West, but when he received word that the Missourians—and not the Mormons— were causing the disturbances, he marched back to Jefferson City.[27] Though untrue, this report was readily believed by the Saints, who knew of the governor's past animosity toward the Church. The Mormons' experiences in September 1838 added further evidence, from their perspective, that they would not receive protection or justice from government officials.

Instead of being relieved that the Saints had pledged to obey the law, many Missourians doubted their sincerity. They believed the Mormons had submitted to trial because of intimidation by General Atchison's troops. "Yes sir, when overawed by a military force, they professed a willingness to obey the law," Neil Gilliam remarked sarcastically concerning the Mormons' actions.[28] The Mormons seemed as belligerent as ever, their secret Danite organization continued to operate, and they could still rally over a thousand armed men to their support. The steady migration of Mormon settlers to Daviess County heightened fears. Many Daviess citizens did not believe the Mormon problem had been satisfactorily resolved.

A few days after Atchison returned home, Daviess settlers proposed that a committee meet with the Mormons at Diahman and offer either to buy or sell out to the Saints. The Mormons agreed and set the meeting for 26 September. General Parks reported on the day before the meeting that if no agreement

26. *Appeal*, p. 26.
27. Rockwood, "Journal," p. 3 (Rockwood recorded this report in his journal on 6 October 1838); and Parley P. Pratt, *History Of The Late Persecution Inflicted By The State Of Missouri Upon The Mormons* (Detroit: Dawson & Bates, Printers, 1839), p. 30.
28. *Missouri Argus*, 15 February 1839, speech by Cornelius Gilliam. See also McGee, *Story of the Grand River Country*, n.p.

was reached, the Daviess County men intended "to drive the Mormons with powder and lead" from the county. [29]

The Missourians did not want to sell out to the Mormons, nor did the Mormons desire to leave. All Mormon accounts of the meeting at Diahman report that the Missourians agreed to sell their claims. [30] The non-Mormons left no known accounts of this meeting, but the evidence suggests that many Daviess settlers did agree to sell. The Saints began immediately to buy the Missourians' farms and property. Some Mormons traded their livestock and wagons; others exchanged their property in nearby counties for farms in Daviess. Mormon leaders also sent representatives to the eastern and southern states to raise funds to buy out the Daviess settlers. Only two weeks previously the vigilantes had threatened to drive the Mormons from the county; it now appeared that the Saints would have the entire county to themselves. Albert P. Rockwood, a Mormon resident of Far West, wrote on 6 October concerning this providential turn of events:

. . . the mob have now retired from Davies County with shame and disgrace, great, very great fear rests on the Missourians, in Davis Co. they were selling their property verry low to the Brethren, in many cases they sell their Real Estate with their houses and crops on the ground, for less than the crop is worth, Davis County is now in the posession of the Brethren, Real Estate of the Brethren has risen while that of the Missourians has fallen 3/4 in 3 months thus the Lord is preparing the way for his children. [31]

Although the Mormons may have seen the hand of the Lord in these transactions, many Daviess citizens believed that, in essence, they were being driven from their homes. The Mormons were moving in at such an alarming rate that the Missourians

29. *Document*, p. 33, General Parks to the Governor, 25 September 1838.
30. See George A. Smith, "History," n.p.; Rockwood, "Journal," p. 2; Owen, "Memorial," p. 3; Daniel D. McArthur, "Journal," pp. 13–14. Photocopy, BYU Special Collections; and Don Carlos Smith, "A Journal Kept By Don C. Smith While On A Mission With George A. Smith, His Cousin," published in Lucy Mack Smith, *Biographical Sketches of Joseph Smith the Prophet* (Lamoni, Iowa: Published by the Reorganized Church of Jesus Christ of Latter-Day Saints, 1912), p. 359.
31. "Journal," p. 2. Joseph Smith and Sidney Rigdon also estimated that the Missourians sold their land to the Saints for as little as one-fourth its value. See p. 36 above.

saw no alternative but to sell and move out.

Newspaper reports of the disturbances demonstrated their editors' desire for fairness and accuracy, but also revealed that facts and information were difficult to come by, especially for eastern Missouri newspapers, which were over two hundred miles from the conflict. Over a week after the vigilantes had dispersed, the *Missouri Argus* reported:

Many rumors are current in regard to the movements of these people in our western counties; but we apprehend that the excitement which has been created, or at least much of it, is without foundation.[32]

Consequently, the *Argus* called for toleration and restraint:

All liberal Americans will bitterly regret any violence towards the Mormons, if hereafter it should appear that public feeling has been inflamed against them, without any other cause than their attachment to a creed which they think it a duty to maintain.

Even newspapers close to the conflict had difficulty obtaining full information regarding the disturbances. "So many reports are in circulation relative to battles fought, and men on both sides being killed and captured, that it is hard to get at the truth," said the *Liberty Western Star*.[33] The truth was that no one had been killed. Still, newspapers printed whatever information they could get, including letters from local citizens, and tried to maintain neutrality. "So far as we have heard, all who went to the scene of troubles, concur in saying that both parties are in the wrong," the *Liberty Far West* reported at the conclusion of the September disturbances; ". . . no difficulty may be expected except it arises from the indiscretion of individuals belonging to each of the belligerents."[34]

At this time the sympathies of the Missouri generals lay clearly with the Mormons. In their reports of the disturbances, Generals Atchison and Doniphan both stated that the Mormons appeared to be acting on the defensive, while Austin's men, despite their claims to the contrary, acted aggressively.[35] Atchison condemned

32. 27 September 1838.
33. Reported in ibid.
34. Reported in the *Jeffersonian Republican*, 6 October 1838.
35. *Document*, pp. 24–28, General Doniphan to General Atchison, 15

the "exaggerated statements of designing or half crazy men" who reported that the Mormons were resisting the law.[36] General Parks also believed the Saints' intentions were peaceful:

Whatever may have been the disposition of the people called Mormons, before our arrival here, since we have made our appearance they have shown no disposition to resist the laws, or of hostile intentions.
I deemed it my duty to visit their town in this county, and as soon as they saw the militia interpose between them and the people of this, and some of the adjoining counties who had assembled in arms, they went to work, abandoned their hostile attitude, and at this time peace and tranquility has every appearance of being restored . . . .
There has been so much prejudice and exaggeration concerned in this matter, that I found things on my arrival here, totally different from what I was prepared to expect.[37]

Although the militia generals did not excuse the militant activities of the Saints, they believed the Mormons' actions had been provoked by the lawless aggression of the vigilantes.

The Siege of DeWitt

Trouble was avoided in Daviess County, but when Austin's troops returned to Carroll County they immediately threatened the Mormons at DeWitt. On 20 September about one hundred fifty armed men rode into DeWitt and ordered the Mormons to leave the county within ten days. Col. George Hinkle, the Saints' military leader at DeWitt, informed the Missourians that they were prepared to fight. The Mormons, however, had no desire for a conflict. On 22 September they sent a petition to Governor Boggs, informing him that the Carroll vigilantes had threatened "to exterminate them, without regard to age or sex, and destroy their chattels, by throwing them in the river."[38]

September 1838; General Atchison to the Governor, 17 September 1838; and General Atchison to the Governor, 20 September 1838.
36. Ibid., p. 34, General Atchison to the Commander-in-Chief, 27 September 1838.
37. Ibid., p. 32, General Parks to the Governor, 25 September 1838.
38. Ibid., p. 30, A petition from certain Mormons to the Governor, 22 September 1838.

About two hundred Mormons now lived in DeWitt, where they had built a makeshift town of tents and wagons in the timbered bluff overlooking the Missouri River. Each new arrival of Mormon emigrants infuriated the Carroll vigilantes, who drilled daily in preparation for battle. "The Mormons increased daily," wrote Joseph Thorp, ". . . and the excitement among the citizens rose to such high pitch that it was hard for those of cooler heads to restrain the others from attacking the Mormon camp." [39]   Many settlers, anticipating civil strife, sold their farms and moved out. "Some of the citizens of Carroll have become so much alarmed as to sell their farms at less than half that they could have got for them one year ago, and a great many others intend leaving the county," E. A. Lampkin wrote from Carrollton on 23 September. [40]   The arrival of two hundred Saints from Canada in late September finally provoked an attack on the Mormon town.

On 1 October a company of one hundred fifty armed men marched on DeWitt, burning the home of one Mormon family and driving out settlers along the way. Both sides began shooting when vigilante scouting parties riding near the town encountered Mormon defenders, with intermittent firing continuing for several days. During the attacks, the Mormons ranged their wagons for a breastwork and placed their women and children in a large house with a white flag flying over the roof so it would not be fired upon. The Missourians attempted a brief assault on Thursday, 4 October, but were easily repulsed by seventy to eighty Mormon soldiers. Only one person, a non-Mormon, was wounded during the skirmishing. The Missourians, reluctant to make a serious attack, sealed off the town and appealed to nearby counties for assistance. "This [is] one of the cases of emergency in which the people ought to take the execution of justice in their own hands . . . ," Carroll citizens informed their neighbors. "We . . . shall expect your co-operation and assistance in expelling the fanatics, who are mostly aliens by birth, and aliens in principle from the county.

39. *Early Days in the West*, p. 84.
40. E. A. Lampkin to Maj. T. G. Bradford, 23 September 1838. Bradford Correspondence. When hostilities finally broke out, Lampkin wrote to Bradford that he and other settlers believed that "Carroll is ruined for some years to come" (14 October 1838).

We must be enemies to the common enemies of our laws, religion and country." [41]

Volunteers poured into the vigilante camp. The recent disturbances in Daviess County and the reports of continued Mormon lawlessness and rebellion had convinced many settlers that the Mormons were a criminal class of people. Some of those who had previously opposed the anti-Mormon violence now rushed to assist their neighbors. Reinforcements from Howard, Clay, Livingston, Ray, Saline, and Jackson counties swelled the force to four or five hundred men. The Jackson volunteers brought a cannon. Dr. Austin relinquished his leadership to experienced military men, and the vigilantes organized into a regular militia battalion. The troops elected Col. Congreve Jackson of Howard County as brigadier-general; Ebenezer Price of Clay as colonel; Singleton Vaughn of Saline as lieutenant-colonel; and Sashel Woods, a Cumberland Presbyterian minister from Carroll, as major. Companies of men cut down and hewed timber for a battery; others prepared cartridges; and some cut up log chains, rod iron, and heavy nails for grape and cannister for their cannon. Carroll settlers living nearby provided food and supplies for the army.

Some counties again sent committees to investigate the disturbances. Representatives from Chariton County, after making a one-day investigation of the conflict, reported that the Carroll citizens were "waging a war of extermination" to drive the Mormons from the county. [42] They found the Mormons acting entirely on the defensive, begging for peace, and waiting for the civil authorities to intervene. William F. Dunnica, reporting for a committee from Howard County, confirmed these observations and added that the Mormons were determined to defend their town to the death. "It was our unanimous opinion," Dunnica wrote to the citizens of Howard County, "that if some force

41. *Document*, p. 40. "To the Citizens of Howard County, October 7, 1838." Information about the first days of the siege of DeWitt is found in Murdock, "Affidavit, January 10, 1840." Petitions, U.S. Archives; Smith Humphrey, "Affidavit, January 8, 1840." Petitions, U.S. Archives; *Document*, pp. 34–35, General Lucas to the Governor, 4 October 1838; *Missouri Republican*, 11 October 1838, William Dunnica letter, 7 October 1838; and *History of Carroll County*, pp. 251–53.

42. *Document*, p. 36, Report of the Committee of Chariton County, 5 October 1838.

sufficient to suppress them does not interpose immediately, there will be great slaughter, and many valuable lives lost— some of our first citizens have engaged in it. Our country is under great excitement in consequence of it, and there is no telling where it will end." [43]

The disturbances presented a troubling dilemma for many of the Saints at DeWitt. Some of the Mormons, having endured several months of abuse from the Carroll settlers, stood ready to fight eye-for-eye and tooth-for-tooth against the vigilantes. Other Mormons, especially those who had just arrived from Canada and who knew little about the long-developing conflict, were reluctant to turn so quickly to guns and violence. Zodak Judd described the situation at DeWitt:

This state of affairs was very trying to some of our sober, serious Christians that had been taught that it was wicked to fight; it almost rocked their faith in the Gospel; to take up arms and try to kill their fellow mortals was a new doctrine that some could hardly endure and it was reported some feigned sickness and stayed in their wagons, while on the contrary some of the roughest of the company that cared, seemingly nothing for religion, were always ready and even anxious to make battle with the mob . . . . [44]

Many of the DeWitt Saints probably reacted like Christopher Merkley, who arrived from Canada in late September. Merkley stated that he at first refused to bear arms because he was "rather religious," but after a week of fighting, in which he saw that the Missourians intended to drive the Mormons from their homes, he decided to take up arms with the others. [45] By week's end most of the Mormons at DeWitt had resolved to fight.

The Saints suffered terribly during the siege. With most of them having just arrived and living in tents and wagons, they lacked sufficient shelter and provisions. Though well protected in DeWitt, they could not safely venture outside the town to secure food or other supplies. Those who tried, even the non-Mormons, were detained or imprisoned, and upon release

43. *Missouri Republican*, 11 October 1838, William Dunnica letter, 7 October 1838.
44. "Autobiography of Zadok Knapp Judd," pp. 8–9. Typescript, LDS Archives.
45. *Biography of Christopher Merkley* (Salt Lake City: J. H. Parry & Company, 1887), p. 4.

were ordered to leave the county. Enos McHall, a non-Mormon resident of DeWitt, was held seven days in the Carrollton jail "on an accusation of being friendly to the Mormons." [46] In order to keep from starving, the Mormons butchered the Missourians' livestock that strayed near town. So desperate was their condition that the Mormons viewed the straying livestock as sent from God. "We were sustained as the children of Israel in the desert, only by different animals," Sidney Rigdon wrote, "they by quails, and we by cattle and hogs, which came walking into the camp." [47] Reinforcements from Far West, which included Joseph Smith and Sidney Rigdon, bolstered momentarily the Saints' spirits; but the Missourians, seeing the Mormons fortifying the town, became more incensed and determined to drive them from the county.

The Mormons, though equally determined to repel the vigilantes, wanted to resolve the conflict peacefully. They appealed repeatedly to the civil authorities, requesting them to intervene to end the crisis. When the siege began, the Mormons had not yet heard from Governor Boggs regarding their 22 September petition. On 1 October, the Mormons sent Henry Root, a non-Mormon, to petition Judge King to disperse the Carroll army. [48] King sent Root directly to General Parks (General Atchison was away on business in Boonville and would not be back for several weeks), after which Parks ordered two companies of troops to march to Carroll. On 6 October, the Mormons dispatched another non-Mormon, A. C. Caldwell, to ride to Jefferson City to make a personal appeal to Governor Boggs for assistance. [49] He carried with him affidavits and statements describing the situation in Carroll.

The Ray County militia, commanded by General Parks, arrived in Carroll on 6 October, shortly before Mormon soldiers from

46. "Affidavit, January 6, 1840." Petitions, U.S. Archives. See also Thomas Hollingshead, "Affidavit, May 6, 1839." Petitions, LDS Archives; and Merkley, *Biography*, p. 5.

47. *HC* 3:452, Sidney Rigdon, affidavit, 1 July 1843.

48. John Taylor, *A Short Account of the Murders, Roberies, Burnings, Thefts, and Other Outrages Committed by the Mob and Militia of the State of Missouri Upon the Latter Day Saints* (Provo, Utah: Published by Martin Pamphlet Reprints, 1975; reprint of Springfield, 1839 pamphlet), p. 3; and *Document*, pp. 35–36, General Parks to General Atchison, 3 October 1838.

49. *HC* 3:153; Murdock, "Affidavit, January 10, 1840." Petitions, U.S. Archives.

Far West reinforced DeWitt. Parks ordered Col. Claude Jones of Carroll to raise three companies of soldiers to quell the vigilantes, but the Carroll troops refused to muster out.[50] Jones, in fact, had joined the vigilante army, as had probably most of his men. Upon arriving in Carroll, Parks found the hostile forces numbering several hundred, with both sides expecting reinforcements. Believing that his small force could do little to prevent or discourage a clash between such large armies, Parks sent for two companies from his brigade in Livingston County (which he doubted would come because of their anti-Mormon sympathies) and called upon General Doniphan to raise five companies in Clay. Parks sent a report of the situation to General Atchison in Boonville:

Should these troops [from Doniphan's brigade] arrive here in time, I hope to be able to prevent bloodshed. Nothing seems so much in demand here (to hear the Carroll county men talk,) as Mormon scalps—as yet they are scarce. I believe Hinkle, with his present force and position, will beat Austin with five hundred of his troops. The Mormons say they will die before they will be driven out, &c. As yet they have acted on the defensive as far as I can learn. It is my settled opinion, the Mormons will have no rest until they leave—whether they will, or not, time only can tell.[51]

Parks concluded his letter with a request that Governor Boggs come to Carroll. "He need not order out any forces," Parks wrote, "those already ordered by me I deem sufficient. You know a word from his Excellency would have more power to quell this affair than a regiment." [52]

Despite the relatively small size of his force, Parks might have halted the escalating hostilities if his own troops had not openly sympathized with the vigilantes. The Ray troops, like many Missourians, considered the Mormons to be the aggressors and the cause of the trouble. While the Mormons expected the militia to disperse the vigilantes, which is what Parks wanted to do, the Missouri troops wanted to disperse the unauthorized and "hostile" Mormon forces that were gathering

50. *Document*, p. 37, General Parks to General Atchison, 7 October 1838.
51. Ibid.
52. Ibid., p. 38.

at DeWitt. The Ray troops, angry with the general's sympathetic attitude toward the Mormons, refused to follow his command. Acting without orders, they attempted on several occasions to prevent Mormon soldiers from reinforcing DeWitt. "The militia have been called out to suppress the mob, but I believe they intend helping to kill [the Mormons]," E. A. Lampkin wrote concerning the Ray troops. [53]   Parks's men became so rebellious that he finally decided he must withdraw them from the conflict to prevent them from joining the vigilante army. After staying only a few days in Carroll County (until perhaps 8 or 9 October), Parks marched his soldiers back to Richmond to wait for General Doniphan and his troops from Clay County.

Governor Boggs and the Surrender of DeWitt

Judge James Earickson and William F. Dunnica, sent from Howard County to investigate the disturbances, meanwhile attempted to effect a compromise between the warring parties. The officers and leading citizens from each of the counties consulted with Earickson and Dunnica and then proposed the following terms: the Mormons should move out of the county and pledge never to return, and they should pay for the citizens' cattle and hogs they killed during the siege. In return, the Missourians should pay the Mormons the original cost of their property, plus ten percent, and they should also pay the Saints' expenses moving in and out of the county.[54] Judge Earickson thought these terms were too stringent; the majority of the army opposed the offer as too liberal. The Mormons at first rejected the Missourians' proposal, but the next day they received news that destroyed their hopes of withstanding the vigilantes. A. C. Caldwell, the non-Mormon sent to appeal to Governor Boggs, returned to DeWitt on 9 October and reported that Boggs had refused to give assistance. According to Caldwell, the governor said "the quarrel was between the Mormons and the mob" and they must

53. E. A. Lampkin to Thomas G. Bradford, 14 October 1838. Bradford Correspondence. See also *Document*, p. 39, General Atchison to the Governor, 16 October 1838; and ibid., pp. 41–42, Captain Bogart to the Governor, 13 October 1838.
54. "History of Carroll County," p. 13; and *Missouri Republican*, 11 October 1838, Dunnica letter, 7 October 1838.

fight it out themselves. [55]

Governor Boggs later denied making this statement. He also insisted that local militia officers had been fully authorized to restore order and preserve the peace.[56] The *Missouri Republican* reported that Boggs told the Mormons "that already the State had been put to a great deal of expense on account of these difficulties, and that he could see no cause to interpose . . . ."[57] The governor may have also been thinking of his embarrassment when he called out and then immediately withdrew three thousand troops in September. If he ordered another march to Carroll, he risked further waste of government time and expense, and he risked additional embarrassment, for the local militia might again resolve the conflict before the soldiers arrived. He perhaps considered riding to Carroll without his troops; both Atchison and Parks had requested that he come. But even if Boggs could dissuade the vigilantes from their violent course, he would be taking an extremely unpopular stand that would cost him many votes in western Missouri. Politically, it would be wiser to allow local officials to have responsibility for the difficult task—they had successfully resolved the crisis in Daviess County. The governor probably told A. C. Caldwell that the Mormons should rely on local officials to quell the disturbances. By the time Boggs's message reached the Saints in DeWitt, however, the state militia had withdrawn from the conflict, and his reply left the Mormons and vigilantes to fight it out themselves.

Judge Earickson returned to DeWitt on 10 October to warn the Mormons that the Missourians were preparing to attack. The judge emphasized to Mormon leaders the serious danger they faced, warning that if one Missourian was killed, hundreds would rush to avenge the death. The Mormons, he said, would be driven from the state "by the power of an enraged people."[58] Henry Root and David Thomas, the two men who had invited the Saints to settle in DeWitt, also attempted to persuade them

55. *HC* 3:157; Owen, "Memorial," p. 3; James M. Henderson, "Affidavit, January 6, 1840." Petitions, U.S. Archives; and numerous other Mormon sources report the alleged reply of the governor.

56. Corrill, *A Brief History*, pp. 35–36; and *Document*, p. 14, the Governor to the General Assembly, 5 December 1838.

57. 9 November 1838.

58. "History of Carroll County," p. 13.

to surrender. [59]   Thomas said he had received assurances that the Mormons would not be harmed, and they would be paid for all their losses. Some of the more militant Saints still wanted to fight, but George Hinkle, who had previously declared that he would rather die than be driven from the town, saw the hopelessness of their position. Without support from state or local officials, and especially without the protection of the militia, the Mormons could not hope to defend the town. Hinkle believed his people had suffered enough. Just as the vigilante troops prepared to advance, Judge Earickson returned to their headquarters with the message that the Mormons had agreed to surrender.

The Mormons and Missourians spent most of the day making arrangements for the surrender. [60]   Committees representing each side assessed the value of the Mormons' property and coordinated efforts for the safe removal of the Saints. Because they had invited the Mormons to settle in DeWitt, Henry Root and David Thomas were also required to leave the county. [61] The Mormons, still suffering from lack of adequate provisions and shelter, left DeWitt on Thursday afternoon, 11 October. During the first night at least one Mormon, weakened by the two-week siege, died of exposure, and a woman named Jenson died while giving birth. [62]   Several young children would later succumb to illnesses contracted during the ordeal. Some DeWitt Saints moved to Caldwell County, others went to Daviess. Tired, weak, and discouraged, they marched wearily to their new homes. Although the Mormons later sold their town lots back to the Missourians, they were never paid for losses incurred during the siege.

59. Rigdon, *Appeal*, p. 30.

60. For a description of the arrangements presented here, see Rigdon, *Appeal*, p. 30; "History of Carroll County," p. 13; *Missouri Republican*, 18 October 1838, William Dunnica letter, 12 October 1838; and *Missouri Republican*, 1 November 1838.

61. Root went with the Saints to Quincy, Illinois, where he became a prominent banker. He also signed an affidavit describing the mistreatment of Mormons in DeWitt. *HC* 4:62–63.

62. There are many sources documenting these two deaths. Some Mormon leaders also reported that several other persons died from starvation, and that some were killed by the vigilantes during the siege (e.g., Rigdon, *Appeal*, p. 30; Pratt, *Autobiography*, p. 175; and *HC* 3:407, Hyrum Smith, affidavit, 1 July 1843). No substantial evidence has been found to verify these claims.

The Missourians exulted in their victory. Triumphant Carroll citizens pledged to assist any county that had assisted them if they were needed to expel the Saints. Members of the Carroll army now turned their attention to Daviess County. It angered them to see many of the DeWitt Saints—Canadians—moving to Daviess, where Mormons appeared to be forcing settlers to sell and move out. Some Missourians contended that the Mormons were violating their agreement not to settle outside of Caldwell County. Spurred on by their success in Carroll, vigilante leaders decided to march to Daviess and restore the citizens to their homes. "I am inclined to believe," William Dunnica wrote the day after the Mormons left DeWitt, "that the adjoining counties to Caldwell, will never be contented until they [the Mormons] leave the State." [63]

The Missourians believed they must act swiftly. A group of Daviess settlers told John D. Lee (not knowing he was Mormon) that unless the Mormons were driven out soon "they will be so strong that we cannot compel them to go, [and] unless we force them away, they will be so strong in a few years that they will rule the country as they please." [64] The approaching land sales focused additional attention on the county, because few of the Daviess Saints held title to their land. The Mormons, like their Missouri neighbors, were "squatting" on their claims, waiting to purchase the land from the government. The principal Mormon settlements in Daviess County, including Diahman, would become available for public purchase on 12 November. Sidney Rigdon claimed that, shortly after the Saints left DeWitt, Sashel Woods called his men together and told them, "if they could get the Mormons driven out, they could get all the lands entitled to pre-emptions." [65] The Carroll vigilantes hurried their preparations, hoping to reach Daviess and drive the Mormons from the county before they could make good their claims to the land.

63. *Missouri Republican*, 18 October 1838, Dunnica letter, 12 October 1838.

64. *Mormonism Unveiled*, p. 67.

65. *Appeal*, p. 31. Although a few of the Daviess County Saints qualified for preemption claims under the Preemption Act of 1838 (which required occupancy on the land at the time the act was passed, 22 June 1838), no Mormons filed claims. This seems odd, but studies of United States land records show that settlers did not generally use the preemption right after

Upon learning of the vigilantes' intentions, Doniphan and Parks organized their troops for a march to Daviess County to prevent hostilities. Atchison, still in Boonville, wrote to Governor Boggs and informed him of the continuing anti-Mormon violence. Atchison appealed to the governor either to visit the scene of conflict, issue a strong proclamation, or take some type of action to "put down this spirit of mobocracy."[66] The tone of the letter reveals an impatience, perhaps even a disgust, with the governor's seeming indifference, as if Atchison believed that Boggs's failure to act was encouraging the vigilantes to continue their course of lawlessness and violence. "The state of things which have existed in the counties of Daviess and Carroll for the last two months, has been, in a high degree, ruinous to the public, and disgraceful to the State," he wrote.[67] Only the strongest measures within the governor's power, Atchison contended, could now restore order.

1837, because most settlers felt confident of obtaining their claims at the public sale. Daviess County land records show that few non-Mormons filed preemption claims in 1838. See Paul W. Gates and Paul W. Swenson, *History of Public Land Law Development* (Washington, D.C.: U.S. Government Printing Office, 1968), pp. 234–46.

66. *Document*, p. 39, General Atchison to the Governor, 16 October 1838.
67. Ibid.

7

The Mormons Retaliate

The disturbances in Carroll had threatened to engulf the upper counties in conflict. The settlers from nearby counties, many of whom disapproved of the lawlessness of the vigilantes as much as they did the perceived fanaticism of the Mormons, received with great relief the news of the compromise in Carroll County. But the Saints did not view the settlement as a compromise: they had been forced to surrender. The Mormons were now firmly convinced that the judges, the militia generals, and the governor sympathized with the anti-Mormon vigilantes. When the Saints in Far West heard that the Carroll army was marching to Daviess County, Mormon leaders announced their intention to follow Governor Boggs's advice and fight the vigilantes themselves.

Joseph Smith now assumed leadership of the Mormon military operations. He was always the undisputed leader among Mormons; but previously he had accepted a lesser role in military matters, often stepping into the ranks and allowing Col. Lyman Wight and Col. George Hinkle, both commissioned officers in the state militia, to direct Mormon troops. In addition, religious and administrative duties had occupied Smith's time. During the several months of conflict, he had continued to call and ordain church officers, send out missionaries, preach sermons, and attend to the myriad duties that devolved on the Church president. But the anti-Mormon violence now threatened the entire Church in Missouri. Smith's revelations proclaimed that the Lord would establish Zion in Missouri; he intended to fight for their fulfillment. Shortly after Smith took command of the Mormon troops, Albert P. Rockwood proudly noted: "You may ask if the Prophet goes out with the Saints to Battle? I answer he is a Prophet to go before the people as in times of old . . . ."[1] Joseph Smith declared his determination

1. "Journal," p. 11.

"to put down the mob or die in the attemp[t]." [2]

On 14 and 15 October, Joseph Smith and Sidney Rigdon rallied the Mormons in Far West and called for them to fight in defense of their people in Daviess County. Several hundred Mormons gathered at the town square and listened as Smith and Rigdon vented their seething anger and frustration.[3] The Prophet reviewed the many occasions on which Missouri officials had failed to protect them: in Jackson County, Clay County, and now Carroll County, the Mormons had been driven from their homes. "Who is so big a fool as to cry the law! the law! when it is always administered against us and never in our favor?" Joseph Smith asked derisively. [4]   Sidney Rigdon denounced those Mormons who opposed their efforts to defend themselves, calling them "Oh Don't Men" because, instead of falling in the ranks, they stayed at home, crying "O dont! O dont! you are breaking the law you are bringing ruin on the society . . . ."[5] These people, he said, undermined the unity needed to withstand their enemies. Smith and Rigdon then called for volunteers to march to Daviess County. The Prophet proclaimed:

We will take our affairs into our own hands and manage for ourselves. We have applied to the Governor and he will do nothing for us, the militia of the county we have tried and they will do nothing, all are mob; the Governor is mob, the militia are mob, and the whole state is mob.

We have yielded to the mob in DeWitt and now they are preparing to strike a blow in Daviess, but I am determined that we will not give another foot and I care not how many come against us, ten or ten thousand. God will send his Angels to our deliverance and we can conquer ten thousand as easily as ten. [6]

2. Foote, "Autobiography," p. 30.

3. Descriptions of these speeches are found in Corrill, *A Brief History*, pp. 36–37; Peck, "Manuscript," pp. 18–20; *Document*, pp. 98–99, 110, 112, 115, 117, 122–23, testimonies of Sampson Avard, Morris Phelps, John Corrill, John Cleminson, Reed Peck, and W. W. Phelps; and Foote, "Autobiography," pp. 29–30. The information in Warren Foote's autobiography is extremely important because Foote, who later joined the Church, was a believer in Mormonism, and also because his autobiography was apparently written from notes he kept while he lived in Missouri.

4. Peck, "Manuscript," p. 18.

5. *Document*, p. 117, testimony of Reed Peck; and Peck, "Manuscript," p. 19.

6. Peck, "Manuscript," pp. 18–19 (this excerpt edited for clarity).

Smith also proposed that they confiscate the property of Mormons who refused to fight, to be used by those who did. Sidney Rigdon added that the dissenters should be put upon their horses with bayonets and pitchforks and forced to ride to Daviess with the Mormon army. The Prophet instructed the soldiers to live off the land—the livestock, crops, and property of the Missourians—while they battled their enemies in Daviess County. The Mormon men overwhelmingly supported these proposals. John Corrill, Reed Peck, and others who objected kept quiet and pretended to "take hold" with the rest, afraid of what punishment they might otherwise receive.[7]

The anticipated conflict allowed the Danites to expand their role among the Mormons. Sampson Avard called together his Danite captains and outlined their duties in the coming war:

My Brethren, as you have been chosen to be our leading men, our captains to rule over this last kingdom of Jesus Christ, who have been organized after the ancient order, I have called you here today to teach you and instruct you in the things that pertain to your duty and to show you what your privileges are and what they soon will be.

Know ye not brethren that it soon will be your privilege to take your respective companies and go out on a Scout on the borders of the settlements, and take to yourselves spoils of the goods of the ungodly Gentiles, for it is written "The riches of the Gentiles shall be consecrated to my people, the House of Israel;" thus waste away the Gentiles by robbing and plundering them of their property and in this way we will build up the Kingdom of God and roll forth the little stone that Daniel saw cut out of the Mountain without hands, until it shall fill the whole earth. For this is the very way

---

7. Corrill, *A Brief History*, p. 37; and Peck, "Manuscript," p. 20. There is no evidence that, in their speeches, either Smith or Rigdon referred to previous revelations in which the Prophet proclaimed that God would help the Saints withstand their enemies and establish Zion. Nevertheless, the Saints were undoubtedly aware that their planned defense had considerable scriptural support, including an 1833 revelation that stated God would justify the Saints' military efforts and give them power over their enemies if they were attacked a fourth time (*Doctrine and Covenants*, Section 98:23–32, "Revelation through Joseph Smith the Prophet, at Kirtland, Ohio, August 6, 1833"). The Saints' expulsion from DeWitt represented the third time they had been driven from their homes in Missouri, a fact noted by Albert Rockwood ("Journal," p. 12) and Abraham Palmer, who wrote concerning the matter: "We have been smitten twice, yes, three times and had borne it, but we said, we would bear it no longer without resistance" (Letter to Brother and Sister, 26 June 1839, in "Sketch of the Life of Patience Delila Pierce Palmer," p. 14. Typescript, LDS Archives).

that God destines to build up His Kingdom in the last days. [8]

Morris Phelps, a member of the Danites, later reported that the Danite officers rejected Avard's counsel. [9] The evidence suggests otherwise. Avard's instructions complemented the Prophet's instructions to Mormon soldiers that they live off their enemies. Moreover, the subsequent looting by the Mormon troops reveals that they saw nothing amiss in Avard's teachings.

On the night of 15 October, Mormon soldiers prepared to march to Daviess County. That evening General Doniphan rode through Far West with about sixty men. Doniphan had been ordered out a week earlier by General Parks, who requested that Doniphan bring his troops to Carroll County. The Mormons at DeWitt surrendered before Doniphan could raise the troops, but he now marched to Daviess to prevent hostilities there. Another company of men from Doniphan's brigade had passed through Far West the day before and was waiting for the general just outside the town. Doniphan spoke with Mormon leaders in Far West and confirmed the reports that the Carroll army was advancing toward Daviess County. He informed the Mormons that his troops were mutinous and would probably be of little help. After learning that the Mormons planned to march to Daviess, Doniphan advised them to go unarmed and in small groups because it was illegal for large bodies of armed men to pass from one county into another without proper authorization, which he could not give. The general instructed the Mormons to wait at Diahman until they received further orders or the militia arrived. [10]

The Mormons later tried to justify their activities in Daviess County by claiming that Doniphan ordered them to march to Daviess and disperse the vigilantes. The Mormons thus contended that they acted as legitimate state troops. [11] Although Doniphan probably advised the Mormons to fight in self-defense (he sympathized with their plight), these claims by

8. Phelps, "Reminiscences," p. 4.
9. Ibid.
10. *HC* 3:454–56, Rigdon, affidavit, 1 July 1843; and Phelps, "Reminiscences," p. 7.
11. See, e.g., *HC* 3:406, 425, 433, Hyrum Smith, Parley P. Pratt, and Brigham Young, affidavits, 1 July 1843.

Mormon leaders are misleading. First, the Mormons planned and organized the expedition before Doniphan arrived. Second, the Caldwell County militia did not belong to Doniphan's brigade. He did not have the authority—no one in Caldwell County had the authority—to order the Mormon troops to march to Daviess County. Third, the Mormon soldiers were not organized strictly into their state militia units. Finally, Doniphan did not order the raiding and plundering activities subsequently carried out by the Mormon soldiers. The evidence supports the statements of Sidney Rigdon and Morris Phelps, who reported that Doniphan instructed the Mormons to march unarmed to Daviess County and wait for further orders. Mormon leaders ignored his advice.

Doniphan passed through Far West and joined the troops camped outside of town. The Clay troops were supposed to continue on to Daviess County, where General Parks, then organizing his brigade in Richmond, would join them. But Doniphan found such a rebellious spirit among his men that he could not proceed; he reportedly described them as "damned rotten hearted." [12]   The following morning, 16 October, he marched his troops back to Clay County.

During the next two days over three hundred Mormon soldiers marched from Caldwell to Daviess County, bringing the total number of troops at Diahman to about five hundred. The Mormons, enraged by the treatment of their people at DeWitt and inspired by the fiery speeches of their leaders, resolved to drive out their enemies once and for all.

A severe snowstorm on 17 October, however, prevented the men from going out on patrol and threatened to dampen fighting spirits on both sides. "The snow and cold weather will be the best mediator of peace between the parties," said a grateful *Liberty Far West*, which reported eighteen inches of falling snow in thirty-six hours. "We believe they'll all take to their scrapers for home, and 'suspend' hostilities for the present at least." [13]   But the respite was short-lived. Mormon soldiers entertained themselves during the storm by staging

12. *HC* 3:369, Joseph Smith, "A Bill of Damages," 4 June 1839. Other Mormon sources also state that the militiamen harbored anti-Mormon sympathies and refused to march against the vigilantes. See Rigdon, *Appeal*, pp. 31–32; and Samuel Miles, "Affidavit, January 3, 1840." Petitions, U.S. Archives.

13. Reported in *Missouri Argus*, 1 November 1838.

snowball fights, organized by the Prophet to keep their spirits up; and on Thursday, 18 October, when a lighter snow began to fall, they prepared for battle. As the troops assembled on the Diahman square, Lyman Wight rode through the ranks, his sleeves rolled back despite the cold, exhorting his men to fight bravely against their Missouri enemies. "It would be only a breakfast spell to whip the Missourians," Wight declared. "Many of them will be drunk and if they come against us we will hew them down like old stumps." [14]

Mormon Depredations in Daviess County

Mormon apostle David W. Patten led a company of one hundred fifty men to the county seat of Gallatin, about seven miles south of Diahman, where fifteen to twenty Missourians were gathered at the local saloons. Mason Cope had warned the men that the Mormons were planning an attack, but "the boys laughed at him and told him that it was only [his] imagination," recalled Joseph McGee, who ran a store in Gallatin. [15]   Fortunately for the Missourians, they spotted the troops before the Mormons galloped into town, and all but three escaped; many of the men simply cut their horses' reins and left them hanging on the fence posts, such was their fright and desperation. The Mormon soldiers, finding themselves in possession of the town, looted the small shops, piling clothes, bedding, and other merchandise in the street, and then loaded the plunder on their horses and wagons to haul back to Diahman. Before leaving they set fire to the town. At Diahman young Oliver Huntington, whose brother Dimick rode with Patten's company, stood on Tower Hill and "saw the smoke rising towards Heaven." [16]

The Mormons dispatched similar scouting and raiding parties throughout Daviess and into nearby Clinton County. Lyman Wight led a company of about eighty men to Millport, but they found all the cabins in and around the town deserted. They encountered no enemy troops. After Wight's company

14. Graybill, "Testimony," p. 106; and Stevenson, "Life and History," p. 32.

15. McGee, "The Mormon War In Missouri," written 18 October 1891, published in *Daviess County Centennial Edition* (Gallatin, Mo.: Published by the Gallatin North Missourian, 1937).

16. "History," p. 31.

returned to Diahman, Mormon leaders sent back a group of men to retrieve the property from the empty Missourian homes. About one hundred men, led by Seymour Brunson, rode to Grindstone Forks, in Clinton County, where Col. Neil Gilliam was reportedly organizing a large vigilante force. Along the way Brunson's men drove Daviess settlers from their homes, plundered, and burned, but they found no army gathering against them in Grindstone. Some of the Mormon soldiers pretended to be vigilantes from Carroll and were given food, guns, and ammunition by a local settler. While these cavalry units searched the countryside for vigilantes, Jonathan Dunham led a company of about fifty foot soldiers foraging for food and pillaging abandoned cabins. Dunham's company also captured prisoners and drove suspected enemies from their homes, but their main responsibility was to gather provisions for the Mormon army. At the end of the day these companies returned to Diahman with cattle, hogs, and an abundance of property, but they had encountered no enemy troops.

Most Missourians were ill prepared for the Mormon attacks. Eight inches of snow lay on the ground and more was falling. The settlers often fled from their homes with nothing but the clothes they wore, and in some cases fled in their bare feet. After fleeing with her small children from Millport, Milford Donaho's wife gave birth prematurely to a child who reportedly suffered permanent damage as a result. Another woman with a four-day-old baby also fled from her home. A horrified Taylor family watched as Mormon soldiers plundered and burned their home because guns and ammunition were found hidden in the cornfields. The Mormons allowed the Taylors to keep just what they could carry, and only through the forceful intercession of Benjamin F. Johnson, a young Mormon soldier, was Mr. Taylor able to retain a horse for his pregnant wife and children to ride. [17]

17. The Mormon activities in Daviess County are well documented in the reports of Daviess citizens sent to Governor Boggs, in the reports of the militia generals sent to quell the alleged Mormon uprising, and in the testimony given at the Richmond hearing. See *Document*, pp. 42–46, 55–57, for sworn statements of Daviess citizens; ibid., pp. 67–68, 78–79, 87–88, for reports of Gen. John B. Clark and Gen. Robert Wilson on conditions in Daviess; and ibid., pp. 97–151, for the testimony at the Richmond hearing. In addition, loyal Mormon sources also provide information regarding the

Fear pervaded the Missourians' encounters with Mormon soldiers. Benjamin Johnson reported that when he captured Mr. Taylor,

I learned then something of the influence of fear upon the human heart; for as we put our hands upon his shoulders there was such a look of expectant death, and such a begging for his life and then to see a fine looking married man so filled by fear that as he sank upon the ground his bowels seemed to pour all their contents into his linen pantaloons and into his sockless shoes.[18]

Daniel McArthur, a member of Jonathan Dunham's company, reported that when the Mormon soldiers detained two Missourians traveling through the county, both men desperately pleaded their innocence, claiming they had never done anything against the Mormons. "A Scarter man then one of them was I never Saw," McArthur said.[19]

Some of the Missourians who were threatened or had their homes plundered and burned were actually friends of the Mormons. Jacob Stollings, a Gallatin merchant, had sold goods to the Saints on credit, to be paid for when their crops were harvested. When Captain Patten's company attacked Gallatin, they plundered and burned Stollings' store and confiscated his receipt books, which he never recovered.[20] Two others who befriended the Saints, Judge Josiah Morin and Solomon McBrier, were also threatened and driven from their homes.[21] McBrier, in fact, had his home burned by the Mormons. Conceivably,

―――――

burning and plundering that occurred. See Huntington, "History," pp. 31–33; Benjamin F. Johnson, *My Life's Review* (Independence, Mo.: Zion's Printing and Publishing Company, 1947), pp. 37–43; Foote, "Autobiography," p. 30; Nathan Tanner, "Journal of Nathan Tanner," p. 5. Typescript, LDS Archives; and David Lewis, "Excerpt From The Journal," p. 5.

18. "A Life Review," p. 32. Photocopy, LDS Archives.

19. "Journal," p. 16.

20. Hunt, *Mormonism*, p. 186. Stollings reportedly ransacked the Prophet's home after the surrender, apparently looking for his stolen books (*HC* 3:288). On 12 April 1839, Stollings wrote to Joseph Smith and promised to cancel all debts owed to him by the Mormons if they returned his books. Smith told Stollings that Sampson Avard might have the books (*HC* 3:316–17, 378–79).

21. Lee, *Mormonism Unveiled*, p. 72; and *Document*, pp. 52–53, Report of Messrs. Morehead, Thorton, and Gudgel. Judge Morin is referred to as a friend in several reminiscences of the Saints.

many others driven from Daviess County had also been friendly to or tolerant of the Saints.

The Mormons deposited most of their spoils in the bishop's storehouse at Diahman. Oliver B. Huntington, a teenage boy living at Diahman, and Benjamin F. Johnson, a member of the Mormon militia, both claimed that the decision to plunder the Missourians' food and possessions was prompted by the necessities of war. "It should not be supposed ... that we were common robbers because we took by reprisal that with which to keep from starvation our women and children," Johnson wrote. "Ours was a struggle for our lives and homes...."[22] The Mormon soldiers developed secret names for their stolen goods, perhaps so they would not have to admit directly to stealing. They referred to honey as "sweet oil," hogs as "bear," and cattle as "buffalo." In addition, they called the stolen goods "consecrated property"; many soldiers believed that they were not really stealing if they deposited their plunder in the common storehouse for the use of all the Saints. And the rumor spread among them, particularly among Danites under Sampson Avard's tutelage, that "the time had come when the 'riches of the Gentiles' should be consecrated to the Saints," thus fulfilling an 1831 revelation to Joseph Smith.[23] The Mormon soldiers believed their pillaging was divinely sanctioned.

Although the Mormon depredations in Daviess County are well detailed both by Mormon dissenters and by non-Mormon victims, many Mormons subsequently denied that their people committed any crimes, contending instead that Daviess settlers, in hopes of inciting the public against the Saints, set fire to their own homes and then reported that the Mormons had

22. *Life's Review*, pp. 42–43. See also Huntington, "History," p. 33. Warren Foote stated that "in order to sustain themselves, the mormons took their enemies corn, cattle, hogs &c according to the usages of war" ("Autobiography," p. 30).

23. *Document*, pp. 113, 115, 118, 128, 143, testimonies of James C. Owens, John Cleminson, Reed Peck, George Hinkle, and Porter Yale; Corrill, *A Brief History*, p. 38; and Peck, "Manuscript," p. 20. Joseph Smith's revelation is found in *A Book Of Commandments*, 44:32. The plundering activities engaged in by Mormon soldiers also fulfilled the biblical scripture from which the Danites took their original name, "Daughters of Zion": "Arise and thresh, O daughters of Zion: for I will make thine horn iron, and I will make thy hoofs brass: and thou shalt beat in pieces many people: and *I will consecrate their gain unto the Lord*, and their substance unto the Lord of the whole earth" (Micah 4:13; italics mine). See also p. 18 above.

done it. [24] However, evidence from the reminiscences of loyal Mormons (for example, Oliver Huntington and Benjamin Johnson, cited above) contradicts these claims and confirms the reports that the Mormons were driving settlers from their homes, plundering, and burning. Moreover, Mormon soldiers carried out these activities with the knowledge and approval of their leaders; the hogs, cattle, grain, and abundant spoils were deposited at Diahman in full view of all. No substantial evidence has been found to support the claim that the Missourians burned their own homes.

The desperate crimes committed by the Mormon soldiers can be attributed to several factors. Their militant activities and the belligerent speeches of their leaders during the summer and fall of 1838 had been leading them on a course of increasing lawlessness and violence. Pent-up hostility and frustration, fostered by years of persecution, lay waiting to explode. The Mormons' conviction that they were God's chosen people, that their righteous anger justified retaliation, and that their depredations were helping to build the Kingdom of God encouraged Mormon soldiers to commit crimes they normally would not have perpetrated. Their perception of all Missourians as "enemies" and "mobbers" led the Mormons to believe that their victims deserved their fate, that they had brought the wrath of God upon themselves. Once the Mormon soldiers had begun, many of them discovered that they enjoyed plundering and burning on behalf of the Lord. "It appeared to me also that the love of pillage grew upon them very fast," John Corrill observed. [25] "Men stole simply for the love of stealing," lamented John D. Lee. Necessity had prompted them to take up arms in self-defense; anger, frustration, fear, devotion to God, and love of plunder stimulated and sustained their acts of violence and crime.

Mormon depredations in Daviess County outraged local citizens. Angry mobs began to retaliate that night. Groups of Missourians roaming the countryside around Millport burned several Mormon homes, drove off livestock, and stole property. Agnes Smith, wife of the Prophet's brother Don Carlos, was alone with her two small children when a raiding party drove

24. See, e.g., *HC* 3:408–9, Hyrum Smith, affidavit, 1 July 1843; *HC* 3:444, Lyman Wight, affidavit, 1 July 1843; and Pratt, *Autobiography*, p. 181.
25. *A Brief History*, p. 38; and Lee, *Mormonism Unveiled*, p. 72.

her out and burned her home. Carrying a child in each arm, she fled three miles to Diahman, where she waded the frigid waters of Grand River to reach the safety of the Mormon camp. Nathan Tanner reported that his company rescued a Latter-day Saint woman and her three children, who were hiding in the brush near their burning cabin. [26]   After much persuasion, Tanner's company convinced the family they were friends and escorted them to safety. Many Mormons, fearing similar mistreatment by the mobs, packed their belongings and fled to Diahman during the night.

The state militia never arrived. After learning that the Carroll vigilantes planned to drive the Mormons from Daviess, General Parks organized the Ray militia to counter their activities. On Tuesday, 16 October, Parks marched from Richmond with two companies of troops, but the snowstorm forced them to abandon the expedition. Parks and part of his staff continued to Far West, where they learned that General Doniphan had also dismissed his men and returned home. Parks apparently planned to call out his troops again when the weather improved, but he decided first to go to Daviess and investigate the reported disturbances. He arrived in Daviess on Thursday, 18 October, and after learning of the Mormons' depredations, proceeded directly to Diahman.

Parks reported that he found about five hundred well-armed soldiers, including two hundred cavalry, at Diahman. He questioned Mormon leaders about their activities and intentions:

I asked them their motive in appearing in arms—their answer was: "they intended to defend that place; they had been driven from DeWitt and other places, and here they were determined to stand and die, rather than be driven from that place." [27]

While Parks conferred with the Mormons, Agnes Smith and some of the others who had been driven from their homes straggled into Diahman. The general now realized that a full-scale civil war had broken out in Daviess County. "That county is in a worse state than at any former period, and I believe that the Mormons are

26. "Journal," p. 4.
27. *Document*, p. 47, General Parks to General Atchison, 21 October 1838.

now the aggressors ... ," he wrote. "The excitement in this county is more deep and full of vengeance than I have yet seen it, and I would not be surprised if some signal act of vengeance would be taken on these fanatics." [28] Yet Parks still sympathized with the Mormons. He had seen their sufferings in Daviess and Carroll counties, and he saw that their enemies continued to molest them. The general advised the Mormons to act defensively, after which he returned to Richmond. From Richmond, he wrote to General Atchison and described conditions in Daviess County, concluding:

I do not know what to do. I will remain passive until I hear from you. I do not believe calling out the militia would avail any thing towards restoring peace, unless they were called out in such force as to fright the Mormons and drive them from the country. This would satisfy the people, but I cannot agree to it. [29]

So Parks did nothing.

The Mormons later tried to justify their activities in Daviess County by asserting that General Parks ordered them into the field during his visit to Diahman. [30] This claim, like the assertion that General Doniphan authorized their expedition to Daviess County, is misleading. First, Parks did not arrive at Diahman until after the Mormons had begun their activities, including the sacking and burning of Gallatin. Second, Parks did not report ordering the Mormons into the field. Finally, although Parks probably advised the Mormons to fight in self-defense, he certainly did not instruct them to drive Daviess settlers from their homes.

During the next week both Mormons and Missourians continued their raids, plundering and burning homes, taking prisoners, and threatening death. Although no one was seriously injured, these encounters frightened the victims on both sides. Additionally, the snow and cold weather increased the suffering of those who were driven from their homes: they often fled with little clothing and no place to go for shelter. The Mormons

28. Ibid., p. 48.
29. Ibid.
30. See, e.g., *HC* 3:408, Hyrum Smith, affidavit, 1 July 1843; *HC* 3:442–44, Lyman Wight, affidavit, 1 July 1843; and *HC* 3:370, Joseph Smith, "A Bill of Damages," 4 June 1839.

outnumbered and easily outfought the Missourians, and they soon drove them from the county. "The Mormons completely gutted Daviess county," recalled Joseph McGee, whose father hid the family furniture and kitchenware in the woods until the war was over. "There was scarcely a Missourian's house left standing in the county."[31]   Altogether, the Mormons burned about fifty cabins and stores, and drove one hundred non-Mormon families from their homes.[32] As many as half of the buildings burned by the Mormons were located in and around Millport and Gallatin, both of which were nearly leveled. The number of cabins (perhaps as few as ten) and the amount of property lost by the Mormons at this time were considerably less than that of their neighbors because the Mormon soldiers completely overwhelmed their foes. Within a week after their arrival at Diahman, they had driven all enemy troops—and nearly all the non-Mormons—from the county.

While the Mormon troops skirmished in Daviess County, those in Caldwell prepared for additional conflicts with the vigilantes. Each morning and night the Mormons set out guards; soldiers and cavalrymen paraded constantly through the streets of Far West; and messengers arrived daily with reports from Joseph Smith describing the Mormon successes in Daviess County. One message from the Prophet, read aloud by Sidney Rigdon to the Far West troops, proclaimed that "they had nothing to fear, and that the enemy was in their hands."[33]   Many of the men tore down their house logs and moved their families into Far West for safety. On 20 October, Mormon soldiers met secretly and organized into companies of ten, fifty, and one hundred in preparation for war. At this meeting Avard talked ominously about poisoning the Missourians' crops and then spreading the word that it was the work of the Lord. Mormon soldiers resolved, because dissenters had been spreading inflammatory reports about their teachings and activities, that they would

31. *Story of the Grand River Country*, n.p.

32. John Corrill said it was estimated that Mormon soldiers burned from eighty to one-hundred-fifty cabins (*A Brief History*, p. 38). The lower estimate of eighty is plausible but probably too high. See also Hunt, *Mormonism*, p. 186.

33. *Document*, p. 114, testimony of Nathaniel Carr. See also ibid., pp. 99, 113, 129, testimonies of Sampson Avard, James C. Owens, and George M. Hinkle, for testimony of the same.

not allow dissenters to leave the county. "The last man had run away from Far West that was a going to," Rigdon declared; ". . . the next man who started, he should be pursued and brought back, dead or alive." [34]

The victorious Mormon troops in Daviess County meanwhile prepared to return to Far West. They had rescued beleaguered Mormon families, captured a cannon in Livingston County, and driven their enemies from Daviess. In addition, the First Presidency organized the Mormon militia for an extended conflict. They chose Lyman Wight, George Hinkle, David Patten, and Seymour Brunson as their chief military officers, while Joseph Smith held overall responsibility for the militia. [35] On

34. *Document*, p. 135, testimony of Burr Riggs. Descriptions of this meeting are found in ibid., pp. 124, 143, 144, testimonies of W. W. Phelps, Benjamin Slade, and Addison Green. Additional information is contained in Rockwood, "Journal," pp. 7–8; Amasa M. Lyman, "Amasa Lyman's History," *Millennial Star* 27 (19 August 1865): 520; and *Document*, p. 58, Thomas Marsh, affidavit, 24 October 1838.

35. The evidence is unclear as to whether the Mormon army represented a reorganization of the Danites or the formation of a new military organization. Leland H. Gentry and B. H. Roberts argue that Joseph Smith organized a new military organization, called the Army of Israel, which was distinct and separate from the Danites (Gentry, "A History of the Latter-Day Saints in Northern Missouri from 1836–1839" [Ph.D. diss., Brigham Young University, 1964], pp. 326–30; and Roberts, *A Comprehensive History of the Church of Jesus Christ of Latter-day Saints*, 6 vols. [Salt Lake City: Deseret News Press, 1930], 1:503–4). Evidence exists to support this claim. First, none of the leading Danite officers, such as Elias Higbee, Sampson Avard, Cornelius P. Lott, or George W. Robinson, were chosen as superior officers, while George Hinkle, who was not a Danite, was given significant command. In addition, John D. Lee and Morris Phelps, who were members of both organizations, asserted that the organizations were separate (Lee, *Mormonism Unveiled*, pp. 57, 72; Phelps, "Reminiscences," pp. 3–5).

Gentry and Roberts emphasize the distinction between the two organizations to support their argument that, while the Prophet may have directed the "legitimate" Armies of Israel, he knew nothing about the "unauthorized" Danite organization. This distinction, however, was not so clear—nor so important—to Mormon soldiers at that time. Most Mormons who belonged to the Army of Israel did not regard it as significantly different from the Danites. Many Danites described their group as a defensive military organization. According to Anson Call, all members of the Mormon military belonged to the Danites. In addition, both Lyman Wight and David Patten, who were reportedly lower-ranked Danite leaders, served as chief officers in the new army. Under their new organization, Mormon soldiers continued to practice their Danite military formations and to use their secret signs as passwords. Consequently, many Mormon soldiers believed the two organizations were the same: ". . . both Joseph Smith, jr., and Sidney Rigdon sanctioned and favored the only organization of 'Danites' of which the writer has any knowledge,"

the morning of 20 October, Joseph Smith gathered about three hundred of his men on a ridge near Diahman and covenanted with them never to accept peace at the sacrifice of truth and justice.[36] Afterward, the Mormons fired off three rounds from their newly captured cannon. At each discharge the men waved their hats and shouted "Hosanna to God and the Lamb!" The Prophet then stepped forward, drew his sword, and, lifting it high above his head, proclaimed, "I have drawn my sword from its sheath and I swear by the living God that it never shall return again till I can go and come and be treated by others as they wish to be treated by me."[37]   The Mormon soldiers shouted, "Amen!" The Caldwell troops returned two days later to Far West.

"The Mob disperse by hundreds on the approach of the Danites," Albert Rockwood wrote after receiving news of the Mormon victories in Daviess County.[38]   The Mormon soldiers, emboldened by their success and sustained by their faith, confidently believed the Lord would help them finally to establish their Zion in Missouri. "I thought that one Danite could chase a thousand·Gentiles, and two could put ten thousand to

---

Ebenezer Robinson wrote. "If there were any other 'companies of tens or fifties organized by the brethren for self defense,' aside from those called 'Danites,' we knew nothing of it." Call, "Statement, December 30, 1885," p. 2; E. Robinson, *The Return* 2 (February 1890): 217; Hosea Stout, *On The Mormon Frontier*, 1:141, 197; and Shurtliff, "History," p. 125.

The most important source regarding this issue is Albert P. Rockwood's "Journal," which was written before the Mormons surrendered—and before Mormon leaders attempted to distance themselves from the Danites. Rockwood reported that the Mormon Armies of Israel "are called Dan because Prophet Daniel has said the Saints shall take the Kingdom and possess it forever" (p. 8). Rockwood's account used the appellations "Armies of Israel" and "Danites" interchangeably.

Mormon historians have perhaps made too much of the alleged distinction between the two organizations. As has been shown, Joseph Smith knew and approved of the Danites. Moreover, regardless of whether it was the Danites or the Armies of Israel that operated in Daviess County, the evidence is clear that it was Joseph Smith—and not Sampson Avard—who directed their activities.

36. Accounts of this incident are given in James B. Bracken, Sr., "Verbal Statement, November 6, 1881," pp. 9–10. Typescript, LDS Archives; Duncan, "Biography," p. 37; McArthur, "Journal," p. 19; and Solomon Wixom, "The Journal and Day Book of Solomon Wixom," n.p. Typescript, LDS Archives.

37. Wixom, "Journal and Day Book," n.p.

38. "Journal," p. 8.

flight," said John D. Lee.[39]   Another Mormon soldier, Benjamin F. Johnson, recalled the general feeling of the Mormon troops: "At this time the Saints seemed sanguine of our success in standing off all mobs and of ultimate triumph over our enemies in Missouri."[40]   It is not surprising, given the many promises by the Lord through His prophet Joseph Smith, that the Saints believed He would protect them in accomplishing His work. "Death appears to have lost its terrors among the armies of Israel," wrote a jubilant Albert Rockwood.[41]

Not all Mormons shared this confidence in their military prowess. George Hinkle, who led the Mormon defense at DeWitt, told Joseph Smith "that this course of burning houses and plundering, by the Mormon troops, would ruin us; that it could not be kept hid; and would bring the force of the State upon us . . . ."[42]   When John Corrill questioned the Prophet regarding the propriety of the Mormons' actions,

Smith replied no; they would not have the whole state on them, but only that party which was governed by a mob spirit, and they were not very numerous; and they, when they found they would have to fight, would not be so fond of gathering together against them.[43]

Joseph Smith and other Mormon leaders, most notably Lyman Wight, declared that they would march through the entire state if "pressed too tight," but they apparently did not think such drastic action would be necessary because they believed the honest citizens would support their measures to defend themselves. When James Cobb, a Daviess settler, informed Smith and Wight that the citizens of Clay and Ray counties were turning out against them, "Wight or Smith, observed he did not believe that was true. Lyman Wight said their cause was just; he considered they were acting on the defensive, and he would as soon 50,000 should come as 500."[44]   Mormon leaders believed that only their persecutors would oppose them; but

39. *Mormonism Unveiled*, p. 75.
40. *Life's Review*, pp. 37–38.
41. "Journal," p. 7.
42. *Document*, p. 126, testimony of George Hinkle.
43. *A Brief History*, p. 36.
44. *Document*, p. 140, testimony of James B. Turner.

if that turned out to be the entire state, God would help them to defeat their—and His—enemies. [45]

A Gathering Storm

News of the Mormon invasion of Daviess County traveled quickly. Reports circulated among the settlers that the Mormons intended to sweep through the upper counties and indemnify themselves for losses in Jackson and Carroll. "Blood and plunder appears to be their object," reported agitated citizens from Ray County. [46]   Missouri settlers began immediately to organize and arm themselves against the Saints. In Livingston County the citizens formed vigilante committees and mobilized local militia companies. Settlers from Carroll and Daviess joined them. Large companies of men, fifteen to fifty in number, roamed throughout Livingston County and harassed Mormon settlers and emigrants. The Missourians stopped and searched wagons for weapons, sometimes ordering the Mormons to go back, sometimes detaining them for a day to a week, and at other times allowing them to proceed. Near the Caldwell County border, Missouri troops seized the arms and ammunition carried by John Walker's wagon company, warning the Mormons that "if we went on we would all be killed." [47]   Walker's company crossed into Caldwell and camped a few miles below Haun's Mill for safety.

In Clinton County the Missourians organized under Col. Neil

45. The Mormons, of course, did not intend to overthrow the Missouri state government; but the many statements by Joseph Smith and other Mormons that, if necessary, they would oppose and defeat the entire state were later cited as evidence of treasonous intent by Mormon leaders. Claims that Mormon leaders said they would take the entire state are found in Corrill, *A Brief History*, p. 38; Lee, *Mormonism Unveiled*, p. 90; *Document*, p. 55, Henry Marks (non-Mormon), affidavit, 24 October 1838; *Document*, pp. 57–59, Thomas B. Marsh and Orson Hyde, affidavits, 24 October 1838; *Document*, pp. 129, 137, 138, testimonies of George Hinkle, Jesse Kelly (non-Mormon), and Addison Price (non-Mormon); and Hunt, *Mormonism*, p. 217, testimony of George Walter (Walter's testimony was also given at the Richmond hearing, but was left out of *Document*).

46. *Document*, p. 49, Citizens of Ray County to the Governor, 23 October 1838.

47. William H. Walker, *The Life Incidents and Travels of Elder William Holmes Walker and His Association with Joseph Smith, the Prophet* (n.p.: Published by John Walker Family Organization, 1971), p. 6.

Gilliam, the state senator elect from that region. Gilliam later cited the Mormon depredations in Daviess County as the reason why he called out his regiment. "I saw enough to make any man who had a spark of love for his country, or sympathy for insulted humanity, to take up arms and fight to redress their wrongs," he said.[48] In addition, Gilliam's relatives were among those recently burned out by the Mormons. He now sought to return the favor. Over two hundred men flocked to Gilliam's camp, where they painted themselves with red and black stripes, Indian style, to distinguish themselves from the Mormons. Gilliam called himself the "Delaware Chief" and proposed to his men that the conflict be decided by single combat between the Mormons' champion, Lyman Wight, and himself. The painted soldiers, whooping and yelling like ferocious savages, marched through Clinton and Daviess counties, driving Mormon settlers from their homes, plundering, and burning. As the men advanced into Caldwell, they talked of driving the Mormons to Far West and then out of the state.

Although many of the troops in Livingston and Clinton apparently had been called out by local authorities, the commanding generals of these soldiers refused to authorize or direct their activities. General Parks, who commanded the troops from Livingston County, stated that he could not agree to calling out the militia against the Mormons. General Doniphan, to whose brigade Gilliam's troops belonged, remained at his home in Liberty while the Clinton militia operated without orders or direction from him. General Atchison, commander of all militia units in northwestern Missouri, was the most adamantly opposed to calling upon the troops. In a letter to Governor Boggs written 22 October, Atchison described the conditions in Daviess County, stating that both the Mormons (who he said were acting like "mad-men") and the vigilantes were committing numerous crimes and outrages. The general said, however, that he did not intend to call upon his troops to intervene because he believed they would disgrace the state and themselves by acting with the vigilantes: "If the Mormons are to be driven from their homes, let it be done without any color of law, and in open defiance thereof; let it be done by

48. *Missouri Argus*, 15 February 1838. See also Lockley, "Reminiscences of Martha Elizabeth Gilliam," p. 360.

volunteers acting upon their own responsibilities." [49]

Many settlers were angered by the militia generals' refusal to act. Dissatisfaction with the generals' performance had been growing for several weeks. Following the disturbances in Carroll County, Captain Bogart, a member of Parks's brigade, wrote to Governor Boggs and criticized Parks's apparent pro-Mormon bias. "Too many of our officers are seeking popularity with the Mormons, supposing their votes in time would be of some service to them," Bogart said, probably referring to Atchison and Doniphan as well as Parks. [50]   Col. William Peniston of Daviess County also wrote to the governor and condemned the "political juggling" of Atchison and others. Their favorable reports of the conduct and character of the Mormons, Peniston said, were "prompted by the hope of interest or emolument." [51]   Bogart and Peniston, both bitter opponents of the Saints, expressed what many of their fellow citizens probably suspected: the generals had allowed their political and business connections with the Mormons to affect their judgment and handling of the disturbances. No evidence exists to support these claims; nevertheless, Atchison, Doniphan, and Parks found themselves caught in the middle of the conflict. Mormon leaders condemned them for not taking stronger, more determined steps to disperse the vigilantes, while Missourians criticized the generals for not acting against the Mormons, who they believed were the aggressors.

Following the Mormon invasion of Daviess County, Missouri citizens sent letters and petitions to Governor Boggs, describing for him the Mormon depredations and pleading that he send assistance. Detailed eyewitness accounts from Daviess settlers gave damaging testimony concerning the activities of the Mormon soldiers. [52]   It would be several days, however, before the governor would receive and act upon this information.

49. *Document*, pp. 46–47, General Atchison to the Governor, 22 October 1838.
50. Ibid., p. 42, Captain Bogart to the Governor, 13 October 1838. Atchison and Doniphan were both prominent politicians and lawyers for the Saints.
51. Ibid., p. 44, Col. Peniston to the Governor, 21 October 1838.
52. See ibid., pp. 42–46, 55–57, for affidavits written 21 and 22 October by Daviess citizens and sent to Governor Boggs.

8

Open Warfare

The disturbances and excitement increased following the return of the Mormon soldiers to Far West. Hundreds of Missouri troops and volunteers continued to harass the Saints in Livingston and Clinton counties, and their raids into Caldwell became bolder and more destructive. When reports reached Far West that Ray County citizens were planning to invade Caldwell County, Mormon leaders dispatched a company of spies to Ray to watch for unusual movements by the Missourians.[1] Mormon leaders instructed the spies that, if the people of Ray began driving the Saints from their homes, the spies were to retaliate in a similar manner.

Excitement in Ray County

The citizens of Ray County did not intend to attack the Mormons, but they had become alarmed by the Saints' activities in Daviess County. They feared that their county, which contained twenty-five to thirty Mormon families along its northern border, would become the new focus of Mormon military operations. Reports of Mormon oppression also increased tension. "Mormon dissenters are daily flying to this county for refuge from the ferocity of the prophet Jo Smith, who, they say, threatens the lives of all Mormons who refuse to take up arms at his bidding or to do his commands," reported Thomas C. Burch, the circuit attorney from Ray County, in a letter to Governor Boggs.[2] Shortly after the Mormons organized their spy company, dissenters informed Ray citizens of its existence.

On Monday, 22 October, in response to reports of Mormon lawlessness, the people of Ray sent three of their leading citizens

1. The ten-man spy company was organized at the 20 October meeting in Far West.
2. *Document*, p. 50, T. C. Burch to the Governor, 23 October 1838.

to investigate the situation in Daviess County.[3]   The next day fourteen Ray citizens wrote to Governor Boggs, describing the reported destruction in Daviess and claiming that the Mormons threatened other counties as well. "Unless a military force is brought to act against them, and that shortly, they will destroy as far as they are able," the citizens warned.[4]   Prompted by these reports, Capt. Samuel Bogart, a local Methodist minister, called out his militia company to prevent an invasion by the Mormons.

"Captain Bogard was not a very discreet man, and his men were of much the same character," said Peter Burnett, a resident of Liberty who knew these men.[5]   They had sided with the vigilantes during the Carroll disturbances, forcing General Parks to dismiss the troops and return to Ray County. Because of Bogart's insubordination, Parks reportedly tried to discharge him from the militia. Some of the other officers told Mormon leaders that Bogart "was as lawless, if not more so, and as mobocratic as the worst of the mob."[6]   Bogart had earlier written to Governor Boggs and warned that the Mormons would drive the Daviess settlers from the county.[7]   He now asserted that the Mormons, having resolved to carry out Rigdon's war of extermination against their enemies, planned to invade Ray County. An anonymous letter written from Bogart's headquarters the day before he marched for Caldwell ominously stated that "we believe that in less than six days, Far West will be burnt and her fugitives driven from the borders of the State."[8]

Captain Bogart, impetuous and self-assured, acted aggressively to halt the alleged Mormon rebellion. On 23 October, Bogart assembled thirty-five men and marched to the Caldwell line,

3. Ibid., p. 52, Report of Messrs. Morehead, Thorton, and Gudgel. Reed Peck states that despite the flood of testimony from Daviess citizens, most settlers from the surrounding counties hesitated to believe the reports of Mormon depredations until they first sent representatives to investigate those reports ("Manuscript," pp. 21–22).

4. *Document*, p. 49, Citizens of Ray County to the Governor, 23 October 1838.

5. *Recollections*, p. 58.

6. Rigdon, *Appeal*, p. 32. See also Phelps, "Reminiscences," p. 2; and *HC* 3:444, Lyman Wight, affidavit, 1 July 1843.

7. *Document*, p. 41, Captain Bogart to the Governor, 13 October 1838.

8. *Missouri Argus*, 1 November 1838, letter from the "Occidentalist," 22 October 1838.

picking up another twenty to thirty volunteers along the way. Earlier that day he had written to General Atchison and requested permission to patrol the county line. Seeing that the Ray troops intended to act, Atchison granted permission and ordered Bogart "to range the line between Caldwell and Ray counties, with your company of volunteers, and prevent, if possible, any invasion of Ray county by any persons in arms whatever."[9] The Ray troops, however, exceeded their orders.

Bogart and his men split up into several parties and disarmed Mormon settlers in northern Ray, ordering many of them to leave the county. On 24 October a company of men led by Captain Bogart crossed into Caldwell and disarmed Mormons in that county as well. Bogart's men presented a hard, menacing appearance; some wore white blanket coats and carried large bowie knives attached to their leather belts with scabbards. Thoret Parsons and Arza Judd, Jr., reported that Bogart ordered them from their homes and threatened to give Far West "thunder and lightning" when he joined up with Neil Gilliam's troops from Clinton County.[10] Within two days the Missourians had disarmed or driven from the county most of the Saints in Ray.

Later Mormon accounts asserted that Bogart's company burned numerous homes and destroyed and plundered much property.[11] No substantial evidence supports these claims. All eyewitness accounts by Mormon settlers state that they were either disarmed or ordered to leave their homes, but they do not report any burning or plundering by the Ray County troops. The exaggerated reports of destruction, however, were readily believed by Mormon leaders.

9. For the exchange of letters between Bogart and Atchison, see *Document*, p. 48, Captain Bogart to General Atchison, 23 October 1838; and ibid., p. 108, General Atchison to Captain Bogart, 23 October 1838. The line "between Caldwell and Ray" probably referred to the disputed six-mile strip of land in northern Ray County.

10. Arza Judd, Jr., Thoret Parsons, and Mary Judd Eaton give the only eyewitness accounts of Bogart's activities in Caldwell County. *Document*, pp. 148–49, testimony of Arza Judd, Jr., and Thoret Parsons; Arza Judd, Jr., "Affidavit, January 6, 1840." Petitions, U.S. Archives; and "Temple Lot Case," *In The Circuit Court Of The United States, Western Division At Kansas City. Reorganized Church of Jesus Christ of Latter Day Saints versus The Church of Christ* (Lamoni, Iowa: Herald Publishing House and Binding, 1893), p. 268, testimony of Mary Eaton Judd.

11. See, e.g., *HC* 3:407, Hyrum Smith, affidavit, 1 July 1843; *HC* 3:457, Sidney Rigdon, affidavit, 1 July 1843; and John P. Greene, *Facts Relative*

During the afternoon of 24 October, while Captain Bogart harassed Mormon settlers in Caldwell, a small company of his men patrolling Ray County captured two Mormon spies, William Seeley and Addison Green, at the home of Nathan Pinkham, Sr., where the spy company quartered.[12] The Missourians stripped and searched the prisoners for weapons and dragged them from the house. Green said his captors threatened to "blow out my brains and swore that if I was a Mormon they would hang me without further ceremony."[13] Seeley said they told him "he would never see home again."[14] The Missourians confiscated their weapons, horses, and equipment, then took the two spies and Pinkham's son, Nathan, Jr., to their camp on Crooked River. Before leaving, the soldiers warned the elder Pinkham that if he and his family were not gone by the next morning they would be killed.

At the Missourians' camp, the Mormon prisoners were interrogated and again threatened by their captors. William Seeley stated that the volunteer troops were especially abusive and cried loudly to have them executed. The prisoners, however, were not harmed, and the evidence indicates that the Missourians intended to release them the next day.[15]

The same day, 24 October, two Mormon apostles, Thomas B. Marsh and Orson Hyde, signed affidavits in Richmond that described the militant activities of the Saints and alleged that

---

To The Expulsion Of The Mormons From The State Of Missouri, Under The "Exterminating Order" (Cincinnati: Printed by R. P. Brooks, 1839), p. 12. Compare with accounts of those who were driven from Ray and Caldwell counties: James M. Henderson, "Affidavit, January 6, 1840." Petitions, U.S. Archives; Tunis Rappleye, "Affidavit, January 7, 1840." Petitions, U.S. Archives; Elijah Reed, "Affidavit, January 9, 1840." Petitions, U.S. Archives; Pierce Hawley, "Affidavit, May 6, 1839." Petitions, LDS Archives; and accounts by Parsons and the Judds, cited in the preceding footnote.

12. For evidence that Green and Seeley were spies, see *Document*, p. 144, testimony of Addison Green; and Rockwood, "Journal," p. 9. Lyman, "History," p. 520, states that the Mormon spies quartered at Pinkham's home.

13. *HC* 4:65, Addison Green, affidavit, 17 March 1840.

14. Seeley, "Affidavit, January 20, 1840." Petitions, U.S. Archives.

15. Addison Green testified at the Richmond hearing that the Mormon prisoners were released that night and told to go home, but "I thought proper to remain with them [Bogart's company] in camp that night" (*Document*, p. 144). In a later statement, Green merely asserted that he was released the next day (*HC* 4:65). Seeley does not state if or when the Missourians intended to release the prisoners.

Mormon leaders intended to continue their lawless course. [16] Both Marsh and Hyde had been disturbed by the intolerant and belligerent spirit that had developed among the Saints. Earlier in the year, Marsh had opposed radical measures for dealing with dissenters. He also believed the Mormons had overreacted to threats of violence from Missourians, an attitude that other Mormons found incomprehensible. "He [Marsh] expressed unbounded charity for our enemies—said he did not think they intended us much harm—they were not naturally inclined to wickedness, etc.," Lorenzo Snow remarked following a conversation with Marsh. [17] Snow considered the Mormon apostle to be "utterly blind in relation to the condition of things and the spirit of the times." After Mormon soldiers burned and plundered homes in Daviess County, which Marsh witnessed, he and Orson Hyde decided that they had had enough of Mormonism. "I have left the Mormons [and] Joseph Smith Jr for conscience sake, and that alone, for I have come to the full conclusion that he is a very wicked man; notwithstanding all my efforts to persuade myself to the contra[ry] . . . ," Marsh told friends in Far West. "For the burning the Post Office in Galiton, for pillaging goods &c in Davise, The Government will undoubtedly take notice, & I fear that many innocent among you will have to suffer." [18] "I felt like taking no part whatever in the Danite movement . . . ," Hyde said regarding his disaffection. The two men loaded their property and families into a wagon and together with a number of other dissenters fled secretly from Far West during the night.

The affidavits, which Marsh wrote and they both signed, detailed the Mormon military operations in Daviess County, confirmed the existence and activities of the Danite band, and told of the threats against dissenters and others who refused to take up arms in the conflict. The affidavits also confirmed the existence of the spy company (which Marsh called the "Destruction Company") and alleged that the spies had been

16. *Document*, pp. 57–59, Thomas Marsh and Orson Hyde, affidavits, 24 October 1838.

17. Quoted in Eliza R. Snow, *Biography and Family Record of Lorenzo Snow* (Salt Lake City: Deseret News Company, Printers, 1884), p. 31.

18. Thomas B. Marsh to Brother and Sister Abbot, 25 October 1838. Photocopy, BYU Special Collections; and Orson Hyde to Brigham Young, 30 March 1839. Photocopy, LDS Archives. Hyde also stated that he was sick and feeling mentally depressed at the time of his departure.

instructed to burn Buncombe and Richmond if Ray citizens first attacked the Mormons. Marsh then wrote an inflammatory description of Joseph Smith's intentions:

The plan of said Smith, the prophet, is to take this State, and he professes to his people to intend taking the United States, and ultimately the whole world. This is the belief of the church, and my own opinion of the prophet's plans and intentions. It is my opinion that neither said Joseph Smith, the prophet, nor any one of the principal men, who is firm in the faith, could be indicted for any offence in the county of Caldwell. The prophet inculcates the notion, and it is believed by every true Mormon, that Smith's prophecies are superior to the law of the land. I have heard the prophet say that he should yet tread down his enemies and walk over their dead bodies; that if he was not let alone he would be a second Mahomet to this generation, and that he would make it one gore of blood from the Rocky Mountains to the Atlantic Ocean; that like Mahomet, whose motto, in treating for peace, was "the Alcoran, or the Sword," so should it be eventually with us, "Joseph Smith or the Sword."[19]

No one claim or accusation in the Marsh-Hyde affidavits proved as damaging as the overall effect. The affidavits, written by leading Mormon officials, seemed to confirm what many Missourians had suspected: the Mormons were a violent and fanatical people, led by an equally fanatical and ruthless prophet, Joseph Smith.

Later that day the Ray committee, which had been sent to Daviess County to investigate the disturbances, returned to Richmond and reported "that much more had been done by the Mormons than the people of this county had been informed of."[20]   The committee received the bulk of its information from Judge Josiah Morin. Morin, who lived about a mile from Millport, informed them that Millport and Gallatin were almost entirely in ashes, Peniston's horsemill had been torn down and its parts scattered, and nearly all the Daviess settlers had been driven from the county, their possessions seized, and their homes burned. Morin had previously counted himself as

19. *Document*, p. 58, Thomas Marsh, affidavit, 24 October 1838. Other Mormon dissenters also stated that Joseph Smith compared himself to Mahomet: ibid., pp. 111, 128, testimonies of John Corrill and George Hinkle; and Hunt, *Mormonism*, p. 217, testimony of George Walter. Corrill, *A Brief History*, p. 38, also called the spy company the "Destructionists."

20. *Document*, p. 52, Report of Messrs. Morehead, Thorton, and Gudgel.

a friend of the Saints and had performed for them numerous services. But he now informed the Ray committee "that he, too, had been ordered to leave; he appeared very anxious that we should not be seen at his house by any Mormon—that it should not be known that he had given any information, or expressed any thing unfavorable towards them, until he got away." [21]

The Marsh-Hyde affidavits and the report of the Ray committee caused near panic. The Missourians believed the Mormons were planning an *immediate* invasion of Ray County. Non-Mormon settlers in northern Ray abandoned their homes and fled southward. Following a public meeting in Richmond, Ray citizens dispatched Amos Rees and Wiley C. Williams to Jefferson City with a formal petition and letters imploring Governor Boggs to send aid. [22]   In one letter, Judge Austin A. King described the reported activities of the Saints, adding, "until lately, I thought the Mormons were disposed to act only on the defensive, but their recent conduct shows that they are the aggressors, and that they intend to take the law into their own hands." [23]   Ray citizens called for volunteers to ride north to guard the county against attack.

Captain Bogart, after receiving word of the expected attack, moved his camp on 24 October to a ford on Crooked River, about one and one-half miles south of the Caldwell County line, and blocked the crossing on the main road to Richmond. That night he placed sentinels along the road about one-quarter mile north of camp to watch for advancing troops. The rest of Bogart's men pitched their tents and slept on top of a slough-bank that ran alongside Crooked River.

The Battle of Crooked River

On 24 October, Mormon settlers fleeing north to Far West brought news of Bogart's activities in Ray County. In the late afternoon a messenger reported that the Ray troops had crossed into Caldwell County and were threatening to attack Far West.

---

21. Ibid., p. 53.

22. Ibid., pp. 51–52, Proceedings of a Public Meeting in Ray County, 24 October 1838.

23. Ibid., p. 53, Hon. A. A. King to the Governor, 24 October 1838.

At midnight Joseph Holbrook and David Judy, two members of the spy company, galloped into town with the news that the Missourians had taken three prisoners, including two spies, and threatened to execute them in the morning. Mormon leaders quickly decided to raise a company of men to rescue the prisoners and disperse the Missouri troops. "Go and kill every devil of them," the outraged Mormon prophet advised.[24] The sound of the bugle and the beating of drums summoned the brethren to the public square.[25]

Within minutes more than fifty men reported for duty. Mormon leaders advised them that if they rode at once, they might surprise the enemy while it was yet dark and rescue the prisoners without bloodshed. Elias Higbee, a Caldwell County judge, authorized the volunteers to act as Missouri state troops. It is not certain whether the Mormon soldiers realized they would be riding against another militia unit, but given the circumstances and nature of the conflict, it probably would not have mattered.[26] Command of the expedition was given to Captain and Apostle David W. Patten.

Known as "Captain Fearnought" among his soldiers, Patten had gained a reputation as a skilled and fearless leader. Reportedly

24. *The Return* 2 (February 1890): 216, letter from C. Hall and Richard Hill. Hill and Hall said that David Judy was their source for this quotation.

25. The ensuing battle at Crooked River is described by a dozen Mormon participants. The most detailed descriptions include: Holbrook, "Life," pp. 23–24; Pratt, *Autobiography*, pp. 177–81; Charles C. Rich, Statement, pp. 1–3. LDS Archives; Hosea Stout, "Autobiography of Hosea Stout 1810 to 1844," edited by Reed A. Stout, *Utah Historical Quarterly* 30 (Fall 1962): 335–39; and Lorenzo D. Young, "Lorenzo Dow Young's Narrative," *Fragments of Experience: Sixth Book of the Faith-Promoting Series* (Salt Lake City: Juvenile Instructor Office, 1882), pp. 50–52. Descriptions by Missouri and Mormon participants are found in *Document*, pp. 108–10, 133–34, 142, testimonies of Nehemiah Odle, Samuel Bogart, Wyatt Cravens, Morris Phelps, Freeburn H. Gardner, and John Lockhart.

26. The question regarding whether the Mormons knew they were attacking official state troops became an important issue at a subsequent examination of Mormon participants. Captain Bogart and Lt. Asa Cook testified that they informed the Mormons that their company was militia (*Document*, pp. 108, 149). A Mormon dissenter, Burr Riggs, also testified that the Mormons knew Bogart's company was militia (ibid., p. 136). Most Mormon sources claim they did not discover that they had attacked state troops until a few days later (see Corrill, *A Brief History*, p. 39; Owen, "Memorial," pp. 3–4; and Green, *Facts Relative To The Expulsion*, p. 12). Joseph Holbrook stated that the mobs were "calling themselves militia," which probably expressed the Mormons' perception of Bogart's troops ("Life," p. 23).

a captain in the Danite organization, Patten had led Mormon troops in the burning and sacking of Gallatin. Many of those with Patten in the Gallatin expedition, Parley P. Pratt, Dimick Huntington, Morris Phelps, and others, now rode with him to Crooked River. John D. Lee described him as a brave, impulsive man who "rushed into the thickest of the fight, regardless of danger . . . . "[27]   Ebenezer Robinson said that Patten, highly esteemed and loved by his brethren, "seemed reckless of his life, as though it was scarce worth preserving."[28]   The Mormon apostle reportedly told Joseph Smith that he would rather die than allow the persecution to continue. His courageous but impetuous nature seemed destined to lead him toward that end. Captain Patten wore a conspicuous white blanket overcoat that night as he led his men into battle.

The company left immediately for Crooked River, stopping only briefly to pick up twenty-five volunteers from the settlements along Goose and Log creeks. Drusilla Hendricks remembered the messenger who alerted James, her husband:

. . . Bro. C. C. Rich called at the door for him and told him what he wanted. . . . I got up and lit a fire for it was cold, while he [James] brought his horse to the door. I thought he was slower than usual. He told me where they were to meet. I got his overcoat and put his pistols in the pockets, then got his sword and belted it on him. He bid me goodnight and got on his horse and I took his gun from the rack and handed it to him and said, "Don't get shot in the back."[29]

At about 3:00 a.m., shortly after they crossed into Ray County, the Mormon troops dismounted and proceeded on foot. They had marched to within a mile of the militia camp when one of Bogart's sentries, John Lockhart, suddenly ordered them to halt. A few words passed between Lockhart and the Mormons, but Lockhart thought he heard a gun snap, as if someone were shooting at him, so he fired into the crowd of Mormon soldiers, his shot hitting Patrick O'Banion. Lockhart and the

27. *Mormonism Unveiled*, p. 73.
28. "Items of Personal History," *The Return* 2 (January 1890): 202.
29. "Historical Sketch of James and Drusilla Doris Hendricks," p. 19. Typescript, LDS Archives.

other sentry, who did not fire, scurried back to their camp. [30]

Bogart's men, warned by the gunfire and the shouts of their sentries, scrambled from their tents and hurriedly took up positions behind the slough-bank along Crooked River. Moments later the Mormon troops could be seen emerging from the woods at the top of a small hill, about eighty yards above the riverbank. Captain Patten, upon spotting the Missourians, marched his men halfway down the hill and formed a battle line.

The Mormons attacked from an extremely inferior position. It was now daybreak and they stood on nearly open ground, making excellent targets in the early morning light, while the Missourians lay well hidden behind the trees and bushes along the riverbank below. Three or four of Patten's men fell during the first round of fire, two more on the second, but he was unable to determine what damage, if any, had been inflicted upon the Missourians. Realizing that his men could not long endure such withering fire, Patten ordered a precipitate charge upon the Missourians' camp. The Mormon troops, shouting their watchword, "God and Liberty," drew their swords and flung themselves into the enemy's ranks.

Bogart's men panicked. Most of them immediately fled across the river, and those who remained were soon routed after brief hand-to-hand combat. Many of the soldiers shouted "We are brethren" as they waded the river, hoping to halt the Mormons' fire until they could escape.[31] Hosea Stout, a Mormon participant, later remarked that "many a mobber was there baptised without faith or repentance under the messingers of lead sent by the brethren."[32] Two Mormon soldiers intercepted Samuel Tarwater as he ran to the river and gave him several piercing cuts with their corn-cutter swords. One of the Mormons, Lorenzo D. Young (brother of the future Mormon prophet), said he saw an angel's hand hold Tarwater's arm so he could not return

30. Lockhart's testimony of the incident is found in *Document*, p. 142. Although some words passed between the Mormons and Lockhart (see H. Stout, "Autobiography," p. 336; Burnett, *Recollections*, p. 58; and Corrill, *A Brief History*, 39), there is not enough evidence to conclude that the Mormon soldiers attempted to shoot Lockhart. The Mormons claimed Patten's company was fired upon without provocation.

31. H. Stout, "Autobiography," p. 337.

32. Ibid., p. 336.

the blows. [33] The Missourian suffered a severed jaw and cuts about the throat and had his skull cut open and his upper teeth destroyed. [34] Within minutes the Mormons had routed the Missouri troops and sent them fleeing desperately to their homes.

The Mormon soldiers quickly regrouped, reloaded, and gathered their wounded. They suffered nine men wounded, including Captain Patten and William Seeley, one of the captured spies. Seeley reported that the Missourians, when they saw that the Mormons were going to attack, placed the three prisoners in front of their line so they would be shot in the crossfire. The prisoners broke for the Mormon line as soon as the firing began. Seeley was shot in the shoulder, but the other two escaped unharmed. Also among the wounded was James Hendricks, who lay face down, shot in the neck and unable to move. The Mormon soldier who discovered Hendricks did not recognize him. "Which side are you on?" the soldier asked. "God and Liberty," Hendricks replied. [35]

The Mormons captured one prisoner, Wyatt Cravens, whom they released before they reached Far West. Soon after release he was mysteriously shot. Cravens and a number of others claimed that he was "set up" and deliberately shot by the Mormons. [36] Morris Phelps, a member of Patten's company, said that Cravens was accidentally shot by another Missourian while returning home. Although the shooting was probably accidental, it is more likely that a Mormon soldier rather than a Missourian did the shooting because Cravens was shot while in territory under Mormon control. Cravens recovered and testified against the Mormons at the Richmond hearing.

The Mormons confiscated the Missourians' baggage and horses and placed their wounded in one of the wagons left

33. Young, "Narrative," pp. 51–52; and Little, "Biography of Lorenzo Dow Young," p. 55.

34. "Mormon Troubles in Ray County," *Richmond Missourian* (Richmond, Mo.), 7 November 1901; and *History of Ray County, Missouri* (St. Louis: Missouri Historical Company, 1881), p. 657. Because he was serving as a state militiaman, Tarwater received a pension for the injuries he sustained at the Crooked River battle.

35. Hendricks, "Historical Sketch," p. 20.

36. See *Document*, p. 109, testimony of Wyatt Cravens; Lee, *Mormonism Unveiled*, p. 73; Peck, "Manuscript," pp. 23, 31; and Morris Phelps, "Reminiscences," p. 4.

behind. [37]   The journey back to Far West proved too painful for Patten, who frequently begged the brethren to lay him down by the road. They finally stopped at the home of Stephen Winchester, about four miles south of town, where Joseph Smith and other Mormon leaders rushed to pronounce blessings on his wounds. They sensed, however, that the wounds were fatal. "Brother David, when you get home I want you to remember me," Heber C. Kimball said. [38]   Patten replied, "I will." Turning to his wife, who was also present, the dying apostle implored, "Whatever you do else, O, do not deny the faith." He died shortly after, Mormonism's first apostolic martyr.

Patrick O'Banion died the next night at the home of Sidney Rigdon. The Mormons later discovered that Gideon Carter had also been killed in the battle, raising the number of casualties to three killed and seven wounded. [39]   The Saints buried their dead with military honors. "There lies a man that has done just as he said he would—he has laid down his life for his friends," said Joseph Smith of the fallen apostle. [40]   At Patten's grave Mormon soldiers made a solemn covenant to avenge his death.

37. The *Missouri Argus*, 8 November 1838, printed a letter to the editor reporting that the Mormons took about $4,500 worth of horses and equipment.

38. Heber C. Kimball, *President Heber C. Kimball's Journal* (Salt Lake City: Juvenile Instructor, 1882), p. 55.

39. Carter had been left on the battlefield, mistakenly identified as a Missourian (Pratt, *Autobiography*, p. 179).

40. *HC* 3:175; and E. Robinson, "Items of Personal History," *The Return* 2 (January 1890): 202.

9

War Against the Saints

"You can hardly find in the annals of history a more severe battle[,] when taking into consideration the smallness of the number, & the shortness of the engagement," Albert Rockwood wrote shortly after the conflict at Crooked River.[1] Drusilla Hendricks, whose husband fought in the battle, supported Rockwood's claim, stating that when the Mormon soldiers returned from Crooked River their weapons "bore blood from hilt to point."[2] Rockwood, Dimick Huntington (a participant in the battle), Silas Hillman, and Vinson Knight each estimated that between twenty and thirty Missourians had been killed.[3] Hosea Stout, another participant, reported that the Mormons put to death all of Bogart's men who did not run away and then shot many more as they fled across the river.[4] He estimated that the Missourians lost thirty or forty men. The Mormons believed they had nearly destroyed Bogart's company.

The Missourians actually had only one man killed and six wounded, but they had fled so rapidly and in such confusion that they too believed their company had been wiped out. Wandering home one by one, Bogart's men stopped in nearby settlements, recounting details of the battle and reporting that very few of their company had survived.

Panic in Upper Missouri

News of the battle spread swiftly. The first reports stated that nearly all of Bogart's company had been massacred by the

1. "Journal," pp. 10–11.
2. "Historical Sketch," p. 21.
3. Rockwood, "Journal," p. 10; Huntington, "Journal," n.p.; Hillman, "Autobiography," p. 21. Photocopy, LDS Archives; and Knight to William Cooper, 3 February 1839. Ephraim Owen reported that Bogart's company was almost entirely destroyed ("Memorial," p. 4).
4. "Autobiography," pp. 336–37.

Mormons.[5] Later reports said that ten had been killed and most of the rest taken prisoner—and probably put to death. The seemingly unprovoked attack on state troops terrified Missouri settlers, who envisioned hordes of Danite soldiers sweeping down upon them. The Mormons, reports said, planned to continue their acts of lawlessness by marching through the entire northwestern portion of the state. Ray County settlers evacuated the women and children from Richmond and sent them across the Missouri River to Lexington. Volunteers rushed north to hold off the Mormon armies.

Carroll County settlers expected immediate retaliation for their expulsion of the Saints from DeWitt. Alexander Blackwell, who had served as secretary for Carroll's vigilance committee, described conditions in Carrollton:

Everything at the County seat was in confusion. Merchants had packed their goods and books, and sent them to a place of safety, in anticipation of an attack. Many families were preparing to leave the place, while others had already sought refuge elsewhere. The citizens, fearing the houses would be burned, had moved goods and furniture to the brush, or wherever protection or concealment could be obtained.[6]

Col. William Claude Jones called out the Carroll militia, but the men were too panic-stricken to respond. According to Blackwell, many of the men spent their time at a Carrollton dram shop, drinking themselves into a stupor. This continued until the Rev. Sashel Woods purchased the remaining whiskey, rolled the barrel into the street, knocked in its head, and emptied the contents into the gutters. Jones then organized the troops while Woods and Joseph Dickson, the county clerk, appealed to neighboring counties for assistance. "We know not the hour or minute we will be laid in ashes—our county is ruined," they wrote. "For God sake give us assistance as quick

5. For early reports of the battle see *Document*, p. 60, Letter from Woods and Dickson, 26 October 1838 (this letter is incorrectly dated 24 October in the text); ibid., pp. 61–62, E. M. Ryland to Messrs. Rees and Williams, 25 October 1838; *Missouri Republican*, 1 November 1838, letters from George Woodward (aide to General Parks) and Col. Claude Jones, 25 October 1838; and *History of Caldwell and Livingston Counties*, p. 131.

6. "History of Carroll County," p. 16.

as possible." [7]

After learning of the Crooked River battle, Generals Atchison, Doniphan, and Parks decided they must act to prevent further violence. Although they still contended that the conflict had been provoked by the Missourians, the generals believed the militia should protect the innocent citizens from further Mormon depredations. Writing to Lt.-Col. R. B. Mason, commander of the federal troops at Fort Leavenworth in Kansas, Atchison and Doniphan reported:

We regret that the State of (the) country in Upper Missouri is such as to make it necessary for each man to become a soldier; and each town to be guarded to protect them from arson and plunder. The citizens of Daviess, Corroll, and some other northern counties have raised mob after mob for the last two months for the purpose of driving a community of fanatics, (called mormons) from those counties and from the State. Those things have at length goaded the mormons into a state of desperation that has now made them aggressors instead of acting on the defensive. This places the citizens of this whole community in the unpleasant attitude that the civil and decent part of the community have now to engage in war to arrest a torrent that has been let loose by a cowardly mob, and from which they have dastardly fled on the first show of danger. [8]

The generals requested that Colonel Mason send two hundred weapons for the citizens to use against the Mormons, but Mason replied that he did not have authority to release the weapons for civil or religious disputes.

The attitudes of the generals reflected the opinions of many Missouri settlers who hitherto had remained neutral. John Parsons, a non-Mormon traveling through the upper counties at this time, described the general opinion of local citizens:

Altho the Mormons are in arms against the civil authorities of the state of Missouri & have already killed individuals & destroyed their property,—yet, it is believed (without countenancing or favoring in

7. *Document*, p. 60, Letter from Woods and Dickson, 26 October 1838.
8. David R. Atchison and Alexander W. Doniphan to Lt. Col. R. B. Mason, 27 October 1838. Photocopy, LDS Archives. For Mason's reply, see Lt. Col. R. B. Mason to Gens. D. R. Atchison and A. W. Doniphan, 28 October 1838. Photocopy, LDS Archives. The fact that Doniphan voluntarily called out his troops against the Mormons further suggests that the Mormon troops were not acting under orders from him.

the least their present measures or conduct,) that they have been purposely abused by private persons and delt with in an unwarrantable manner.[9]

Even those who opposed the vigilantes now armed in self-defense to suppress the apparent Mormon insurrection. Arthur Bradford, a resident of Carrollton in Carroll County, wrote:

I did not at first approve of [the vigilantes], but I finally believed they were right and I joined in with them. I am convinced history does not afford a deeper laid scheme of vallainy than that which has just developed itself in regard to the course persued by that sect.[10]

Significantly, neither Atchison, Doniphan, nor Parks attempted to contact Mormon leaders, as they had done in the past, to ascertain the Mormons' real intentions. They began immediately to prepare for battle.

Hundreds of Missourians volunteered for militia duty. Atchison and Parks set up headquarters in Richmond, where they organized the soldiers for an assault on Far West. Doniphan stationed his brigade near Crooked River, about a mile south of the Caldwell line. Many of the soldiers were undisciplined and eager to punish the Mormons. Some of them had previously been dismissed because they refused to act against the vigilantes. Many vigilantes now enrolled in the militia and continued their anti-Mormon activities under the guise of restoring order. Most of the militiamen sincerely wanted to do their duty, but the logistics of the situation, the rapid call-up of troops, the lack of training of both officers and soldiers, and the fear of continued Mormon assaults made it difficult for the officers to organize and control the large military force.

Among the volunteers was Maj.-Gen. Samuel D. Lucas, reputedly one of the chief persecutors of the Saints in Jackson County. During the disturbances in Carroll, Lucas had visited Dewitt, after which he had urged Governor Boggs to take some kind of action lest a massive civil war erupt. On 4 October, Lucas wrote:

If a fight [at DeWitt] has actually taken place, of which I have

9. John Usher Parsons, Diary, n.p., entry 1 November 1838. LDS Archives.
10. Arthur I. H. Bradford to Maj. T. G. Bradford, 13 November 1838. Bradford Correspondence.

no doubt, it will create excitement in the whole upper Missouri, and those base and degraded beings will be exterminated from the face of the earth. If one of the citizens of Carroll should be killed, before five days I believe that there will be from four to five thousand volunteers in the field against the Mormons, and nothing but their blood will satisfy them.[11]

The expected battle at DeWitt did not occur, but now, only two days after a Missourian had been killed at Crooked River, Lucas and his men marched toward Far West in fulfillment of his warning to the governor.

While the generals prepared for the march to Far West, militia and vigilante companies continued to harass Mormon settlers, taking prisoners and ordering the Saints from their homes. Joseph Thorp, a member of Doniphan's brigade, said the soldiers were ordered to "bring in all the stragglers they found that couldn't give a good account of themselves."[12] Some of these companies subsisted on the Saints' crops and livestock and destroyed much property as they roamed the countryside. Mormons migrating from the east were stopped on the outskirts of Caldwell and ordered to turn back. Militia officers and local officials frequently had to intervene to prevent Mormon settlers and emigrants from being harmed.[13] David Osborn, a Mormon taken prisoner by Colonel Gilliam's troops in Clinton County, reported concerning his captors:

I never was in such a crowd before—many of them had never seen a mormon till they saw me . . . they had been stirred up to anger by designing men & were made to believe the mormons were a dangerous set of desperadoes & their own safety depended on their present action. They would curse old joe Smith . . . dam him. I'll shoot him the first sight I get of him.[14]

When a few of Osborn's non-Mormon friends informed the

11. *Document*, pp. 34–35, General Lucas to the Governor, 4 October 1838.

12. *Early Days in the West*, p. 87.

13. For Mormons who were protected, see Osborn, "Autobiography," p. 33; L. D. Young, "Narrative," pp. 47–49; Emma Anderson, "An Incident of the Past," *Autumn Leaves* 8 (July 1895): 316; Elijah Reed, "Affidavit, May 6, 1839." Petitions, LDS Archives; A. J. Stout, "Journal," p. 9; Palmer, "Sketch of the Life," p. 6; and Walker, *Life Incidents and Travels*, p. 7.

14. "Autobiography," p. 34.

others that he was an "honest Mormon," Gilliam instructed his men not to abuse or insult their prisoner.

Not all Mormons, however, were as fortunate. Among the thirty or forty prisoners taken by the Missourians, at least two, John Tanner and William Carey, were beaten. John Tanner and his son Myron were driving their wagon to a mill to obtain provisions for the Mormon army when they spotted a company of Missourians riding toward them. Tanner told his twelve-year-old son to hide in the woods and make his way home as best he could. Although the elder Tanner made no attempt to escape, Myer Odell, captain of the militia unit, shot twice at the Mormon as he rode toward the wagon, his gun misfiring each time. Upon reaching the wagon, Odell called Tanner a "god damned old Mormon" and struck him on the side of the head with the butt of his rifle.[15]   Tanner suffered a large, ugly gash, but his thick felt hat partially cushioned the blow and prevented more serious injury to the sixty-year-old man. The stunned Mormon was taken as a prisoner to the Missourians' camp.

William Carey was gathering corn with John Smith when the two men were captured by a militia patrol. A recent convert from Canada, Carey had arrived in Far West only four weeks previously. One of the militiamen, Milford Donaho, thought he recognized Carey as a member of the Mormon company that had burned his home and driven his family from Daviess County. "You will make a damned good wagoner for us," he told Smith. "But for that damned son of a bitch," he said, pointing to Carey, "all that he is fit for is sausage stuffings, and the quicker he is used for it the better."[16]   The Missourians placed several guns in the back of the wagon and escorted the Mormons to their camp. When Donaho retrieved the guns from the wagon, he found one of them cocked and ready to fire. "You damned son

15. Elizabeth Beswick Tanner, "Reminiscences," p. 3. Accounts of this incident are also found in John Tanner, "Sketch of An Elder's Life," *Scraps of Biography: Tenth Book of the Faith-Promoting Series* (Salt Lake City: Juvenile Instructor Office, 1883), p. 15; and Myron Tanner, *Biography of Myron Tanner* (Salt Lake City: The Deseret News, 1907), p. 6.

16. John Smith, "Affidavit, January 8, 1840." Petitions, U.S. Archives (excerpt edited for clarity). Other accounts of this incident are found in John Loveless, "Affidavit, January 7, 1840." Petitions, U.S. Archives; Nancy Cary [*sic*], "Affidavit, May 6, 1839." Petitions, LDS Archives; *History of Daviess County* (1882), p. 205; Thorp, *Early Days in the West*, p. 88; and Corrill, *A Brief History*, p. 44.

of a bitch, you have cocked your gun to shoot us," he screamed at Carey. Carey denied the accusation. "Don't you contradict me you damned son of a bitch," replied the enraged Missourian, who then struck Carey across the head with the breach of his rifle. Knocked unconscious, Carey pitched forward but was caught by John Smith before he fell from the wagon. The company surgeon later washed and dressed the wound, but the ailing Carey, whose brains oozed from his skull, lay senseless and unable to speak. Donaho continued to harass others captured by his militia unit, and he reportedly plundered several Mormon homes during the march toward Far West.

Nearly all the Mormon accounts that describe in any detail the 1838 events in Missouri report that the vigilantes and militia committed similar acts of violence and destruction throughout the brief conflict. According to many accounts, the Missourians engaged in widespread plundering and burning of homes, drove off livestock, destroyed property and crops, and indiscriminately beat and murdered Mormon men.

These claims, however, are not verified by eyewitness accounts. In the hundreds of petitions, journals, letters, and reminiscences written by the Saints, not one Mormon settler reported seeing a Missourian or group of Missourians burn another Mormon's home, nor did any Mormons report that their own homes had been burned, *before the surrender*— except in the instances described in this book. The accounts of Mormons who did report personal encounters with the vigilantes and militia units indicate that the Missourians were primarily concerned with disarming the Mormons and stopping them from migrating into the northern section of the state. The attack on Haun's Mill was a notable exception. The Missourians often threatened the Mormons and sometimes treated their prisoners roughly by pushing or shoving them, but there is no record of any Mormons (except Tanner, Carey, and the residents of Haun's Mill) being harmed or physically abused prior to the surrender. In the absence of eyewitness accounts from the hundreds of Mormon sources, the historian must conclude that widespread plundering and burning of homes and beating of Mormon settlers did not occur. Most of the destruction of property and subsequent suffering the Mormons associate with this period occurred after the surrender.

The Missourians, nevertheless, represented a real danger: random acts of violence occurred often enough to pose a threat to all Mormons. Within a few days after the Crooked River battle, more than two thousand troops collected against the Saints, some organizing under their militia generals in Richmond, some stationed in their own counties to prevent incursions by the Mormons, and others harassing and driving Mormon settlers from their homes. On 28 October, Atchison and Lucas, apparently acting as joint commanders of the large army, wrote a brief description of the situation to Governor Boggs and urged him to come to the "seat of war" as soon as possible.[17] Unknown to these men, Boggs had already signed orders initiating more extraordinary measures to restore civil order.

Governor Boggs's Extermination Order

As previously mentioned, Richmond citizens dispatched Amos Rees and Wiley C. Williams to Jefferson City on 24 October, the day before the Crooked River battle, to inform Governor Boggs of conditions in Daviess County and to request that he send assistance. On the night of 25 October, while they hastened to the state capital, Williams and Rees received an express from Judge E. M. Ryland of Lexington reporting that the Mormons had attacked Bogart's company at Crooked River, killing ten, wounding many more, and taking the remainder prisoner. After stating that the people expected Richmond to be sacked and burned that night, Ryland concluded:

You will see the necessity of hurrying on to the City of Jefferson, and also of imparting correct information to the public as you go along. My impression is, that you had better send one of your number to Howard, Cooper and Boone counties, in order that volunteers may be getting ready, and flocking to the scene of trouble as fast as possible. They must make haste and put a stop to the devastation which is menaced by these infuriated fanatics, and they must go prepared and with the full determination to exterminate or expel them from the State enmasse. Nothing but this can give tranquility to the public mind, and re-establish the supremacy of the laws.

17. *Document*, p. 76, Generals Atchison and Lucas to the Governor, 28 October 1838.

There must be no further delaying with this question any where. The Mormons must leave the State, or we will—one and all. And to this complexion it must come at last.[18]

After receiving Ryland's express, Williams and Rees stopped only long enough to write a brief letter to Maj.-Gen. John B. Clark of Howard County, informing him of the Mormon outrages and urging the strongest measures against them. "These creatures will never stop until they are stopped by the strong hand of force," they said, "and something must be done and that speedily."[19]

Reports of the Mormon depredations in Daviess County had already reached Governor Boggs when Williams and Rees arrived in Jefferson City on Saturday, 27 October. The day before, the governor had ordered General Clark to lead several divisions of troops to Daviess to restore the citizens to their homes.[20]   Upon receiving the letters and petitions brought by Williams and Rees, and learning that the Mormons had attacked state troops and were threatening to overrun all of northwestern Missouri, Boggs sent a new, more drastic set of orders to General Clark:

Head Quarters of the Militia
City of Jefferson, Oct. 27, 1838

Gen. John B. Clark

Sir:—Since the order of this morning to you, directing you to cause four hundred mounted men to be raised within your Division, I have received by Amos Rees, Esq. of Ray county and Wiley C. Williams, Esq. one of my aids, information of the most appalling character, which entirely changes the face of things, and places the Mormons in the attitude of an open and avowed defiance of the laws, and of having made war upon the people of this State. Your

18. Ibid., p. 62, E. M. Ryland to Messrs. Rees and Williams, 25 October 1838.
19. Ibid., p. 60, Williams and Rees to General Clark, 25 October 1838. It is of more than passing interest that Amos Rees served on this mission to request aid against the Mormons and that he advocated the strongest measures possible against them. In 1833 he opposed the anti-Mormon vigilantes and served with Atchison and Doniphan as a lawyer for the Saints (*HC* 1:424–25). In 1836 Rees joined with Atchison and Doniphan to help the Saints settle in Caldwell County (Peck, "Manuscript," p. 3). Ironically, after the Mormons surrendered, he again served as one of their lawyers.
20. *Document*, pp. 62–63, Commander-in-Chief to Gen. John B. Clark, 26 October 1838.

orders are, therefore, to hasten your operations with all possible speed. *The Mormons must be treated as enemies, and must be exterminated or driven from the State if necessary for the public peace—their outrages are beyond all description.* If you can increase your force, you are authorized to do so to any extent you may consider necessary. I have just issued orders to Maj. Gen. Willock, of Marion county, to raise five hundred men, and to march them to the northern part of Daviess, and there unite with Gen Doniphan, of Clay, who has been ordered with five hundred men to proceed to the same point for the purpose of intercepting the retreat of the Mormons to the north. They have been directed to communicate with you by express, you can also communicate with them if you find it necessary. Instead therefore of proceeding as at first directed to reinstate the citizens of Daviess in their homes, you will proceed immediately to Richmond and then operate against the Mormons. Brig. Gen. Parks, of Ray, has been ordered to have four hundred of his Brigade in readiness to join you at Richmond. The whole force will be placed under your command.

> I am very respectfully,
> your ob't serv't,
> L. W. BOGGS, Commander-in-Chief [21]

Clark began immediately to organize the expedition to Richmond.

Governor Boggs said that his main desire was to quell the Mormon insurrection without bloodshed; he therefore called out several thousand troops to "awe them into submission."[22] The Mormons, and some Missourians too, condemned his proclamation as excessive and harsh.[23] As General Clark later observed, Boggs "was too decided, too fast."[24] The order was issued in an environment of hostility and fear. Recent studies of anti-Mormon violence suggest that the constant labeling of the Saints as fanatics, creatures, and degraded human beings dehumanized them and created an atmosphere that allowed

21. *Document*, p. 61, the Governor to General Clark, 27 October 1838 (italics mine).

22. Ibid., p. 14, the Governor to the General Assembly, 5 December 1838.

23. For criticism by Missourians, see *Missouri Republican*, 27 December 1838, speech by David Atchison; *Missouri Argus*, 20 December 1838; and Gordon, "Public Career of Lilburn W. Boggs," pp. 106–9.

24. Quoted in Walter B. Stevens, *Centennial History of Missouri*, 4 vols. (St. Louis & Chicago: S. J. Clarke Publishing Company, 1924), 2:119, "Gen. John B. Clark's Narrative."

the governor to treat them as subhuman beings who could be exterminated or driven from the state. [25]   Boggs himself referred to the Mormons as a "deluded people." Nevertheless, whatever underlying motives or forces influenced his decision, Boggs acted from a genuine belief that the Mormons had rebelled against state authority. Even Atchison and Parks, who had previously defended their activities, now reported that Mormon soldiers had run amuck. And Judge Austin A. King, who represented the highest civil authority in northern Missouri, informed Boggs that the conflict had escalated beyond local control—"that it is utterly useless for the civil authorities to pretend to interpose"—and therefore the citizens looked to him for protection. [26]   In view of the information he had received, Boggs believed drastic measures were required to halt the Mormon onslaught.

The governor's order, though of questionable legality, was supported by the unwritten—but often affirmed—right of American citizens to expel unwanted persons or groups from their communities. Americans asserted this right when they drove abolitionists, gamblers, Catholics, free Blacks, and others from their communities. Missourians asserted this right when they drove the Mormons from Jackson, Clay, and then Carroll counties. Mormons asserted this right when they drove dissenters from Caldwell County. After receiving word that Mormon soldiers were planning to sweep through Missouri's upper counties, Governor Boggs asserted this right by ordering that the Mormons be exterminated or driven from the state.

Preparations for Battle

The Mormons did not intend to attack Richmond or any Missouri settlements, but they expected trouble. For several months Joseph Smith had instructed the Saints to move to the larger settlements and towns for safety. About this time Jacob Haun visited Far West to seek counsel regarding the Mormon village of Haun's Mill, which lay on the eastern border of

25. See Arrington and Bitton, *Mormon Experience*, pp. 60–62; and Alma R. Blair, "The Haun's Mill Massacre," *BYU Studies* 3 (Autumn 1972): 65–66.
26. *Document*, p. 54, Hon. A. A. King to the Governor, 24 October 1838.

Caldwell County.

"Move in, by all means, if you wish to save your lives," Smith advised.[27] When Haun protested that the settlers would surely lose their homes and property if they moved to Far West, the Prophet replied, "You had much better lose your property than your lives." Haun continued to press his point and insisted that the villagers could protect themselves from attack. Seeing that Haun could not be persuaded, Smith finally relented. "You are at liberty to do so if you think best," Smith concluded.

Upon returning to the village, Haun informed the residents that Smith had said they could move into Far West if they desired. But Haun did not report that the Prophet had commanded them to move. "We thought from the way the thing was represented [we] would be cowards to leave and not try to maintain it," wrote David Lewis, a Haun's Mill resident, regarding Jacob Haun's message from Joseph Smith; ". . . we did not know that it was Joseph's decided council for us to do so."[28] The Mormon villagers organized a militia company and remained in their homes.

Smith also encouraged migration to northwestern Missouri to bolster the Mormon army. William Draper reported that in August the Prophet instructed the Saints in Huntsville, Missouri, "to break up our organization and come to Caldwell County, as there was a strong indication of hostilities by the mob."[29] John Pulsipher said Mormon leaders were heartened by the arrival of a company of two hundred fifty emigrants from Ohio in early October, because they needed reinforcements for the anticipated conflict.[30] The doctrine of "gathering" thus assumed military as well as religious significance for the Saints, who now prepared to battle the Missourians from their two major towns, Far West and Diahman.

Both towns overflowed with refugees. The disturbances of the past several months had prevented the Mormons from constructing many homes or buildings in either Far West or

27. Lee, *Mormonism Unveiled*, p. 78.
28. Lewis, "Excerpt From The Journal," p. 2.
29. "A Biographical Sketch Of The Life And Travels And Birth And Parentage Of William Draper," p. 4. Typescript, LDS Archives.
30. Pulsipher, "A Short Sketch of the History of John Pulsipher," p. 3. Typescript, Utah State Historical Society Library.

Diahman. Over a thousand people gathered at Diahman, where only thirty to forty homes stood. Most families lived in tents or wagons. At Far West, which had a normal population of about two thousand, between three and four thousand Mormons filled the town to overflowing. Col. Lyman Wight commanded approximately three hundred men at Diahman; Col. George Hinkle led the six to seven hundred troops at Far West. At Diahman the Mormons loaded their cannon with small iron slugs and pointed it at the crossing on Grand River where they expected the Missourians to attack.[31] Mormon leaders continued to send out spies and guards to watch the movements of their enemies, while soldiers at Diahman and Far West remained on constant alert. "I slept in my clothes with my rifle in my arms nearly one Month," William Huntington, Sr., reported concerning his activities at Diahman, "day times we labored What we could with our arms and Amunition by our sides . . . ."[32]

The Saints at first believed the forces operating against them were large companies of mobs, but on 28 or 29 October word began to filter into Far West that these supposed mobs were actually Missouri state troops. By that time, however, the information made little difference to the Mormons. The lawless activities of the Missourians, whatever their official status, branded them as mobs. On the morning of 30 October, Joseph Smith assembled the Mormon soldiers and announced his intention to fight whoever came against them. "They pretended to come out as militia, but . . . they were all a damned set of mobs," Smith said of the Missouri troops. "God should damn them."[33] After promising the Saints that God would send angels to fight on their side, Smith declared, "If the mob persisted in coming upon us, we will play hell with their applecart."[34]

Chaos prevailed throughout the upper counties. Thousands

31. Zerah Pulsipher, "History of Zerah Pulsipher," Nora Lund and Terry Lund, compilers, *Pulsipher Family History Book* (Salt Lake City: Reprinted by Terry and Nora Lund, 1963), p. 16.

32. "Diaries," p. 4. Typescript, LDS Archives.

33. *Document*, p. 113, testimony of James C. Owens. Other accounts of this speech are recorded in E. Robinson, "Items of Personal History," *The Return* 2 (January 1890): 206; and *Document*, pp. 100, 128, 138, testimonies of Sampson Avard, George Hinkle, and Samuel Kimbel.

34. Robinson, "Items of Personal History," p. 206; and *Document*, p. 128, testimony of George Hinkle.

had fled or been driven from their homes. Daviess County was a scene of desolation, while Caldwell and northern Ray counties, except for the larger settlements, were mainly occupied by soldiers and vigilantes. Mormons could not safely venture outside of Caldwell or Daviess counties; Missourians could not safely enter the Mormon strongholds of Far West and Diahman. The *Missouri Republican* reported concerning these conditions:

Every account from that quarter shows an existing state of agitation in the public mind truly alarming. Every stranger is watched with jealousy, and every man compelled to take sides for or against the Mormons.[35]

Neutral participants on both sides were forced to take up arms in the conflict: many did so to avoid the distrust and enmity of their neighbors. One Missourian, after informing Lorenzo Young that a company of forty men was coming to burn his house, explained, "I have come to give you this warning as a friend. Should it be found out that I have done so, I might lose my own life!"[36] Both the Mormons and Missourians detained and arrested suspected enemies and persons of unknown loyalty. The fact that the Mormons and Missourians could not physically be distinguished from one another increased tension and fear. A Carroll settler told two Mormons (who did not reveal their religious affiliation) that he hated Mormons worse than Indians because "he could tell an Indian when he saw him, but he could not always tell a Mormon."[37] Desperate Mormon and Missouri leaders seized horses, wagons, mills, and other property to use in the expected hostilities.[38] Parley P. Pratt recorded that the Mormon soldiers resolved to fight to the last "in defence of our houses, homes, wives and children, and the cause of our country and our God."[39] On the Missouri side, Col. Neil Gilliam

35. 1 November 1838.
36. Young, "Narrative," p. 49.
37. George A. Smith, "History," n.p.
38. See, e.g., Hunt, *Mormonism*, pp. 218–19, testimony of George Walter; *Document*, p. 136, testimony of Elisha Cameron; Foote, "Autobiography," pp. 29–30; Shurtliff, "History," pp. 131–32, cf. Murdock, Journal, p. 106; and David Whitmer, "Letters from David and John C. Whitmer," *Saints' Herald* 34 (5 February 1887): 90.
39. *Autobiography*, p. 176.

admonished his troops "to be valiant and remember the blood & treasures spent by their revolutionary fathers to purchase the liberty which they were now called on to defend." [40] Both groups believed their extraordinary actions were necessary for the preservation of their lives, property, and American rights.

General Atchison Relieved of Command

On 29 October, Atchison and Lucas began a two-day march to Far West with their troops. The next day, before they resumed their march, they received Governor Boggs's orders of 26 and 27 October calling out the militia against the Mormons. Generals Lucas, Doniphan, and Parks were called out by these orders, but General Atchison was not. [41] Governor Boggs had given command to General Clark, who was then marching toward Richmond. Upon receiving these orders, Atchison returned with his staff to Liberty.

Governor Boggs later said that he relieved Atchison of command because he was a member of the state legislature, which would soon be meeting, and because of the numerous complaints from local citizens about Atchison's handling of the crisis. [42] A degree of enmity existed between the two men. Atchison believed the governor should have used his authority to suppress the anti-Mormon vigilantes; but it possibly appeared to Boggs that Atchison, by refusing to call out the militia against the Mormons, had allowed the conflict to escalate beyond the control of local officials. Boggs may have believed a more resolute commander was needed to quell the Mormon rebellion. But whatever his reason, Missouri's western newspapers questioned the governor's action. "The course of Gov. Boggs, in superseding Gen. Atchison, we hear much complaint about. Why the Gov. did this we are at a loss to know," said the *Western Star*. "So far as we have heard an expression of opinion, the people appear to be satisfied with

40. Osborn, "Autobiography," p. 35.
41. *Document*, p. 77, the Governor to General Clark, 1 November 1838; and ibid., p. 72, General Lucas to the Governor, 2 November 1838. General Lucas was given the "privilege" or option of taking the field with the troops from his division, but he was to be subject to the orders of General Clark.
42. Ibid., p. 69, the Governor to General Clark, 6 November 1838.

Mr. A. as a General." [43]

Although the governor's order relieved Atchison of command, it is uncertain whether the order also obligated him to retire before Clark arrived. Clark did not think so. On the same day, 30 October, Clark wrote to Atchison and Lucas and instructed them "to act for the best" until he arrived. [44] It was later said, though not by Atchison, that he voluntarily withdrew because he objected to the severity of Governor Boggs's decree. [45] This may be true: Atchison vehemently condemned the order in the next session of the state legislature, stating that the governor had no constitutional authority to issue such a proclamation. [46] In addition, Atchison may have been offended by the order, which relieved him of his rightful responsibility. By giving command to Clark, Boggs implied that Atchison was incompetent. Perhaps these personal objections to the governor's order prompted Atchison's seemingly unnecessary withdrawal from the conflict. After his departure, Lucas resumed the march toward Far West.

The Siege of Far West

During the several months of conflict, Mormon leaders had vacillated between aggressive resistance and a willingness to compromise. Although Joseph Smith announced on the morning of 30 October that the Mormons would fight whoever came against them, mob or militia, he wanted to avoid hostilities if he could. Later that day he dispatched a company of one hundred fifty men under Colonel Hinkle to search out the Missouri troops and learn their intentions. Smith asked John Corrill and Reed Peck, both friends of General Doniphan, to

43. Reported in the *Missouri Republican*, 17 November 1838. The *Republican* also carried a report from the *Far West* similar to that in the *Western Star*. After the disturbances, Liberty citizens held a dinner in Atchison's honor, paying tribute to his "meritorious and prudent course in the late difficulties with the Mormons."

44. *Document*, p. 76, General Clark to the Governor, 30 October 1838.

45. See *Missouri Republican*, 9 November 1838. See also Phineas Richards, Letter to Wealthy Richards, 21 January 1839. Photocopy, BYU Special Collections; and Francis Gladden Bishop, *A Brief History Of The Church Of Jesus Christ, Of Latter Day Saints, from their rise until the present time; Containing An Account Of, And Showing The Cause Of Their Sufferings In The State Of Missouri, In The Years 1833–1838* (Salem, n.p.: Printed by Blum and Son, 1839), pp. 7–8.

46. *Missouri Republican*, 27 December 1838.

accompany the Mormon troops and seek an interview with the general. [47]

While Hinkle's company was searching for the Missouri troops, those troops marched to Far West by a different route. The Mormons at Far West spotted the Missouri army about an hour before sunset as the army crossed a small creek two miles south of town. One of the Mormon guards called for his company to retreat as the large army approached. "Retreat! where in the name of God shall we retreat to?" exclaimed Joseph Smith, who quickly led three hundred soldiers to the edge of Far West and formed a battle line. [48]   As the Missourians approached to within a mile of town, Hinkle returned with his company of soldiers. Lucas dispatched Doniphan with two hundred fifty men to intercept Hinkle's company, but the Mormons eluded their pursuers and galloped safely into Far West, where they joined the other soldiers in line. Seeing that the Mormons intended to stand, Lucas decided to postpone the attack and wait for reinforcements. He withdrew his troops and camped about one-and-a-half miles south of Far West. [49]

As soon as the Missourians retreated, Reed Peck rode to their camp with instructions from Smith to seek a compromise. Peck met with Doniphan, to whom he gave the Prophet's message. An opponent of the Mormon military operations, Peck also tried to convince the general that many innocent people would be killed if the Missourians attacked. He informed Doniphan:

. . . there were many individuals among the Mormons who were as warmly opposed to the wicked transactions in Daviess County and the oppressive influence by which the church is led as any man in his army could be and that those men were now compelled to stand in the Mormon rank where in the event of battle their blood would flow

47. Peck, "Manuscript," p. 24; Corrill, *A Brief History*, p. 40; and *Document*, p. 127, testimony of George Hinkle.

48. John Taylor, "Discourse, March 5, 1882," *Journal of Discourses*, 23:37.

49. *Document*, pp. 72–73, General Lucas to the Governor, 2 November 1838; and ibid., p. 127, testimony of George Hinkle. Some Mormons later reported that Lucas decided to withdraw his obviously superior forces because hundreds of angels, bearing the appearance of "legions of armed men," stood beside the Mormon soldiers, visible only to the Missouri troops. See, e.g., "Elder John Brush, By Two Friends," *Autumn Leaves* 4 (April 1891): 173.

in defence of measures to which they had ever been averse.[50]

Assuring Peck that the Missourians wanted to punish only the guilty, Doniphan agreed to meet with some of the leading citizens of Far West the next morning and named John Corrill and W. W. Phelps to return with Peck. The general promised to hold off the attack until after their meeting, but said that he could not guarantee the good behavior of Colonel Gilliam's troops.[51]

After his interview with Doniphan, Peck felt confident that the innocent among the Saints had no need to fear unless the Mormon soldiers provoked an attack. Joseph Smith and other Mormon leaders, however, had no such confidence in the honorable intentions of the militia officers. They expected the Missourians to attack.

The Mormons prepared all night for battle. The men desperately threw up a breastwork of house logs, fence rails, floor planks, wagons, and any other materials that could be spared. Luman Shurtliff, a Mormon soldier at Far West, reported that he worked the entire night in a blacksmith shop, hammering out spears.[52] While the men worked on fortifications, the women packed their possessions in case the Missourians set fire to the town. Mormon leaders also sent an express to Diahman requesting more troops. Lyman Wight arrived the next day with one hundred fifty soldiers. By morning the Mormons at Far West had constructed a breastwork that extended three-quarters of a mile, covering the southern side of town (facing the army) and portions of their flanks.[53]

50. Peck, "Manuscript," p. 25.

51. Ibid., pp. 24–25; and Corrill, *A Brief History*, p. 40, describe Peck's meeting with General Doniphan. See *HC* 3:410, Hyrum Smith, affidavit, 1 July 1843, for Doniphan's comment regarding Gilliam's troops.

52. "History," p. 130.

53. Pratt, *Autobiography*, pp. 184–85; Rockwood, "Journal," pp. 11–12; and Draper, "Biographical Sketch," p. 6. John Corrill reported that during the summer and fall, rumors circulated throughout the upper counties that the Mormons were building blockhouses and fortifying their towns in preparation for war. The hastily constructed barricade built this night at Far West, when later discovered by the Missourians, served as apparent evidence for these otherwise unfounded rumors (*A Brief History*, p. 40).

10
Surrender

Mormon leaders still hoped to negotiate a compromise with the militia. Reed Peck, John Corrill, and W. W. Phelps, named by General Doniphan to return to the militia camp for discussions with the officers, were opponents of the Mormons' recent military activities. Joining them in the discussions were Col. George Hinkle and Arthur Morrison, apparently added by Smith to balance the representation on the Mormon committee. Hinkle was a religious and military leader among the Mormons, while Morrison served as a captain in the militia and as a Caldwell County judge. It is not known why Smith and his counselors did not negotiate directly with the officers; perhaps they feared their lives would be in danger outside of Far West.[1] Responsibility for settling the conflict peacefully thus fell upon Hinkle and the others.

On Wednesday morning, 31 October, the Mormons requested an interview with the Missouri militia officers. General Lucas replied that he was too busy organizing his troops and suggested that they meet at 2:00 p.m. instead.[2] The committeemen were able to speak briefly with General Doniphan, who informed them that General Atchison had been relieved of command and that Lucas now directed the troops. Doniphan also informed them that the militia had been called out by order of the governor, but he did not give them the particulars of the extermination order. According to both Corrill and Peck, Doniphan told

1. Smith believed that his enemies had been plotting to kill him from the time he arrived in Missouri in early 1838 (*HC* 3:368, Joseph Smith, "A Bill of Damages," 4 June 1839; cf. Swartzell, *Mormonism Exposed*, p. 36). He later hesitated to go to the militia camp (when General Lucas demanded that he surrender as a hostage), partly because he believed it unsafe. Both Peck and Hinkle believed their own lives were in danger outside of Far West (Peck, "Manuscript," p. 32; Hinkle, "Letter to W. W. Phelps, August 14, 1844," published in S. J. Hinkle, "A Biographical Sketch of G. M. Hinkle," *Journal of History* 13 [October 1920]: 449–50).

2. *Document*, p. 73, General Lucas to the Governor, 2 November 1838.

them that the militia officers delayed their negotiations with the Mormons because they were still waiting for Boggs's orders.[3] Apparently the orders received by the officers the previous day did not contain specific instructions regarding what action to take against the Mormons. The governor's extermination proclamation was sent only to General Clark, who then forwarded it to the other generals.[4] The Mormon representatives returned to Far West with only a limited amount of information. And while they waited to begin negotiations, the Missouri forces continued to grow, swelling to over twenty-five hundred men.

The situation grew worse for the Mormons throughout the day. The news that General Lucas had taken charge of the militia distressed Mormon leaders, for Lucas had been one of their chief persecutors in Jackson County. The Missourians allowed some of their Mormon prisoners to return to Far West that day. The prisoners carried into town William Carey, who lay speechless and suffering, having been struck over the head by one of his captors. Carey died a day or two later. During the early afternoon Charles Rich and a small company of Mormons parading under a white flag escorted two non-Mormon prisoners out of Far West. During their return they were fired upon by Captain Bogart, who recognized Rich as one of his assailants at the Crooked River battle.[5] Although no one was injured, the Mormons believed this incident portended the kind of treatment they could expect from the Missouri troops. About this time a messenger brought news to Far West confirming the worst Mormon fears. A large company of Missourians had attacked and destroyed the Mormon village of Haun's Mill.

The Haun's Mill Massacre

Haun's Mill was located on the eastern edge of Caldwell County, bordering Livingston County, about sixteen miles east

3. Corrill, *A Brief History*, pp. 40–41; and Peck, "Manuscript," p. 25.

4. See *Document*, pp. 61, 72, 76, the Governor to General Clark, 27 October 1838; General Lucas to the Governor, 2 November 1838; General Clark to the Governor, 30 October 1838; and Thorp, *Early Days in the West*, pp. 88–89.

5. Rich, Statement, p. 3; Josiah Butterfield to Mr. John Elden, 17 June 1839. Typescript, LDS Archives; and many other sources describe this incident.

of Far West. Ten to fifteen Mormon families lived at or near the village; another twenty emigrant families had stopped there during the disturbances and were living in their wagons. For two weeks a company of troops from Livingston County, led by Capt. Nehemiah Comstock, had harassed the Saints at Haun's Mill, driving off livestock and ordering the residents to leave their homes. After the 25 October battle at Crooked River, both the Mormons at Haun's Mill and the Livingston troops became fearful of an attack from the other. Consequently, their leaders signed a peace treaty halting the raids on the village. Joseph Smith repeatedly warned the Haun's Mill Saints to move into Far West for safety, but due to a misunderstanding of the Prophet's instructions, they chose to remain at the village, trusting in the Lord and their recently signed treaty to protect them. "None had ever been killed who abode by my counsel," Smith later said. "At Hauns' Mill the brethren went contrary to my counsel; if they had not, their lives would have been spared." [6]

No one knows who ordered the attack on Haun's Mill. The militia companies that participated in the assault belonged to General Parks's brigade, but he did not issue the order. [7] The troops organized under the command of Col. Thomas Jennings, who apparently acted on his own initiative in leading the attack. [8] It is possible that the Missourians received word of Governor Boggs's extermination order and took it upon themselves to carry out the decree, but they never offered this as a reason for the raid. [9] One of the attackers, Charles Ashby, a state legislator from Livingston, said the Missourians attacked because Mormon dissenters fleeing into Livingston warned them

6. *HC* 5:137.
7. Parks was with the troops that marched from Richmond to Far West. No evidence from Mormon or non-Mormon sources suggests that he ordered the attack.
8. *History of Caldwell and Livingston Counties*, p. 151; and Carrie P. Johnston and W. H. S. McGlumphy, *History of Clinton and Caldwell Counties, Missouri* (Topeka-Indianapolis: Historical Publishing Company, 1923), p. 240; both assert that Colonel Jennings, as commanding officer of the expedition, held responsibility for the attack on Haun's Mill. Jennings was a resident of Livingston County.
9. One problem with this theory is that there is no evidence indicating when Governor Boggs's order became known to the Missourians. Generals Atchison, Doniphan, and Lucas did not receive their orders from the governor until the afternoon of 30 October, and they did not receive an official

that the Saints at Haun's Mill were planning an invasion of their county. Local citizens decided they must act to prevent Mormon soldiers from overrunning Livingston as they had Daviess. "We thought it best to attack them first . . . ," Ashby told fellow legislators. "What we did was in our own defence, and we had the right to do." [10]

The Livingston troops were joined by companies from Daviess and Carroll counties. Many of the Daviess men wanted to even the score for Mormon depredations in their county. Capts. Nehemiah Comstock and William Mann, whose troops had been harassing Mormon emigrants and settlers, also brought their companies into the field. Prior to the attack, the Missourians blackened their faces and attached red cloths to their hats and shirts to distinguish themselves from their Mormon enemies. On the afternoon of Tuesday, 30 October, about 200 to 250 Missouri troops swept down upon Haun's Mill. [11]

The Mormons at Haun's Mill were not planning an attack

---

copy of the extermination order until 31 October. According to Burr Joyce, "The Haun's Mill Massacre," *St. Louis Globe-Democrat*, 6 October 1887, the decision to attack the Mormon village was made on 29 October.

10. *Missouri Republican*, 24 December 1838, speech by Charles Ashby.

11. Numerous descriptions were written by Mormon survivors of the attack. Petitions located in the U.S. Archives: Mosiah Benner, David C. Deming, Catherine Fuller, David Fullmer, Mahlon Johnson, Moses Kelley, Nathan K. Knight, Isaac Leany, Tarlton Lewis, Philanda Merrick, Reuben Naper, Ruth Naper, Alma Smith, Amanda Smith, Hannah York, and Joseph Young. Petitions in the LDS Archives: Jacob Fouts, Nathan K. Knight, Catherine McBride, Jacob Potts, Levi Stilts, and Joseph Young. Detailed accounts in later statements and reminiscences: Olive Ames, statement, *History of the Reorganized Church of Jesus Christ of Latter Day Saints*, 8 vols. (Independence, Mo.: Herald House, 1967), 2:234–37; Margaret Foutz, "Haun's Mill Massacre," LDS Archives; William Leany, "Autobiography of William Leany." Typescript, LDS Archives; David Lewis, "Excerpt From The Journal"; David Lewis, statement, *Times and Seasons* 1 (August 1840): 147–50; Ellis Eamut, statement, Journal History, 30 October 1838; and James McBride, "Autobiography." Photocopy, LDS Archives. The only known description by a non-Mormon participant is found in *Document*, pp. 82–83, D. Ashby's statement of the Battle at the Mill, 23 November 1838. Charles Ashby, also a participant, mentioned the incident in a speech in the state legislature, reported in the *Missouri Republican*, 24 December 1838. The *Missouri Republican*, 12 November 1838, published an account of the battle. The author of the Caldwell County history interviewed participants and local citizens for his account in the *History of Caldwell and Livingston Counties*, pp. 145–59. Joyce, "The Haun's Mill Massacre," also presents details of the incident.

upon Livingston settlers. They had set guards around the village, but because of their recent treaty they were not expecting an attack. The Missouri troops were first seen as they emerged from the woods about one hundred yards from the village. The Mormons, who were simply going about their daily tasks, did not react with alarm, but stared cautiously as the Missourians formed into three companies for their attack. Many of the Saints thought the troops were reinforcements from Far West. Captain Comstock fired his rifle into the air, after which ten seconds of silence followed. During the silence—described by Joseph Young as a "solemn pause"—the Mormons began slowly to grasp the meaning of the soldiers' appearance as they anxiously searched for wives, husbands, children, and the nearest shelter. The Missouri troops raised their guns, and with a thunderous roar broke the spell of silence by firing at the Mormon villagers.

From T. B. H. Stenhouse, *The Rocky Mountain Saints* (New York: D. Appleton and Company, 1881).

As soon as the shooting started, David Evans, the commander of the small militia force at Haun's Mill, ran to the center of the village, waved his hat, and yelled for quarter. So did a number of other Mormons, but the Missouri troops ignored their appeals and continued firing. Mothers frantically gathered their children and fled into the woods. A rifle ball pierced Mary Stedwell's hand as she attempted to jump a log. Her dress caught the log, and she fell over it, protected, as another twenty balls peppered the fallen tree. Fifteen men and three boys ran into a blacksmith shop, where the Mormons had previously determined to fight if they were attacked. They thought the shop would provide a shelter from which to defend the village, and their brief stand doubtless saved the lives of their fleeing neighbors because they attracted most of the Missourians' fire. But the shop also became a deathtrap, for the Missourians' musket balls easily passed through the large, unchinked cracks between the logs of the shop's walls.

Inside the shop the three boys crawled under the bellows for safety while the men frantically loaded, fired, reloaded, and fired again. The Missourians poured round after round into the shop while the Mormons' fire proved entirely ineffective as one-by-one the Mormon men fell. The Missourians slowly advanced toward the shop until they simply shoved their muskets through the logs and fired into the crowd of bodies. David Lewis attempted to fire through an open window, but, as he raised his gun, saw a Missourian preparing to fire. Lewis ducked just as another Mormon, stepping to the window to fire his musket, was shot in the face. Eventually, the crush of the Missourians' guns through the shop walls was so great that the defenders could not return fire, but could only desperately parry and dodge as the Missourians continued firing into the shop.

About half the Mormon men had fallen when Captain Evans ordered the rest to flee, but most of them were cut down as they ran the gauntlet of soldiers. Thomas McBride, a sixty-two-year-old Mormon who was wounded as he ran from the shop, surrendered his gun when the Missourians came upon him. Jacob Rogers, who ran a ferry in Daviess County, took McBride's loaded gun and discharged it into the old man's breast. Rogers then hacked at McBride with a scythe until his body was mangled from head to foot. Isaac Leany, after having the breach of his rifle shot off, crawled through a window and ran for the woods. He received two shots in the chest, one in the hip, and one in each arm before reaching the safety of the brush. His clothes were torn to shreds by a dozen other balls that grazed his body. Inside the blacksmith shop the Missourians found ten-year-old Sardius Smith hiding under the bellows. Young Smith, whose father lay mortally wounded on the floor, begged for his life, but William Reynolds of Livingston County put a gun to the boy's head and blew off the top. "Nits will make lice, and if he had lived he would have become a Mormon," Reynolds reportedly said in justification of his act. [12] After the firing ceased, some of the Missourians looted the homes and bodies of the Saints—several of the wounded were stripped as they feigned death—and then rode off. The Missourians suffered three wounded in the attack.

Few of the Saints returned to Haun's Mill until after dark. Some did not wander back until the next day. Amanda Smith returned to find her husband, Warren, and her son Sardius lying dead in the blacksmith shop. She discovered her seven-year-old son, Alma, wounded and feigning death under a pile of bodies (where he had lain since being shot), afraid to move or make any noise until he heard his mother calling several hours later. Bodies lay scattered throughout the village: eighteen had been killed or mortally wounded, twelve to fifteen others wounded. [13] All but one were men or boys. The floor of the blacksmith's shop was almost entirely covered by a pool of blood. The women who came back the night of the massacre tended to the wounded, but left most of the dead where they had fallen. "All through the night we heard the groans of the dying," Amanda Smith recalled. "Once in the dark we crawled over the heap of dead in the blacksmith's shop to try to help or soothe the sufferers' wants; once we followed the cries of a wounded brother who hid in some bushes from the murderers and relieved him all we could." [14] Late that night Isaac Leany crawled back to the village, where the Mormon women blessed him and then hid him under the floor of a cabin. A few of the men returned the next day, but, fearing the Missourians would

12. *History of Caldwell and Livingston Counties*, p. 149. Several different persons were named by the Mormons as having killed young Smith, but the author of the Caldwell County history, who investigated the incident, insisted that Reynolds was the assailant.

13. One of those killed was a non-Mormon named Walker. Walker was apparently a resident of Haun's Mill or a member of a Mormon emigrant company, because he did not belong to the militia. Blair, "The Haun's Mill Massacre," p. 64.

14. "Some Highlights in the Life of Amanda Barnes Smith," n.p. Typescript, BYU Special Collections.

attack, did not take time to bury the dead. Instead, they helped the women gather the bodies, frozen stiff, and threw them into an old well, some feet first, others head first, after which they filled in the well with dirt and straw. Although some of the women stayed to care for the wounded, most of the men fled back into the woods for safety after they disposed of the dead.

The messenger who brought news of the attack to Far West did not know how many had been killed or wounded; he could only report that the Missourians had overrun Haun's Mill and massacred a great number of its inhabitants.

Negotiations and Dictated Terms

News of the massacre seemed to change Joseph Smith's perception of the conflict. He not only saw that the Mormons could not win an all-out war with the Missourians, but he also realized that his people would be utterly destroyed if such a war occurred. He now pressed the five representatives to work out a compromise with the militia. Both Reed Peck and John Corrill wrote that Smith instructed them to "beg like a dog for peace." [15]   Hinkle reported that Smith told them to obtain a treaty "on any terms short of a battle." [16]   According to Corrill, Smith said he would go to prison for twenty years or even die rather than allow his people to be exterminated. [17]   When the appointed time arrived, the Mormon representatives, with clear instructions from Smith to seek a compromise, rode out to meet the Missouri officers.

The negotiators met between Far West and the militia camp. [18] Colonel Hinkle spoke for the Mormons, General Lucas for the Missourians. The militia officers, having now received a copy of Governor Boggs's extermination order from General Clark, were ready to negotiate. After a brief discussion, during which Hinkle

15. Corrill, *A Brief History*, p. 41; and Peck, "Manuscript," p. 24.

16. Hinkle, "Letter to W. W. Phelps, August 14, 1844," p. 449.

17. *A Brief History*, p. 41.

18. Descriptions of the discussions between the Mormon representatives and the militia officers are found in *Document*, p. 73, General Lucas to the Governor, 2 November 1838; Corrill, *A Brief History*, pp. 41–42; Peck, "Manuscript," pp. 25–27; Hinkle, "Letter to W. W. Phelps, August 14, 1844," pp. 448–53; and Arthur Morrison, "Affidavit, January 9, 1840." Petitions, U.S. Archives. Morrison's statement is brief. W. W. Phelps left no known account of this incident.

expressed a desire to settle the conflict without a fight, Lucas read the order to the Mormon representatives. They were shocked by its severity. "I expected we should be exterminated without fail," John Corrill recalled of this moment. "There lay three thousand men, highly excited and full of vengeance, and it was as much as the officers could do to keep them off from us any how; and they now had authority from the executive to exterminate . . . ."[19]

Lucas assured the representatives that he would not be as harsh as the governor had stipulated. The matter could be settled without bloodshed, he said, if the Mormons would accede to four demands:

1st. To give up their leaders to be tried and punished.
2d. To make an appropriation of their property, all who had taken up arms, to the payment of their debts, and indemnify for damage done by them.
3d. That the balance should leave the State, and be protected out by the militia, but to be permitted to remain under protection until further orders were received from the Commander-in-Chief.
4th. To give up the arms of every description to be receipted for.[20]

Lucas made it clear that the Mormons who participated in the attack on Bogart's company at Crooked River as well as those who committed the depredations in Daviess County would be liable to trial and punishment.

Hinkle objected strenuously to the demands to surrender their weapons and leave the state. He contended that if the Mormons had committed any crimes, they should be tried and punished according to the law. "But to give up our arms and leave the State, would be virtually throwing away our most sacred rites as citizens of a republican state," he said.[21] Lucas became enraged by Hinkle's obstinacy and declared that no other terms would do. He allowed no discussion of the matter. Still hesitant to agree, Hinkle requested that the Mormons be given until the morning to decide. Lucas agreed, but demanded that Joseph Smith, Sidney Rigdon, Lyman Wight, Parley P. Pratt, and George W. Robinson be surrendered as hostages to insure the Mormons' faithful compliance with the terms. The general

19. *A Brief History*, p. 42.
20. *Document*, p. 73, General Lucas to the Governor, 2 November 1838.
21. Hinkle, "Letter to W. W. Phelps, August 14, 1844," p. 451.

promised that these men would be returned to Far West the next morning if the Mormons decided to reject the surrender terms. [22]

It made little difference to the Missourians whether they attacked Far West then or on the next morning, but they were afraid the Mormon leaders would escape while they waited for Hinkle's decision. Consequently, they demanded that these men be surrendered at once. Arthur Morrison reported that Lucas threatened the Mormon negotiators, warning "that if Joseph Smith Jr. with a number of others was not given up to them, that the city of far-West would be consumed by fire and that it with its contents would soon be in ashes." [23]   Faced with this ultimatum, the Mormon representatives agreed to surrender the hostages as required. "We knew that General Lucas had no authority, and his requirements were illegal; for he was out of the bounds of his division, and the Governor's order was to General Clark, and not to him," Corrill said regarding their decision, "but there was no other way for the Mormons but to submit." [24]

Lucas gave them until one hour before sundown, about thirty minutes to an hour away, to deliver the hostages. As they were leaving, one of the Missourians warned Corrill that if the Mormon leaders escaped or could not be found, Far West would be destroyed and the Mormons exterminated.

The Mormon representatives, frightened by the threats of the militia officers, rushed back to Far West to inform their leaders of what had transpired. They hurriedly rounded up the hostages and tried to persuade them to surrender. The representatives brought with them copies of Boggs's extermination order and Lucas's surrender terms, which they read to Joseph Smith and

22. In his report to Governor Boggs, General Lucas said that Colonel Hinkle "agreed readily" to the surrender terms but asked the general to postpone the surrender until the next morning. Lucas thus implies that Hinkle made no objections to the terms (see *Document*, p. 73, General Lucas to the Governor, 2 November 1838). It is apparent, however, that since Lucas gave the Mormons until the morning to decide whether to accept the terms, there must have been some question or hesitation on the part of the Mormon representatives. Hence, Colonel Hinkle did not readily agree but actually objected to the terms, as Hinkle contends in his own account of this incident.

23. "Affidavit, January 9, 1840." Petitions, U.S. Archives.

24. *A Brief History*, p. 42.

the others. Confusion and disagreement occurred as the Mormon leaders hesitated to give themselves up. "There is no time for controversy," Colonel Hinkle argued with much agitation in his voice. "If you go not into the camp immediately, they are determined to come upon Far West before the setting of the sun . . . ."[25] During the brief discussion the representatives told their leaders that they might be able to arrange more favorable terms; if not, they could still return to Far West in the morning.

While the Mormon leaders and their representatives debated their options, they received word that the Missouri army, in full battle array, was marching toward Far West. Knowing the excitement that prevailed among the Missouri troops, the representatives pressed even harder for their leaders to surrender. Finally, Smith decided that he and the others would give themselves up and comply with whatever terms the militia officers required.[26] Corrill recorded, "Smith said if it was the Governor's order, they would submit, and the Lord would take care of them."[27] Besides, as Parley P. Pratt, another of the hostages, explained, "there was no alternative but to put ourselves into the hands of such monsters, or to have the city attacked, and men, women and children massacred."[28]

Lucas had waited only fifteen to thirty minutes after his meeting with the Mormon representatives before he organized his army and began marching toward Far West. He had worked out his battle strategy with the other officers and intended to attack immediately if the hostages were not produced.[29] He brought over twenty-five hundred men into the field, and one cannon, with which he planned to bombard the Mormon town. When the Mormons spied the Missouri army, they sounded the alarm and prepared for battle. Outnumbered more than three to one, the Mormon troops, their heads bound with handkerchiefs, took

25. *HC* 3:445, Lyman Wight, affidavit, 1 July 1843.

26. Corrill, *A Brief History*, p. 42; Peck, "Manuscript," p. 27; and Hinkle, "Letter to W. W. Phelps, August 14, 1844," p. 451. Statements by the hostages confirm the representatives' claim that they would not resist the militia. See Pratt, *Autobiography*, p. 186; and *HC* 4:34, Joseph Smith, Sidney Rigdon, and Elias Higbee, The Saint's [*sic*] Petition to Congress.

27. *A Brief History*, p. 42.

28. *Autobiography*, p. 186.

29. Lucas described his intended strategy in *Document*, pp. 73–74, General Lucas to the Governor, 2 November 1838.

their places along the makeshift breastwork. Few of the Mormon soldiers knew their leaders were contemplating surrender. They expected the long-anticipated battle to begin within minutes. "We knew their determination was to exterminate us," Albert Rockwood wrote of the approaching troops, "& [we] made up our determination to defend the City until the last man should fall to the ground."[30]   It was about this moment that Joseph Smith and the other hostages decided to give themselves up. Fearing the conflict would begin before their leaders could surrender, Reed Peck and John Corrill rushed out to meet the advancing army and informed the officers that the hostages were on their way. Lucas halted his troops about six hundred yards from Far West.

Colonel Hinkle escorted the Mormon leaders to the general. "Here, general, are the prisoners I agreed to deliver to you," Hinkle said.[31]   Both Smith and Wight asked Lucas if they could postpone the matter until morning, but he refused their request. "You are my prisoners, and there is no time for talking at the present," Lucas responded curtly. "You will march into the camp." As Hinkle and the others rode off, the Missouri troops closed around the prisoners and began shouting triumphantly. Some of the men, guns cocked, rushed in and threatened to shoot the hostages. General Doniphan and several other officers rode up and, with swords drawn, drove the men back, threatening to cut them down if they did not uncock their guns and move away. At camp, many of the Missouri soldiers continued to insult and threaten the Mormon prisoners; consequently, Lucas placed a guard of thirty soldiers in a double ring around the Mormons to protect them.[32]   The Mormon leaders spent the entire night on open ground, in the cold and rain, surrounded by thousands of hostile troops. They were given no opportunity

30. "Journal," p. 12. Similarly, John D. Lee reported that "our men were confident that God was going to deliver the enemy into our hands, and so we had no fears" (*Mormonism Unveiled*, p. 79).

31. *HC* 3:445, Lyman Wight, affidavit, 1 July 1843.

32. Mormon accounts of the mistreatment of the hostages are often exaggerated (with claims of blasphemy and attempted murder by the troops), but evidence from Missouri sources confirms that the hostages were threatened and it was necessary to place a guard around them (*Missouri Republican*, 24 December 1838, speech by Mr. Bowring; and Thorp, *Early Days in the West*, p. 89).

to discuss the surrender terms with the militia officers.

Contemplations of Battle
and Preparations for Surrender

The Mormon soldiers at Far West expected the Prophet to return in the morning. Although they understood that legitimate state troops—not vigilantes—surrounded their town, they still intended to fight. Some of the men had covenanted with Joseph Smith in 1836 to seek revenge against their enemies if any more of the Saints were slain or driven from their Missouri homes. Many also covenanted to avenge the death of Apostle David W. Patten. Sidney Rigdon had declared in his Fourth of July oration that the Mormons would wage a "war of extermination" against any mobs that molested them. And recently the men

Charles C. Rich (ca. 1852). Courtesy LDS Historical Department.

Sarah Rich (ca. 1879). Courtesy LDS Historical Department.

had covenanted with the Prophet never to surrender or accept terms of peace at the sacrifice of truth and right. That night Albert Rockwood wrote to his father and described the gravity of their situation, stating that they intended to defend their families and homes to the death. "You may now imagine to yourself the solemnity that rests upon us," he wrote; "we have the promise that but little blood will be shed at this time. But God only knows how we are to be delivered." [33]

Hyrum Smith, Brigham Young, and some of the other Mormon leaders in Far West knew that Joseph Smith intended to surrender. They also understood the nature of the Missourians' demands. [34]   Late the same night Hyrum Smith and Brigham Young met with Charles C. Rich, Lorenzo Young, and a number of others who had fought in the Crooked River battle and warned them that the Missourians had demanded they be surrendered and tried for murder. "Gather all the Crooked river boys you can and take them out of the state," Hyrum Smith told them, "for, if found, they will be shot down like dogs." [35]   Mormon leaders asked Phineas Young, a skilled woodsman, to guide the soldiers to safety. [36]   Lorenzo Young's wife, taking a sheet from their bed, hastily sewed a new pair of pants for her husband to wear on the long journey. Hosea Stout and Charles Rich bade a quick but emotional goodbye to their wives, and the two men and two women covenanted that they would not separate until they again reunited with their spouses. At about midnight twenty-five men fled on horseback north toward the Iowa Territory. Others, also warned by Hyrum Smith, left during the remainder of the night. Altogether, about seventy men escaped.

Soldiers in the militia camp waited restlessly for morning to arrive. Two Mormons, John L. Butler and Elijah Averett, reported that during the night one of their men crept outside Far West and shot his pistol to scare the Missourians. According to Averett, the man tormented the soldiers all night. Lyman Wight, who spent the night in the militia camp, reported that the Missourians were called to arms three times in expectation of an attack by the Mormons. [37]

33. "Journal," p. 12.

34. Hyrum Smith, a member of the First Presidency and one of the Prophet's closest associates, was probably present when his brother decided to surrender himself as a hostage. Brigham Young and other Mormon leaders may have also been present.

35. Journal History, 1 November 1838, Dimick B. Huntington, "Account of the flight from Far West after the Crooked River Battle."

36. L. D. Young, "Narrative," pp. 52–53. Phineas Young was a brother of Brigham and Lorenzo.

37. Butler, "History," p. 19; Averett, "History," p. 9. Photocopy, LDS Archives; and *History of the Reorganized Church of Jesus Christ of Latter Day Saints,* 2:260.

The Alleged Betrayal

The Mormon hostages spent the entire night surrounded by hostile troops, listening to boasts and threats of violence. The following morning, 1 November, General Lucas informed them that they could surrender and accept the terms offered, or they could fight—and be exterminated by the Missouri troops. According to Joseph Thorp, a member of Doniphan's brigade, Lyman Wight was the only hostage who wanted to return to town. "They were about as badly scared set as I ever saw," Thorp said concerning the hostages, "except old Wright [*sic*], who stood like a lion and said fight, without a sign of fear about him . . . ." [38] At about 8:00 a.m. Joseph Smith sent a message to Far West instructing the Saints to surrender.

The hostages felt betrayed. Their representatives had led them to believe they would be able to discuss the surrender terms with the militia officers, but once in camp they found that the terms had already been set, apparently arranged and agreed to by Hinkle and the others. It is clear from Lucas's report to Boggs that he considered Hinkle—and not Joseph Smith—to be the person who represented the Mormons in this matter. Later, while speaking to the hostages, General Clark referred to the surrender treaty "agreed to by Colonel Hinkle," indicating that Clark also believed Hinkle had been the chief representative for the Mormons at Far West. [39] Joseph Smith, however, never intended that Hinkle should be the final arbiter of his people's fate. It therefore appeared to Smith and the other hostages that the representatives had lured them into the militia camp, where the surrender terms were then forced upon them. Subsequent events, such as the court-martial of the hostages, the disaffection of Hinkle, Corrill, Peck, and W. W. Phelps, and their testimony against Church leaders at the Richmond hearing, seemed to confirm the Mormons' belief that these men had betrayed their leaders.

The Mormon representatives vehemently denied the accusations of betrayal, claiming instead that they faithfully informed their leaders of all propositions and demands made by the

38. *Early Days in the West*, p. 89.
39. See *Document*, pp. 73–74, General Lucas to the Governor, 2 November 1838; and Pratt, *Autobiography*, p. 199.

Missourians. There is much evidence to support their case. The representatives present consistent descriptions of their activities and discussions, while the accusations made by the hostages are inconsistent and contradictory.[40] Moreover, a close examination of the hostages' statements reveals that they understood the basic surrender terms. They knew that (1) they were going to the militia camp as hostages, and that they had the option of returning to Far West the next morning;[41] (2) the governor's order demanded that the Mormons leave the state; and (3) the Missourians intended to punish the Mormons allegedly guilty of crimes. The fact that Mormon leaders warned their soldiers to flee the state supports this contention and indicates that the hostages, before they gave themselves up, intended to surrender—they would not have sent away a large portion of their army if they were planning to fight.

An unresolved point of controversy, however, is the hostages' claim that they were told, falsely, that the militia officers wanted to discuss the surrender terms with them. The evidence, though inconclusive, suggests that the Mormon representatives unknowingly misled the hostages regarding this matter. When Lucas dictated the surrender terms to the representatives, their only viable option was to accede to his demands and hope that their leaders could persuade him to revise the terms. After

40. Statements by the representatives: (1) Corrill, *A Brief History*, p. 42; (2) Peck, "Manuscript," pp. 25, 32–33; and (3) Hinkle, "Letter to W. W. Phelps, August 14, 1844," pp. 448–53. W. W. Phelps and Arthur Morrison made no known statements concerning the alleged betrayal. Compare with accounts by the hostages: (1) Pratt, *Autobiography*, p. 186; *History of the Late Persecution*, pp. 39–40; and *HC* 3: 427, affidavit, 1 July 1843; (2) Wight: "Appeals to Supreme Court of Missouri," p. 203, affidavit, 15 March 1839; *HC* 3:444–45; and *History of the Reorganized Church of Jesus Christ of Latter Day Saints*, 2:259–60, Journal of Lyman Wight; (3) Rigdon: *HC* 3:459, affidavit, 1 July 1843; and (4) Joseph Smith: *HC* 3:371, "A Bill of Damages," 4 June 1839; "Appeals to Supreme Court of Missouri," p. 206, affidavit, 15 March 1839. Also Joseph Smith, Sidney Rigdon, and Elias Higbee, *HC* 4:34, The Saint's [*sic*] Petition to Congress, November 1839. George W. Robinson left no known account of these events.

41. In addition, Mormon soldiers also knew that their leaders had gone voluntarily to the Missourians' camp as hostages. On the night Mormon leaders surrendered themselves to General Lucas, Albert P. Rockwood recorded in his journal that the Missourians had agreed to "delay the attack of the City for the night if we would surrender Joseph Smith, Sidney Rigdon & P. P. Pratt as hostages until tomorrow morning 8 oclock, when they should be returned" (p. 12).

returning to Far West, the representatives probably told Smith and the others that they might be able to arrange more favorable terms. The representatives did not anticipate—how could they have known?—that Lucas would refuse to speak to the hostages.

Misunderstanding on two key issues thus contributed to the hostages' belief that they had been betrayed. The first was the incorrect assumption that the representatives "negotiated" and agreed with the surrender terms. In reality, Lucas dictated the terms to the representatives; they had no more chance to negotiate or arrange the terms than did their leaders. The second misunderstanding arose from the hostages' mistaken belief, apparently conveyed by the representatives, that the militia officers would discuss the surrender agreement with them. When the Missourians declined discussion, it appeared to the hostages that they had been deliberately misled. Blame for the harsh surrender terms fell upon the Mormon representatives, who were consequently denounced as traitors to the Church.

The Surrender

After Colonel Hinkle received Joseph Smith's message, he called together the Mormon troops and informed them of the decision to surrender. He described to the men the terms required by the Missourians and requested all in favor to take three steps forward. [42]

Hinkle's report stunned the Mormon soldiers. Many of the soldiers, probably most, did not want to surrender. "I would have willingly have faught until the last drop of my blood had been spilt," Jesse W. Johnstun later wrote.[43] Luman Shurtliff, who also wanted to fight, stated that "although our numbers ware small I felt confident the victory would be ours and the Lord [would] work out our Escape with our lives and the Kingdom of God roll on . . . ." [44] Zerah Pulsipher, who received news at Diahman of the surrender, said, "If we had not have received word from Joseph we should have been very likely to have sent hundre[d]s of them [Missourians] to *Hell, cross lots* . . . ."[45] But

42. Hinkle, "Letter to W. W. Phelps, August 14, 1844," p. 451; and Peck, "Manuscript," p. 28.
43. "Reminiscences," p. 10. LDS Archives.
44. "History," p. 130.
45. "History," p. 16.

the Mormons trusted their prophet and believed the decision to surrender was the will of the Lord. "That was a tough pill to swallow," William Draper said of the decision, "however, if Joseph says so, all right."[46]   After a slow start, all the Mormon soldiers stepped forward.

At 9:30 a.m. General Lucas marched his troops to the prairie about two hundred yards south of Far West, where they formed a hollow square. The Mormon troops, numbering about six hundred, marched out and formed another hollow square inside the Missourians' square. Some of the Mormon women came out of their homes, crying, claiming their men would all be shot. Inside the square, Maj. Seymour Brunson, speaking low to the Mormon men as he passed around, instructed them not to surrender their powder and bullet accouterments because they had only agreed to give up their weapons.[47]   Even while surrounded, Luman Shurtliff still wanted to fight, believing that the Mormon soldiers could defeat the Missourians "by practicing our Danite order of fighting."[48] When the militia officers ordered the Mormons to ground their arms, some of the men angrily threw them down.[49]   Capt. Jonathan Dunham broke his sword in three pieces over his knee before tossing it on the pile. The towering Alexander McRae, six-and-a-half feet tall, took several flashing cuts with his sword and then staked it in the ground as far as he could send it. Some of the Missouri troops, angered by the belligerent spirit of the Mormon soldiers, began cursing them and threatened to shoot McRae for his insolence. While the surrender continued, the Missourians attempted to intimidate the Mormons by picking their flints and priming their guns, as if they were making ready to fire. After all the weapons had been laid down, Hinkle rode forward and delivered his sword and pistols to Lucas. The Mormons marched back to Far West under heavy guard.

46. "Biographical Sketch," p. 6.

47. E. Robinson, "Items of Personal History," *The Return* 2 (February 1890): 210. Robinson reported that this upset many of the Missourians.

48. "History," p. 131.

49. See Hillman, "Autobiography," p. 22; William Allred, "Biography and Journal," p. 6. Photocopy, LDS Archives; Stevenson, "Life and History," p. 44; Duncan, "Biography," p. 38; Martha P. J. Thomas, "Family Genealogy," in *Daniel Stillwell Thomas Family History* (Salt Lake City: n.p., 1927), p. 20; and Draper, "Biographical Sketch," p. 6.

Later that day Lucas marched his entire force of twenty-five hundred men through the streets of Far West in order to "gratify" his troops and to show the Mormons their strength. [50] The Missourians paraded through the town with obvious satisfaction, and many of the men threw out taunts and insults to the unarmed Mormon soldiers as they swaggered by. "You God damn Danites," some yelled, threatening the Mormons. "Charge, Danites! Charge!" others shouted derisively. [51] The Mormons made no attempts to retaliate or resist.

50. *Document*, p. 75, General Lucas to the Governor, 2 November 1838.
51. Peck, "Manuscript," p. 28; and Averett, "History," p. 9.

11
Terms of Surrender

The disarming of the Mormon soldiers opened the way for widespread plundering and violence against the Saints that continued until they left the state. Missouri soldiers ransacked homes, some looking for property allegedly stolen from them, others simply searching for booty, while the Mormon owners looked helplessly on. William E. McLellin, a former Mormon apostle, led a search of Joseph Smith's home to confiscate books and papers that might prove damaging to the Mormons. The Danite constitution was reportedly found in a trunk filled with the Prophet's personal papers. [1] Josiah Butterfield said the Missourians would enter homes during the night, awaken the Mormons with cocked guns, and then search the houses for weapons and take whatever they pleased. [2] A gang of eight men, catching William Clark alone, beat him up because "your a God Dam Mormon Preacher & we are Determined to kill every mormon." [3] In Carroll County a mob captured Riley Stewart and, holding two pistols at his head, forced him to take off his coat, kneel down, and receive fifty lashes. [4] James Powell, a non-Mormon whose wife belonged to the Church, was clubbed senseless by a group of Missourians when he resisted their attempts to take possession of his property and home. Powell received a six-inch gash in his head, exposing his brain, and a doctor later removed fourteen pieces of bone from his skull. Swearing they would indemnify themselves for Mormon damages in Daviess County, the Missourians warned Powell's wife and her parents, who witnessed the entire affair, "to be gone by early breakfast time the next morning or they

1. *Missouri Republican*, 20 November 1838; and *HC* 3:286–88.
2. Josiah Butterfield to Mr. John Elden, 17 June 1839.
3. William O. Clark, Letter to Friends & Relatives, 21 July 1839. Photocopy, LDS Archives.
4. Lee, *Mormonism Unveiled*, p. 84.

would kill every one of us." [5]

At Far West several Mormon families crowded into each small cabin for shelter. Many lived in tents and slept near fires to keep warm during the night. The Missouri soldiers lived off the Mormons' livestock and crops and used their house logs for fire, while the Mormons ate frozen potatoes and boiled corn. The soldiers reportedly shot hogs and cattle for sport, claiming the animals were "Mormons running away on all fours." [6] According to Mormon reports, the soldiers also raped several women. The accusations of rape, which were promptly denied by Missouri officials, are difficult to verify. [7] Yet, there are at least two eyewitness accounts of attempted rapes, and the evidence indicates that the soldiers brazenly threatened the unprotected Mormon women. Mercy Thompson, whose husband fled the state the night before the surrender, said she lived in such constant terror that "at times I feard to lay my Babe down lest they should slay me and leave it to suffer worse than immediate Death." [8]

General Lucas was more concerned with punishing the leaders of the alleged Mormon rebellion than with protecting the Saints. On 1 November, the night of the surrender, Lucas met with his chief officers and held a court-martial of seven Mormon leaders, including Joseph Smith, Sidney Rigdon, Hyrum Smith, and Lyman Wight. None of the Mormon First Presidency belonged to the

5. Greene, *Facts Relative To The Expulsion*, p. 37, statement by Peter Wimmer; and *HC* 4:61, affidavit of James Powell, 11 March 1840.

6. Draper, "Biographical Sketch," p. 7.

7. Nearly all reports of rape are based on hearsay and rumors. In addition, the reports are generally vague and often exaggerated—Brigham Young, for example, said that several Mormon women were "ravished to death." But it cannot be expected that the victims would readily reveal details of these incidents. Parley P. Pratt said one of the victims verified that she had been raped but "delicacy at present forbids my mentioning the names" (*HC* 3:428, 434, affidavits of Parley P. Pratt and Brigham Young, 1 July 1843). Charles Morehead, the representative to the state legislature from Ray County, said during a debate that "he was in Far West when one of these reports [of rape] was started, and he assisted in attempting to ascertain the truth, and the Mormons themselves admitted that it was false" (*Missouri Republican*, 24 December 1838). For other denials, see *Document*, p. 92, Report of General Clark, 29 November 1838; and Corrill, *A Brief History*, p. 44. The two eyewitness reports come from the petitions of Ruth Naper (an intended victim) and Elijah Reed (affidavits, 3 and 8 January 1840. Petitions, U.S. Archives).

8. Autobiography, p. 3. LDS Archives.

state militia, and therefore they were not legally subject to a military court. Lucas apparently believed, however, that a summary trial and punishment of these men was necessary to impress upon the Saints the severity of their crimes.

Lyman Wight reported that during the proceedings Gen. Moses Wilson of Jackson County called him aside and promised to release him if he provided evidence against the Mormon prophet. Wight promptly refused, but told the general, "If you will give me the boys I brought from Diahman yesterday, I will whip your whole army." [9]

"Wight, you are a strange man," said Wilson, "but if you will not accept my proposal, you will be shot to-morrow morning at 8."

"Shoot and be damned," Wight replied.

Sketchy evidence makes it difficult to determine who attended and the number who voted at the trial. According to Mormon accounts, Judge Austin A. King as well as seventeen ministers attended the court-martial, but this claim is not verified in other sources. General Doniphan, General Parks, Colonel Hinkle, and a number of others argued strenuously for the prisoners, but about two-thirds of the officers voted for conviction. [10]   At midnight, Lucas issued the following order to Doniphan: "Sir: You will take Joseph Smith and the other prisoners into the public square of Far West, and shoot them at 9 o'clock to-morrow morning." [11]   Whatever Lucas's feelings regarding the necessity of this action, he doubtless realized that the court-martial and execution of civilians was illegal. Consequently, if Doniphan carried out the order, it would help to justify Lucas's action and shield him from any subsequent criticism. Had the prisoners' own friend and lawyer carried out the sentence, few would have questioned its expediency.

Doniphan declared he would have none of it. Peter Burnett, a member of his brigade, privately assured the general that "we

9. "History of Lyman Wight," p. 457; and *HC* 3:446, Lyman Wight, affidavit, 1 July 1843.

10. The numbers on the vote vary: (1) Josiah Butterfield to Mr. John Elden, 17 June 1839, reports the vote as 12 to 7; (2) *Times and Seasons* 1 (January 1840): 37, Alanson Ripley, letter to the editor, has 12 to 5; and (3) Eliza R. Snow, "Letter from Missouri, Feb 22, 1839," *BYU Studies* 13 (Summer 1973): 547, has 13 to 4.

11. *History of Caldwell and Livingston Counties*, p. 137.

of Clay County would stand by him." [12]   Doniphan returned
the following note to Lucas:

It is cold-blooded murder. I will not obey your order. My brigade
shall march for Liberty to-morrow morning, at 8 o'clock; and if you
execute those men, I will hold you responsible before an earthly
tribunal, so help me God! [13]

Doniphan's indignant refusal—for which he was never called to
account—prevented the execution of the Mormon prisoners.
Neither Lucas nor the other officers pursued the matter further.
Lucas, perhaps embarrassed by his hasty and unlawful tribunal,
later denied that the court-martial was held. [14]

On the morning of 2 November the tapping of drums called
the Mormons to the town square, not to witness the Prophet's
execution, as Lucas had originally planned, but to sign away
their property to pay for the expenses of the war, as stipulated
in the surrender agreement. Lucas and Hinkle appointed five
commissioners to supervise the transfer of property: William
Collins, G. W. Woodward, and Judge Elisha Cameron, representing
the Missourians; and John Corrill and W. W. Phelps, representing
the Mormons. Five hundred Mormons came forward one by one to
the commissioners' table at the center of a hollow square formed
by the Missouri troops. "Joe Smith could not make the Saints
consecrate, but we can make them consecrate," a Missourian
remarked as the Mormons signed over their property. [15]   After
signing the deeds, the Mormons were also required to raise their
hands and swear that their actions were voluntary. This proved
too much for Nathan Tanner, who raised his hand and mockingly
waved it over the soldiers' bayonets. "It looks like a free volantear

12. Burnett, *Recollections*, p. 63.
13. *History of Caldwell and Livingston Counties*, p. 137.
14. *Document*, p. 64, General Lucas to the Governor, 11 November
1838. Mormon sources also state that General Clark intended to court-
martial and execute the Mormon prisoners (see, e.g., Rigdon, *Appeal*, p.
47; and *HC* 3:417, affidavit of Hyrum Smith, 1 July 1843). Shortly after
his arrival, General Clark said that he was considering a court-martial, but
"only as a dernier resort"–that is, only if local authorities proved incapable
of holding a trial. Boggs promptly replied that the Mormon prisoners must
be turned over to the civil authorities (*Document*, p. 67, General Clark to
the Governor, 10 November 1838; and ibid., pp. 81–82, the Governor to
Gen. Clark, 19 November 1838).
15. Journal History, 24 December 1861, talk by Brigham Young.

act and deed at the point of beyanet," he remarked sarcastically.[16] One of the guards knocked Tanner senseless and he was
carried from the ground.

General Lucas did not remain long in Far West. After dis-
patching General Parks to Diahman to effect the surrender of
Mormon troops there, he appointed several companies of soldiers to guard the Mormons at Far West until General Clark
arrived from the east. Rather than leaving Joseph Smith and the
other Mormon leaders under guard, however, Lucas marched
them with his troops back to Jackson County. As the Missourians
prepared to leave, hundreds of Mormons gathered around the
wagon that carried the Mormon prisoners. Lucy Mack Smith
could get only as close as one hundred yards, so great was the
crush around the Prophet. "I am the mother of the prophet—is
there not a gentleman here, who will assist me to that wagon,
that I may take a last look at my children . . . ," she cried,
fearing that her sons would be executed in Jackson County.[17] A
gentleman led Lucy through the crowd to the wagon, which was
covered with a strong cloth nailed tightly all around. Joseph and
Hyrum reached their hands through the canvas to grab their
mother's hand, but were forbidden conversation. "God bless
you, mother," Joseph sobbed as the wagon drove away.

Lucas apparently took the Mormon leaders to Independence
to show them off as trophies to the people of Jackson County.
Two of the prisoners reported that Lucas ignored an order
from General Clark to return them to Clark's custody.[18] When
they arrived in Independence, hundreds of curious spectators
crowded the streets to welcome both the victors and the
vanquished. Many strained to catch a glimpse of Smith, for
it was rumored that he professed to be the Lord and that
the Mormons worshiped him. The soldiers allowed Smith and
the other prisoners to converse with the people, much to
the delight of all. "We have been protected by the Jackson
County boys, in the most genteel manner, and arrived here
in the midst of a splended perade," Joseph Smith reported in

16. Tanner, "Journal," p. 7.
17. Lucy Mack Smith, *Biographical Sketches of Joseph Smith the Prophet*,
p. 317.
18. Pratt, *Autobiography*, pp. 192–96; and Rigdon, *Appeal*, p. 45.

"The Extermination Of The Latter Day Saints From The State Of Missouri": a Mormon view of the surrender. Courtesy LDS Historical Department. The small numbers visible in this drawing were keyed to the following comments:

1. Genl. Clarke. Gentlemen you shall have the honor of shooting the Mormon leaders on monday morning at 8 oClock!

2. Mr. Cary, had his brains knocked out by the but end of a musket in a general massacre!

3. Revd. S. Bogard. It is my opinion they should all be shot!

4. Genl. Lucas. Your verdict gentlemen is that the mormons shall be shot to morrow morning. I fully concur with you in your sentence!

5. Rev. I. McCoy. It is my opinion also that they should be shot or other-wise disposed of!

6. Genl. Atcheson. I am against shooting men that have committed no crime.

7. Genl. Graham. I am decidedly opposed to the determination of the court Martial!

8. Genl. Doniphan. By God you have been sentenced to be shot by the Court Martial this morning but I'll be dam'd if I'll have any of the honor of it. I consider it to be cold blooded murder and I bid you farewell!

9. Genl. Wilson. Your die is cast, your doom is fixed, you are sentenced to be shot tomorrow morning on the public square in Far West at 8 o'Clock!

10. Lyman Wight. Shoot and be dam'd.

11. Wm. E. McClellan. I think Coln. we ought not to have left the Mormons. I am sorry for it. I hate to be called a Traitor!

12. Coln. Geo. Hinkle. I would rather be called a Mormon traitor than be shot like a squirrel!

13. Brest Work.

14. City of Far West.

a letter to his wife, Emma; ". . . instead of going to gaol we have a good house provided for us and the kindst treatment."[19]   The prisoners stayed two or three days in Independence, lodged at a local hotel, and were allowed to walk the streets freely with but one guard who looked after them. Finally, when Clark's demands could no longer be ignored—and when, perhaps, Jackson citizens grew bored with their Mormon celebrities—Lucas returned them to Clark's custody.

Lucas's behavior throughout the disturbances baffled Missouri authorities. Governor Boggs later asserted that his orders to Lucas did not authorize him to lead the expedition against the Saints. Yet, Lucas directed the siege of Far West, dictated the surrender terms, court-martialed and sentenced Mormon leaders to die, and then marched those leaders back with his troops to Independence—all without orders.[20]   His gentle treatment of Mormon leaders in Independence contrasted so sharply with the harshness of his surrender terms, and with his previous determination to execute Mormon leaders, that the Mormons too were puzzled by his behavior. Whatever the general's motivation, however, Mormon leaders were grateful he spared their lives. Upon leaving Independence, the seven Mormon prisoners wrote a letter thanking General Lucas, General Wilson, and all the citizens of Jackson County for the kind treatment they had received. "Gentlemen, we found you friends at a time when we most needed them . . . ," the prisoners wrote. "For your prosperity in this life, and rest eternal in that which is to come, you have the sincere desire and devout prayer of your prisoners in tribulation."[21]

During this period immediately following his arrest, Joseph Smith wrote two letters to Emma describing his feelings about the unexpected turn of events. The first letter, written 4

19. Joseph Smith to Emma Smith, 4 November 1838. RLDS Archives.

20. The correspondence between Governor Boggs, General Clark, and General Lucas, which contains information regarding Lucas's actions and authority, is found in *Document*, pp. 63–92. The *Missouri Republican* reported on 14 November 1838: "Gen. Lucas and Atchison acted without authority from the commanding officer in attacking Far West . . . . On account of some misunderstanding of the Governor's orders by Gen. Lucas or a disposition to disobey, things have gotten somewhat deranged."

21. This letter, "To The Citizens of Jackson County," 5 November 1838, was published in *The Ohio Statesman* (Columbus, Ohio), 28 November 1838.

November from Independence, reveals that the obviously distraught Prophet was uncertain whether he would be executed:

. . . what God may do for us I do not know but I hope for the best always in all circumstances although I go unto death, I will trust in God, what outrages may be committed by the mob I know not, but expect there will be but little or no restraint Oh may God have mercy on us. [22]

Smith concluded his letter in an equally distressed tone:

Oh Emma for God sake do not forsake me nor the truth but remember me, if I do not meet you again in this life may God grant that we may meet in heaven. [23]

A week later, as the Richmond hearing began, the Prophet was more hopeful and no longer talked about death:

. . . tell the chilldren that I am alive and trust I shall come and see them before long, comfort their hearts all you can, and try to be comforted yourself, all you can, the[re] is no possible dainger but what we shall be set at Liberty if Justice can be done and that you know as well as myself . . . we are in good spirits and rejoice that we are counted worthy to be persecuted for christ sake. [24]

He concluded by asking Emma to visit him in jail, and, if possible, to bring the children with her.

In these letters the Mormon prophet also presented an interpretation of the conflict which, to a large extent, would be adopted by the entire Church. First, Smith claimed he had been betrayed:

Colonal Hinkle, proved to be a trator, to the Church, he is worse than a hull who betraid the army at detroit, he decoyed us unawares God reward him, [John Corrill] told general wilson, that he was a going to leave the Church, general Willson says he thinks much less of him now then before, why I mention this is to have you careful not to trust them. [25]

22. Joseph Smith to Emma Smith, 4 November 1838.
23. Ibid.
24. Joseph Smith to Emma Smith, 12 November 1838. RLDS Archives.
25. Joseph Smith to Emma Smith, 4 November 1838.

In addition, Smith viewed his imprisonment—and the entire action against the Saints—as religious persecution:

> we are prisoners in chains, and under strong guards, for Christ sake and for no other cause, although there has been things that were unbeknown to us, and altogether beyond our controal, that might seem, to the mob to be a pretext, for them to persacute us, but on examination, I think that the authorities, will discover our inocence, and set us free, but if this blessing cannot be obtained, I have this consolation that I am an innocent man, let what will befall me. [26]

The unusually subdued Prophet no longer issued confident assertions that the Mormons would march through their enemies in Missouri. Nevertheless, he had not lost faith in his own prophetic calling, neither did he doubt the righteousness of his cause. And Joseph Smith never understood how Mormon military operations contributed to the conflict, other than in serving as a pretext for persecution.

Gen. John B. Clark arrived in Richmond on 3 November with some fifteen hundred troops. A leading citizen of Howard County, Clark later claimed that Boggs appointed him commander because he was a Whig. "If the campaign turned out wrong, Boggs wanted to lay the blame on the Whig party," explained Clark, who ran unsuccessfully as the Whig candidate for governor in 1840. [27] Reminiscences by Clark's friends and acquaintances describe him as "a kind and generous neighbor" and "a man devoid of fear, whose soul was full of the milk of human kindness." [28] The Mormons have different memories of this man who, Pratt said, "seemed more haughty, unfeeling, and reserved than even Lucas or Wilson had been when we first entered their camp." [29]

Clark began immediately to enforce the terms of surrender dictated by Lucas. He engaged in a series of letters with Boggs and Lucas to have the Mormon leaders returned to his custody

26. Joseph Smith to Emma Smith, 12 November 1838.

27. "General John B. Clark's Narrative," in Stevens, *Centennial History of Missouri*, 2:119.

28. W. D. Vandiver, "Reminiscences of General John B. Clark," *Missouri Historical Review* 20 (January 1926): 235; C. H. Magee, "General John B. Clark," *Missouri Historical Review* 20 (July 1926): 493.

29. *Autobiography*, p. 198.

and then sent Col. Sterling Price to Independence to escort them to Richmond. He dispatched Gen. Robert Wilson to Diahman to supervise a preliminary hearing of suspected Mormon criminals in Daviess County and set to work himself to round up the chief Mormon criminals in Far West.

Clark attempted to gather information from Saints who had become disillusioned with Mormonism—"and there are not a few at this time," he reported. [30]   Although these Mormons supplied much information about general Mormon activities during the disturbances, they apparently revealed few names to the general. It was not until the Missourians captured the former Danite general, Sampson Avard, that they received the information they needed. Fearing for his life, for he certainly would be identified as one of the chief Danite officers and perpetrators of the Mormon crimes, Avard agreed to supply the names of Mormon offenders in return for immunity from prosecution. "But for the capture of Sampson Avard . . . ," Clark reported, "I do not believe I could have obtained any useful facts." [31]

Clark's two-day investigation convinced him that many Mormons had committed treason, murder, arson, robbery, and numerous other crimes. On 5 November his soldiers arrested approximately fifty men believed to have committed the most serious crimes; these men were to be tried with the seven Mormon leaders at a preliminary hearing in Richmond. Prior to their march to Richmond, the fifty prisoners and the remaining Mormon men were assembled at the Far West public square, where Clark demanded compliance with all the stipulations of the surrender agreement:

The character of this state has suffered almost beyond redemption, from the character, conduct and influence that you have exerted, and we deem it an act of justice to restore her character to its former standing among the states, by every proper means. . . . you must not think of staying here another season, or of putting in crops, for the moment you do this the citizens will be upon you. If I am called here again, in case of a non-compliance of a treaty

30. *Document*, p. 65, General Clark to the Governor, 10 November 1838.
31. Ibid, p. 90, Report of General Clark, 29 November 1838. Reed Peck also states that Sampson Avard provided the names of alleged Mormon criminals ("Manuscript," p. 29).

made, do not think that I shall act any more as I have done—you need not expect any mercy, but extermination, for I am determined the governor's order shall be executed. As for your leaders, do not once think—do not imagine for a moment—do not let it enter your mind that they will be delivered, or that you will see their faces again, for their *fate is fixed—their die is cast—their doom is sealed*.

I am sorry, gentlemen, to see so great a number of apparently intelligent men found in the situation that you are; and oh! that I could invoke that *Great Spirit, the unknown God*, to rest upon you, and make you sufficiently intelligent to break that chain of superstition, and liberate you from those fetters of fanaticism with which you are bound—that you no longer worship a man.

I would advise you to scatter abroad, and never again organize yourselves with Bishops, Presidents, etc., lest you excite the jealousies of the people, and subject yourselves to the same calamities that have now come upon you.

You have always been the aggressors—you have brought upon yourselves these difficulties by being disaffected and not being subject to rule—and my advice is, that you become as other citizens, lest by a recurrence of these events you bring upon yourselves irretrievable ruin. [32]

General Clark informed the Mormons that, due to the inclement weather and their pitiful condition, he would allow them until the spring to leave the state. He also pledged the "honor of the State they should not be hurt" if they complied with the terms. [33] The Mormon men were told they would be allowed to return to their farms and homes outside Far West to obtain supplies for their families; but Clark warned them that they must not be found gathering in groups of five or more. "If you are, the citizens will be upon you and destroy you," he said. [34]

None of the Mormon men or women present ever forgot Clark's humiliating speech. Willard Snow commented:

This short address . . . was delivered to a people who have been mob[b]ed out of Jackson forsed to leave Clay driven from Carrol rooted out of Davis and last of all commanded to give up their pleasant possessions in Caldwell and leave the state or be exterminated by its authority their property has been plundered their cattle killed

32. *HC* 3:203–4, "General Clark's Harrangue to the Brethren."
33. *Document*, p. 91, Report of General Clark, 28 November 1838.
34. *HC* 3:436, Brigham Young, affidavit, 1 July 1843.

their provisions distroyed and their dwellings burned down and yet it would appear from this short addres that they had always been the aggressors . . . .[35]

Having endured years of abuse and persecution, the Mormons now stood divested of all they owned and accused of numerous crimes—and they were informed that, as an act of mercy, they would be allowed to remain in their homes for a few more months. "My pen fails to describe the persecutions & afflictions that the unbelieving Missourians are permitted to inflict upon us, the half cannot be told," Albert Rockwood wrote shortly after Clark's visit to Far West, "the Blood of innocence cries from the ground . . . ."[36]

The Surrender at Adam-ondi-Ahman

The one hundred fifty Mormon soldiers at Diahman, having received word of the Prophet's decision to surrender at Far West, capitulated without a fight when the Missouri troops arrived two days later. General Parks effected the surrender at Diahman and then turned over command to General Wilson when he arrived on 8 November. Wilson was shocked by what he found. In a letter to General Clark he wrote:

It is perfectly impossible for me to convey to you any thing like the awful state of things which exist here—language is inadequate to the task. The citizens of a whole county, first plundered, and then their houses and other buildings burnt to ashes, without houses, beds, furniture or even clothing in many instances, to meet the inclemency of the weather. I confess that my feelings have been shocked with the gross brutality of these Mormons, who have acted more like demons from the infernal regions than human beings.[37]

Wilson marveled at the immense piles of stolen property brought into Diahman by the Mormons; local citizens informed him that much more had been taken to Far West. "Under these circumstances you will readily perceive that it would be

35. "Statement," n.d. Petitions, U.S. Archives.
36. "Journal," p. 17.
37. *Document*, p. 78, General Wilson to General Clark, 12 November 1838.

perfectly impossible for me to protect the Mormons against the just indignation of the citizens," he observed.[38]

Daviess citizens did not conceal their hostility. The Mormon men were kept in a pen while angry settlers gathered around, accusing them of stealing their property and threatening summary retribution. Some came at the prisoners with cocked guns and had to be dragged away by the guards. Some of the guards engaged in the same threatening activities. Many Mormons reported that Colonel Gilliam's troops, who accompanied General Parks to Diahman, destroyed much of their property. "A painted company under the command of Cornelius Gilliam, a member of the legislature, rode through the town plundering and taking just what they pleased and abusing men, women, and children, and swearing that they would kill Joseph Smith, Jr., S. Rigdon, and others," reported Elisha Hill.[39] Although no Mormons were hurt, they felt much abused by both the citizens and the troops sent to maintain order. "We could not decide which was most to be dreaded, the Militia or the mob—no property was safe within the reach of either," Eliza Snow wrote concerning their circumstances.[40]

Judge Adam Black, one of the Saints' chief opponents in Daviess County, conducted a preliminary examination to bring the alleged Mormon offenders to justice; but local citizens were unable to identify those who had burned their homes and stolen their property. The Mormons, of course, revealed nothing. Oliver B. Huntington reported that the night before the militia arrived, the Mormons removed the stolen property from their homes and deposited it at Lyman Wight's new block building so that the Missourians would not know who had stolen their property.[41] Huntington also said that, when questioned about their alleged crimes in Daviess County, the Mormons adopted a policy of being as "innocent and as ignorant as

38. Ibid.
39. "Affidavit, January 6, 1840." Petitions, U.S. Archives (excerpt edited for clarity).
40. "Sketch of My Life," p. 10. Photocopy, LDS Archives. Daniel Cathcart reported that when he complained to General Wilson that local citizens had stolen some of his property, Wilson replied, "you mus[t have] took as mutch from some body els[e]" ("Affidavit," 6 January 1840, Petitions, U.S. Archives).
41. "History," p. 34. Lyman Wight was subsequently charged at a preliminary hearing in Richmond with stealing property in Daviess County.

we knew how to be." [42] In addition, the Mormons told the Missourians that those responsible for the crimes were Danites, and that these men fled the state the night before surrender. Huntington, who just a few weeks previously had joined the Danites, wrote:

> . . . every mysterious trick and bold adventure which had been transacted, was planted upon them [the Danites] and every body knew . . . a company of Mormons fled to the Indian territories . . . and they, it was stated, were the Danites, a most daring band of braves, who were bound together like the Masons. Thus they became, in a great measure, the scapegoats of the people, bearing off every charge, unless, it was personal. [43]

The Mormon ploys proved successful. Although many of the men examined at Diahman had participated in the Daviess raids, Judge Black's preliminary investigation found evidence to hold only one man, Benjamin F. Johnson.

The twenty-year-old Johnson was identified by Mr. and Mrs. Taylor, who remembered his benevolent actions during the attack upon their home: when a fellow Mormon soldier tried to steal one of the Taylors' horses, Johnson forcibly removed the horse from the man's grasp and gave it to Mrs. Taylor, who was pregnant, so she could make her escape. The Missourians held Johnson for nearly a week in an outdoor prison of snow and brush, trying to persuade him to reveal the names of other Mormon soldiers. "If you are the only one to answer for all the burnings and raids upon the old settlers then your case is bad indeed," a local settler informed Johnson. [44] Many believed he should be shot if he refused to cooperate. The Mormon men eventually became uneasy and sent William Huntington, Jr., to determine whether Johnson intended to betray others. The young Johnson, upon hearing their fears, felt as if he had been betrayed:

> . . . a sense of injustice came over me not easy to describe. I had stood there alone in prospect of death, or worse, and I had been

42. Ibid.
43. Ibid., p. 36. The company of Danites referred to by Huntington is Captain Patten's company. Many members of this company, including Huntington's brother Dimick, participated in the Crooked River battle and fled Far West the night before the surrender.
44. Johnson, *Life's Review*, p. 45.

true, and now instead of praying for me and giving me their faith they were prophesying evil, or exercising a faith against me. A flood of grief gushed out of my eyes before I could hinder it. I told him to tell the people to have no fears, for with God's help I would stand true . . . .[45]

Johnson eventually received the help he needed from unexpected friends. Two prominent non-Mormons, a government attorney from St. Louis and Dr. Carr, a Gallatin resident, pleaded on his behalf, first to Judge Black and then to General Wilson. Both claimed that Johnson had acted as a moderating influence on his fellow Mormon soldiers. Based upon these reports, and upon his own conversations with Johnson, Wilson concluded that the young Mormon was an honest, decent man whose crimes were attributable to the corrupting influence of Mormonism. "He [Wilson] said that he liked my appearance very much, and would have liked me to go and live with him," Johnson wrote. "If I would leave the Mormon faith and go with him, and make my home with him he had every advantage to give me to become rich, and he would see that I would be one of the richest young men of the state." [46] Johnson declined the offer, explaining that he still had parents back east who would be anxious to see him again. Wilson then supplied Johnson with the necessary provisions to return to his family and allowed him to escape during the night.

General Wilson stayed only ten days at Diahman. He informed the Mormons that, although they did not have to leave until the spring, they would receive no protection once his soldiers returned home. "I am fully satisfied for myself," Wilson informed General Clark, "that no people having any claims to honesty would permit such a band of robbers, as these Mormons have proved themselves to be, to reside among them." [47] The Mormons immediately moved from the county.

45. Ibid., p. 49.
46. Ibid., p. 50.
47. *Document*, p. 88, General Wilson to General Clark, [25 November 1838].

12

The Richmond Court of Inquiry

While Missouri officials diligently enforced the terms of surrender, eastern Missouri newspapers expressed doubts that the Mormons were solely responsible for the conflict. After describing the slaughter of Mormons at Haun's Mill, the *Missouri Republican* asked, "Will the actors in the tragedy be suffered, by the Courts of that District, to go unpunished?"[1]   Another article condemned the aggressive and illegal activities of the anti-Mormon vigilantes and printed a letter to the editor referring to the conflict as "the war upon the Mormons."[2]   "It is said that the leaders are to be put to trial . . . ," reported the *Republican*. "We hope that a searching operation will be applied to the guilty on all sides."[3]

Western Missouri settlers, however, were little inclined to view the disturbances in such an objective manner. A few non-Mormons, such as Atchison and Doniphan, contended that the illegal activities of anti-Mormon vigilantes had instigated the Saints' retaliatory acts of violence and crime. But most settlers viewed the Mormons as the cause of trouble: their secret Danite band, their depredations in Daviess County, their attack on state troops at Crooked River, their fortifications at Far West, and the dissenters' reports of aggressive intentions by Mormon leaders, all stood as evidence that the Mormons had initiated the disturbances. Crimes committed by non-Mormons, they believed, were the unfortunate result of the excitement generated by the conflict. This biased view of the events led Missouri officials to examine the conduct of Mormons only, as if they alone had been responsible for the disturbances. In early November, while General Wilson settled affairs in Daviess County, Judge Austin A. King held a Court of Inquiry

1. 12 November 1838.
2. 10 November 1838.
3. 9 November 1838.

in Richmond, Ray County, to investigate the crimes allegedly committed by Joseph Smith and other Mormons.

The Richmond hearing must be examined in detail for a number of reasons. The testimony given at the hearing was cited by Missourians as evidence that the Mormons were the aggressors (and therefore the guilty party) in the conflict. The Mormons subsequently sought to discredit this evidence by claiming that the testimony against them was false and that the hearing was a sham, a mere pretense of justice. Many of the early Mormon affidavits, petitions, and histories were written to clear Mormon leaders of the charges brought against them at the Richmond court. Consequently, an understanding of the Mormon War requires an understanding of the Richmond Court of Inquiry because the evidence presented at the hearing and the countercharges subsequently presented by the Mormons constitute important source materials for these events. [4]

The Richmond Court of Inquiry

The Richmond Court of Inquiry was not, as its name implies, a military tribunal, but a preliminary hearing conducted by civil officials. The purpose of preliminary hearings has changed little since the 1830s, though in recent years magistrates have increased their concern for the rights of the accused. [5] When defendants are brought before the court at preliminary hearings, the prosecution must demonstrate that a crime has been

4. Most descriptions of the Richmond hearing found in Mormon histories rely on two groups of Mormon sources: (1) pamphlets and histories written by Mormon leaders immediately following the disturbances, describing their suffering in Missouri; and (2) affidavits and petitions written by Church leaders to refute the charges against Mormon prisoners. The pamphlets are described in the Bibliographical Essay, pp. 269–79. The affidavits and petitions are found in *HC* 3:368–74, 403–66, 4:24–38; and in "Appeals to Supreme Court of Missouri," *Journal of History* 9 (April 1916): 200–216.

5. For general information on early preliminary hearings, see *The Revised Statutes of the State of Missouri* (St. Louis: Printed at the Argus Office, 1835), pp. 474–78; and Nathan Dane, *A General Abridgment and Digest of American Law, With Occasional Notes and Comments*, 9 vols. (Boston: Commings, Hilliard & Co., 1823–1829), 7:300–303. For general information on preliminary hearings, see Frank W. Miller, *Prosecution: The Decision to Charge a Suspect with a Crime* (Boston and Toronto: Little, Brown and Company, 1969), pp. 45–109; Stephen A. Saltzburg, *American Criminal Procedure: Cases and Commentary* (St. Paul, Minn.: West Publishing Company, 1980), pp. 684–96; and Charles E. Torcia, *Wharton's Criminal Procedure*, 4

committed and that sufficient evidence exists to bring the accused to trial. Preliminary hearings serve to prevent suspected persons from escaping while safeguarding them from groundless prosecution. Prosecuting attorneys generally present only enough evidence to establish "probable cause" for believing the defendants are guilty of the alleged crimes. Defense attorneys, once they realize that sufficient evidence exists to charge their clients, rarely make an extended presentation of their case.

The judge plays an active role in the preliminary hearing, sometimes taking over the questioning of witnesses in order to establish the essential facts in the case under examination. Because the prosecution must establish only a reasonable cause for believing the accused are guilty, magistrates often evaluate the evidence in a light favorable to the state. Some judges will stop the examination and bind over the defendants for trial—without even allowing the defense to present its witnesses—when they believe enough evidence has been submitted for probable cause. Questions regarding the defendants' motives, the reliability of witnesses, conflicts in testimony, and other problems of evidence are left for juries—not the judge—to decide at later trials. A decision by the judge to charge the defendants does not represent a conviction or judgment of guilt against them. It simply means the judge has found probable cause to believe the defendants committed the alleged crime, thus warranting further investigation within the judicial system.

The Richmond hearing began on 12 November and lasted until 29 November 1838. Fifty-three of the defendants brought to Richmond had been identified during General Clark's two-day investigation in Far West. Eleven others were added during the hearing. The Missourians focused their examination on three main areas of reported criminal activity: first, on the Mormon raiding expeditions in Daviess County, where Mormon soldiers drove settlers from their homes, plundered, and burned; second, on the 25 October battle at Crooked River, where Mormon soldiers clashed with Missouri state troops, killing

---

vols. (Rochester, N.Y.: The Lawyers Co-Operative Publishing, 1974), 1:299–308. Preliminary hearings today generally have fewer witnesses and do not last as long as the Richmond Court of Inquiry, but the purpose and procedures of the hearings remain the same.

one man and wounding several others; and third, on the allegedly treasonous activities of Mormon leaders. For years rumors had circulated that the Mormons were engaged in an Aaron Burr–type conspiracy to establish a theocratic "kingdom" on the Missouri frontier. Civil officials believed the extralegal military operations of Mormon soldiers, the machinations of the secret Danite band, and the reported dictatorial control of Church leaders in Caldwell County evidenced a treasonous plot by Joseph Smith and his cohorts to usurp the functions of government in northwestern Missouri. The Mormon prisoners hired their loyal friend Alexander Doniphan and Amos Rees to defend them.

Large crowds gathered in Richmond during the preliminary hearing. The unfinished, windowless county courthouse served as both prison and courtroom for most of the Mormon defendants, while the small Richmond jail held only those considered the most dangerous Mormons. During the hearing the defendants stood together behind a long pole that separated them from Judge King. Many of those attending the hearing were non-Mormons who had participated in the recent conflict. Captain Bogart and his men, who made no secret of their animosity toward Mormons, served as guards for the prisoners and their witnesses. "Shoot your Mormon. I have shot mine," one of the guards shouted to another.[6] One of the defendants, Morris Phelps, reported that many citizens gathered menacingly around the prisoners:

Another [Missourian] would say—pointing out some one of us,— "There is a red hot Mormon, d—m him, I am acquainted with him,— to another—"That dam rascal was in the battle—or out to Davis,—or to DeWit, such a one is a great preacher and leader amongst them, he ought to be hung, or sent to the penitentiary. Thus they would examine and view us as critical as if we were ravenous wolves, and they were about to purchase us for our fur.[7]

The large and hostile crowd, convinced of the Mormons' guilt, intimidated the witnesses and defendants throughout the

6. E. Robinson, "Items of Personal History," *The Return* 2 (March 1890): 234.
7. "Reminiscences," p. 16.

hearing. "We have Smith, Rigdon and Dr. Avord [*sic*] here, in chains, closely confined under a strong guard," wrote one observer as the hearing began, "and I hope they will never get from here until they satisfy the world, by their deaths, for all the crimes they were instrumental in committing." [8]

The state called Dr. Sampson Avard as its first witness. A talented and persuasive man, Avard had helped organize and direct the secret Danite organization. His appearance as a witness surprised both Mormons and Missourians. Avard had wielded considerable influence among the Saints during the disturbances, and many expected him to be a prime suspect, not a key witness, in the alleged crimes.

The Mormons claimed that Avard's character, motives, and testimony were highly suspect. According to Sidney Rigdon, Avard advised a potential Mormon witness to "swear hard" against the heads of the church, since they were the ones the court wanted to incriminate. "I intend to do it . . . in order to escape," he said, "for if I do not they will take my life."[9] One of the defense witnesses, Nancy Rigdon, later testified that Avard said "he would swear to a lie to accomplish an object; that he had told many a lie, and would do so again."[10] William T. Wood, the assistant prosecuting attorney, reported that Avard became disillusioned with Mormonism when the Prophet's promised victory over the Missourians failed to occur. Avard told Wood that, after receiving word Joseph Smith had surrendered, "I at once lost all faith and am no longer a Mormon." [11]

Avard's testimony covered a wide range of topics and activities. The prosecution questioned him extensively about the Danite organization, which Avard claimed was directed by Joseph Smith and his counselors. The Danites, he reported, considered themselves duty-bound to obey the First Presidency "as to obey the Supreme God." [12] According to Avard, Smith blessed the Danite officers and prophesied "they should be the

8. *Missouri Republican*, 20 November 1838, Letter to A. B. Chambers (the editor).

9. *Appeal*, pp. 47–48.

10. *Document*, p. 147, testimony of Nancy Rigdon. Nancy was a daughter of Sidney Rigdon.

11. "Mormon Memoirs," *Liberty Tribune* (Liberty, Mo.), 9 April 1886.

12. *Document*, p. 98.

means, in the hands of God, of bringing forth the millenial kingdom."[13] Avard presented a copy of the Danite constitution (a relatively harmless document) and described the group's role in driving dissenters from Caldwell County. The letter ordering the dissenters to leave the county, signed by Hyrum Smith and some eighty Mormons, was also presented to the court. In response to other questions about suspected treasonous activity, Avard briefly related Smith's plans for gathering the Saints and building the Kingdom of God in western Missouri and described the Prophet's leading role in Mormon military operations. Finally, Avard identified the defendants who joined the Danites, marched in the expedition to Daviess County, and participated in the attack on state troops at Crooked River.[14]

Avard's testimony, which makes up about one-fifth of the court record, lasted two days. Peter Burnett, a newspaper editor and lawyer who attended the hearing, reported:

He [Avard] was a very eccentric genius, fluent, imaginative, sarcastic, and very quick in replying to questions put by the prisoners' counsel. His testimony was very important, if true; and, as he had lately been himself a Mormon, and was regarded by them as a traitor from selfish motives, his testimony labored under some apparent suspicion. For these reasons he was cross-examined very rigidly.[15]

According to David Pettigrew, one of those who questioned Avard was Joseph Smith. "Doctor, you said that you had unshaken confidence in me as a Prophet of God. What gave you this confidence?" Smith asked. "Was it because I taught you how to lie, steal and murder as you have testified, or because you actually believed me a prophet?" When Avard made no reply, several of the guards cried out, "Kill the damned doctor."[16]

Judge King also played an active role during the examination as he cross-examined Avard and other witnesses regarding Mormon activities and beliefs. After eliciting testimony about the Prophet's teachings regarding the prophecy of Daniel–that

13. Ibid., p. 97.
14. Avard's entire testimony is contained in *Document*, pp. 97–108.
15. *Recollections*, pp. 63–64. Burnett served as a lawyer for the defendants at subsequent hearings in Clay and Daviess counties.
16. "A History of David Pettigrew," p. 8. Typescript, LDS Archives. Pettigrew was a defendant at the hearing.

the Kingdom of God would roll forth like the little stone that destroyed all earthly kingdoms—King turned to the clerk and said, "Write that down; it is a strong point for treason."[17] One of the Mormon lawyers objected but was overruled by King. "Judge, you had better make the Bible treason," he observed.

During the remainder of the hearing the prosecution called forty-one witnesses, twenty Missourians and twenty-one Mormons. At least eleven of the Mormons were men who had become disillusioned with Church policies. Many of them believed the Danites had exerted an oppressive and spiritually unhealthy influence within Mormonism. John Corrill, a stalwart in the Church leadership during previous troubles in Missouri, had openly quarreled with Mormon leaders about these issues. John Whitmer had been excommunicated and driven from Far West by the Danites. The testimonies of Corrill, Whitmer, and other dissenters reflected their disapproval of Mormon policies and activities. [18]

Most of the information provided by the dissenters supported Avard's testimony. Although they were less certain than Avard of the First Presidency's direct involvement with the Danites— they knew of only one or two meetings that Joseph Smith and his counselors had attended—they believed Avard had received his instructions from these men. John Corrill and Reed Peck reported that they were present when the Prophet blessed the Danite officers as Avard described. In addition, the dissenters gave corroborating testimony concerning other alleged Mormon activities and teachings, most of which have been detailed earlier in this history:

(1) The organization of the Danites in early June 1838 and the various meetings and activities (such as Sidney Rigdon's Salt Sermon) that led to the expulsion of the Cowderys, Whitmers, and others from the county.

(2) The 15 October meeting at which Joseph Smith and Sidney Rigdon rallied the Mormons in Far West prior to the

17. Pratt, *Autobiography*, p. 212.

18. Little information exists indicating how the prosecution located Mormon witnesses willing to testify for the state. Avard, of course, turned state's evidence to avoid prosecution. George Hinkle, who did not consider himself a dissenter, claimed he was "legally subpoenaed" ("Letter to W. W. Phelps, August 14, 1844," p. 452). How the prosecution identified Hinkle and other Mormons (both loyal and dissenting) as witnesses for the state is unknown.

march of Mormon soldiers to Daviess County.

(3) The plundering and burning by Mormon soldiers in Daviess County, as carried out under the direction of Joseph Smith and other Mormon leaders.

(4) Joseph Smith's speech to Mormon soldiers on 30 October when the Missouri troops arrived outside Far West.

The prosecution also elicited information regarding Mormon beliefs and activities that indicated a treasonous intent to set themselves outside the law. George Hinkle, another surprise witness for the state, testified:

> The general teachings of the presidency were, that the kingdom they were setting up was a temporal as well as a spiritual kingdom; that it was the little stone spoken of by Daniel. Until lately, the teachings of the church appeared to be peaceable, and that the kingdom was to be set up peaceably; but lately a different idea has been advanced—that the time had come when this kingdom was to be set up by forcible means, if necessary. [19]

Testimony by these witnesses that Mormon leaders were unwilling to submit to legal process during the disturbances—including Joseph Smith's instructions to the Caldwell County clerk not to issue "vexatious" lawsuits against Mormon leaders—supported the prosecution's contention that the Mormons were engaged in some sort of plot to subvert the laws of the state.

The ten other Mormons who appeared as witnesses for the state were loyal Church members who testified reluctantly at the hearing. According to Mormon accounts, these men testified because Missouri officials threatened them with prosecution and imprisonment. Morris Phelps reported that he attempted to testify on behalf of the defendants, but was stopped by Judge King and the prosecuting attorney, who then filed charges against him for his participation in the Crooked River battle. [20] Most of the Mormon witnesses, including Phelps, either emphasized their own nonparticipation in the alleged crimes or asserted that their leaders had forced them to take up arms. "I first refused to go," Phelps replied, when asked whether he participated in the Mormon attack at Crooked River;

19. *Document*, p. 128, testimony of George Hinkle.
20. "Reminiscences of Columbia Prison," p. 1. Photocopy, LDS Archives.

"but, being threatened with force, I consented to go."[21]   The brevity of their testimonies indicates that these witnesses were unwilling to provide as much information as Corrill, Hinkle, and the others. Nevertheless, their testimonies corroborated the dissenters' statements regarding Mormon activities and beliefs and implicated many defendants in the alleged crimes.

Nearly all of the twenty Missourians who testified described their encounters with Mormon troops. Some told of being captured; others reported that they were accosted and threatened by Mormons. Samuel Bogart and four of his men testified regarding their battle with Mormon soldiers at Crooked River. The Missourians' statements, as transcribed for the court record, reveal no prejudice or exaggeration. Joseph H. McGee's testimony is typical:

On Thursday, the 18th day of October, I was at Mr. Worthington's, in Daviess county, when the Mormons made an attack upon Gallatin. Mr. Worthington had a pair of saddle-bags in my shop, (in Gallatin,) with notes and accounts in them; and he requested me to go up to the shop, and try to secure them. When I went up, the Mormons had broken open my shop and taken them out; one of them had put the saddle-bags on his horse, and I asked him for them. He answered, that he had authority from Captain Still to take them, and would not let me have them. He then told me I must go up to the store. I went along; and when I arrived there, Clark Hallett, one of the defendants, told him that he knew little Joe McGee [the witness]; that there was no harm in him, and to let him go. I was then turned loose. While at the store, I saw the Mormons taking the goods out of the store house, and packing many of the articles on their horses; a number of barrels and boxes were rolled out before the door. When these men who had goods packed before them, rode off, I heard a man, who remained at the store, hallo to one of them to send four wagons. I went down to Mr. Worthington's; and, in returning towards the store again, a short time after, I saw the smoke and flames bursting from the roof of the store house, and three men coming out of the house, who immediately rode off. The balance of the company had just previously left, except two, who were at Mr. Yale's, a citizen there, guarding him. I heard Parley Pratt order the men to take out the goods before the house was set on fire. I also saw Joel S. Miles there in the Mormon company.[22]

21. *Document*, p. 110.
22. Ibid., p. 141.

The statements by the non-Mormon witnesses are straightforward and concise, contain only eyewitness descriptions of their experiences, and present evidence generally consistent with other testimony and accounts of these events.

Following the examination of the state's witnesses, the Mormons presented their defense. The court record states that the defendants declined to make any statements but called seven witnesses on their behalf. Each witness testified regarding specific evidence against certain prisoners. Nancy Rigdon testified that her father, Sidney Rigdon, was not involved in the Crooked River battle. She said that George W. Robinson did not have the clock he allegedly stole in Daviess County. Ezra Chipman, Delia F. Pine, and Malinda Porter testified that Lyman Wight did not steal a featherbed, as asserted by a previous witness. Another witness for the defense, Jonathan W. Barlow, reported that Joseph Smith and Lyman Wight did not participate in the Crooked River battle, but rode down to meet the Mormon troops after receiving word of the battle. Finally, Thoret Parsons and Arza Judd, Jr., testified that, prior to the Crooked River battle, Bogart's troops ordered them from Parsons's home in Caldwell County and threatened to give Far West "thunder and lightening" the next day. Very little testimony was given to explain why the Mormons organized their military operations; *nothing was said regarding the Danites.* Instead, the defense witnesses attempted to refute a few of the allegations against some of the prisoners. Following their testimony, the prosecution called one more witness (who denied that Bogart's troops had threatened Mormon settlers), which concluded the presentation of evidence by both sides. [23]

Based on the evidence presented at the hearing, Judge King found probable cause to order twenty-four defendants to stand trial on suspicion of committing arson, burglary, robbery, and larceny. These prisoners were allowed to post bail of amounts ranging from five hundred to one thousand dollars. King committed five prisoners to the Richmond jail on charges of murder for their alleged participation in the Crooked River battle. The six remaining prisoners, Joseph Smith, Hyrum Smith,

23. The testimony of the defense witnesses can be found in ibid., pp. 146–49.

Sidney Rigdon, Lyman Wight, Caleb Baldwin, and Alexander McRae, were committed to the jail in Liberty, Clay County, on charges of treason. [24] Because their alleged crimes were capital offenses, Judge King allowed no bail for the prisoners charged with treason or murder. Grand jury trials for the defendants were scheduled for March 1839.

Some evidence was presented against each defendant charged by King. Most of those charged were identified by several witnesses as having participated in the alleged crimes. Contrary to the Mormons' expectations, twenty-nine prisoners were released due to insufficient evidence.

Nevertheless, King's decision devastated those charged with crimes, for the Mormons did not consider themselves criminals or enemies of the state. Luman Gibbs, a man described by Ebenezer Robinson as "a good honest hearted soul," found his present criminal status very disconcerting. During the hearing, after one of the witnesses identified Gibbs as having participated in the Crooked River battle, the fifty-year-old Gibbs stepped up on a bench and proclaimed to the judge, "I wasn't there at all. I staid back and took care of the horses." [25] Robinson, who was also a defendant, pulled on Gibbs's coat and urged him to keep quiet. But it was too late. Gibbs had implicated himself in the crime and was charged with murder. After the hearing, while the remaining prisoners bedded for the night, Gibbs pushed his feet out from underneath his blanket, exposing them to the cold night air. "Stay there and freeze, it serves you right," he said, scolding his feet; "bring me here all the way from Vermont to be in prison for murder and [I] never thought of killing any body in all my life." [26] Gibbs's remarks brought laughter to an otherwise somber group of Mormon prisoners.

Questions Regarding the Richmond Hearing

Mormon leaders subsequently denounced the hearing and

24. McRae and Baldwin, who were members of the same Mormon militia company, were apparently charged with treason because they allegedly claimed the Mormons intended to take Daviess County, Livingston County, and then the entire state. See *Document*, p. 137, testimony of Jesse Kelly.

25. Ebenezer Robinson, "Items of Personal History," *The Return* 2 (March 1890): 235.

26. Ibid., p. 236.

Judge King's findings. Parley P. Pratt, one of the defendants, wrote:

> In this mock Court of Inquiry the Judge could not be prevailed on to examine the conduct of murderers and robbers who had desolated our society, nor would he receive testimony except against us. By the dissenters and apostates who wished to save their own lives and secure their property at the expense of others, and by those who had murdered and plundered us from time to time, he obtained abundance of testimony, much of which was entirely false.[27]

Joseph Smith and several Mormon petitioners reported:

> . . . Joseph Smith, jr., was deprived of the privileges of being examined before the court, as the law directs; that the witnesses on the part of the State were taken by force of arms, threatened with extermination or immediate death, and were brought without subpoena or warrant, under this awful glaring anticipation of being exterminated if they did not swear something against him to please the mob, or his persecutors; and those witnesses were compelled to swear at the muzzle of the gun, and that some of them have acknowledged since, which your petitioners do testify and are able to prove, that they did swear false, and that they did it in order to save their lives.[28]

According to many accounts, Captain Bogart's troops, who were charged with delivering the subpoenas, cast into prison nearly forty of the defense witnesses and drove the rest from the state. Many defendants reported that neither they nor their witnesses were allowed to testify. A petition by Joseph Smith, Sidney Rigdon, and Elias Smith asserted:

> In this mock court of inquiry the defendants were prevented from giving any testimony on their part, by an armed force at the court house; they were advised by their lawyers not to bring any [witnesses], as they would be in danger of their lives, or be driven out of the county; so there was no testimony examined only against them.[29]

The Mormon defendants thus disputed the court's findings for two main reasons: they alleged that the prosecution's

27. *Autobiography*, p. 211.
28. "Appeals to Supreme Court of Missouri," p. 206, petition of Joseph Smith, Jr., et al., 15 March 1839.
29. *HC* 4:35, The Saint's [*sic*] Petition to Congress, November 1839.

witnesses testified falsely and that Missouri officials prevented the defendants from presenting an adequate defense. These two issues are examined below.

Did the Prosecution's Witnesses Testify Truthfully?

Mormon leaders asserted that their soldiers did not plunder and burn homes or commit other crimes in Daviess County, as testified by the prosecution witnesses. According to Hyrum Smith, the Missourians set fire to their own homes and then blamed the Mormons in order to inflame the excitement against them. Smith states:

> Many people came to see. They saw the houses burning; and, being filled with prejudice, they could not be made to believe but that the "Mormons" set them on fire; which deed was most diabolical and of the blackest kind; for indeed the "Mormons" did not set them on fire, nor meddle with their houses or their fields.[30]

In addition, the Mormons said that their military operations in Daviess County were authorized by Generals Doniphan and Parks of the Missouri state militia.[31]   The generals reportedly mustered out the Daviess and Caldwell county militia units to which the Mormons belonged and ordered them to repel the vigilantes. The Mormons thus asserted that they acted in self-defense, under legitimate state authority, and committed no crimes.

Both of these claims have been dealt with in earlier chapters, and both have been shown to be false. The reminiscences of Oliver B. Huntington and Benjamin F. Johnson, loyal Mormon participants, present detailed information regarding Mormon plundering and burning in Daviess County. The evidence also indicates that the Mormons acted on their own and not under the authority of the state militia. In fact, as a consequence of the Mormon activities, Generals Doniphan and Parks called out their troops to halt the Mormon military operations. The evidence thus corroborates the testimony of the state's witnesses

30. *HC* 3:408–9, Hyrum Smith, affidavit, 1 July 1843.
31. See *HC* 3:406–8, 425, 442–44, Hyrum Smith, Parley P. Pratt, and Lyman Wight, affidavits, 1 July 1843; and *HC* 3:370, Joseph Smith, "A Bill of Damages," 4 June 1839.

regarding Mormon activities in Daviess County.

Mormon leaders made surprisingly few references to the Danites in their public petitions and statements regarding the Richmond hearing. Joseph Smith asserted that Sampson Avard "swore false" concerning the Danite constitution, but neither Smith nor the other defendants disputed the testimony describing the teachings and activities of the Danite organization. Evidence from Mormon sources, particularly Morris Phelps's "Reminiscences," corroborates the testimony about the group's teachings and goals. Contemporary Mormon accounts also reveal that the Danites played an active and influential role in Mormon affairs—such as the expulsion of dissenters from Caldwell County in June, the consecrating of property to the Church, the Fourth of July celebration at Far West, and the Mormon expedition to Daviess County after the Gallatin election battle. The group operated prominently in northern Missouri for nearly five months. Its teachings and activities were known to Missourians as well as to Mormons. The influential role of the Danites and the presence of Mormon leaders within the organization supports the witnesses' testimony that the First Presidency approved of and encouraged the group's activities.

There remains a question, however, regarding the extent to which Joseph Smith actively directed the Danites. In a letter to the Saints, Smith asserted that Avard taught "many false and pernicious things" of which the First Presidency was not aware.[32] In addition, nearly all Mormons claimed that Avard—and not Joseph Smith—directed the Danite organization. Their assertions contradict Avard's testimony, *but not the testimony of other witnesses*. Although Corrill, Peck, and other witnesses believed that Avard received his instructions from Joseph Smith, none of them claimed to have firsthand knowledge of this fact. They all affirmed that Avard was the "teacher and active agent of the society."[33]   The evidence thus corroborates most of the testimony regarding the Danites. Only Avard's assertions that the First Presidency wrote the Danite constitution and directed the organization's activities remain in doubt.

Joseph Smith's role in directing Mormon activities represented

32. *HC* 3:231, The Prophet's Letter to the Church, 16 December 1838.
33. *Document*, pp. 110–17 (quote is from p. 114, testimony of Cleminson).

a central element of the prosecution's case. The charge of treason against the Prophet rested on the assertion that he directed not only the Danite organization, but also Mormon military operations in Daviess and Caldwell counties.

Mormon leaders denied the testimony placing Smith at the head of Mormon troops. Brigham Young stated that Smith "was in no way connected with the Militia of that state [Missouri], neither did he bear arms at all, nor give advice . . . ."[34] Hyrum Smith asserted that his brother "never bore arms, as a military man, in any capacity whatever, whilst in the state of Missouri, or previous to that time; neither has he given any orders or assumed any command in any capacity whatever."[35] Parley P. Pratt further contended that the Prophet "never bore arms or did military duty, not even in self-defense . . . ."[36] The testimony that Joseph Smith played a leading role in Mormon military operations, these men asserted, was false.

Evidence from Mormon journals and reminiscences, however, contradicts these statements. Albert P. Rockwood reported that, following the Gallatin election battle, "Joseph Smith & Lyman White were at the head of the company (Army of Israel) that went up to the relief of the Brethren in Davis Co."[37] Many Mormons reported that the Prophet organized and led the Mormon troops when the Missouri militia first appeared outside Far West. On another occasion, Smith countermanded an order by state militia colonel George Hinkle directing a group of Mormon soldiers to ride to Haun's Mill. James H. Rollins states that Smith "told us that we were his men, and that we must not go[;] if we did go against his will we would not be one of us left to tell the tale tomorrow morning."[38] All Mormons recognized Smith's leading role in temporal as well as spiritual affairs. Shortly after the Mormon expedition to Daviess County, Rockwood wrote:

You may ask if the Prophet goes out with the Saints to Battle? I answer he is a Prophet to go before the people as in times of old . . . . Bro. Joseph has unsheathed his sword & in the name of Jesus declares that

34. *HC* 3:433, Brigham Young, affidavit, 1 July 1843.
35. *HC* 3:404, Hyrum Smith, affidavit, 1 July 1843.
36. *HC* 3:432, Parley P. Pratt, affidavit, 1 July 1843.
37. "Journal," p. 2.
38. "A Sketch of the Life of James Henry Rollins," p. 7. Typescript, LDS Archives.

it shall not be sheathed again until he can go into any country or state in safety and peace.[39]

This evidence from loyal Mormon sources, along with details presented in earlier chapters, confirms the testimony that Joseph Smith actively led the military operations of the Saints.

Related to the issue of Smith's leadership role among the Saints is the testimony regarding his alleged disregard for the law. Again, Mormon sources confirm many of the witnesses' reports of various statements and speeches by the Prophet. Warren Foote stated that, prior to the march of Mormon troops to Daviess County, Smith said "that those who would not turn out to help to suppress the mob should have their property taken to support those who would."[40]   Regarding "vexatious lawsuits," Mormon leaders denounced such proceedings in the Political Motto, and, at the Fourth of July celebration, they publicly warned that they would allow no one to initiate vexatious lawsuits against them. Similarly, the Mormons made no secret of their belief that they were establishing a temporal Kingdom of God, which, as Daniel prophesied, would eventually destroy all other earthly kingdoms. "The Prophet Joseph laid the foundation of our Church in a *Military Spirit*," wrote Benjamin F. Johnson of Mormonism's early years, "and as the Master taught his disiples So he taught Us to 'Sell our Coats and buy Swords.'"[41] This spirit was the one described by the witnesses.

When the testimony of the Mormon defense witnesses is compared with evidence from other sources, one glaring inconsistency arises. Numerous prosecution witnesses testified that Lyman Wight led a company of Mormon troops to Millport. Several witnesses stated that they saw Wight near the town shortly after it was burned. In rebuttal, three defense witnesses testified that Wight did not leave Diahman during the period in question. In a petition written while he was in Liberty Jail, Wight insisted that he never left his house.[42] In affidavits filed in 1843, however, both Hyrum Smith and Lyman Wight stated

39. "Journal," p. 11.
40. "Autobiography," pp. 29–30.
41. Zimmerman, *I Knew the Prophets*, p. 26.
42. "Appeals to Supreme Court of Missouri," pp. 202–3, petition of Lyman Wight, 15 March 1839.

that he commanded Mormon troops in expeditions against the vigilantes. [43] Wight reported that he led a company of sixty men to Millport. The 1843 affidavits confirm the testimony of the prosecution's witnesses.

Source materials for this period do not provide the necessary detail to examine each accusation against the defendants. The evidence that is available, however, substantiates most of the testimony by the prosecution's witnesses regarding key issues and events. The claims by Mormon leaders that the testimony against them was false, and their alternative explanations of these events, are contradicted by evidence from the reminiscences and journals of loyal Mormon participants.

Conduct of the Trial

Evidence from Mormon sources supports the claim by Mormon leaders that their witnesses were intimidated at the Richmond hearing. Missouri officials threatened to prosecute witnesses who refused to cooperate with the investigation. Morris Phelps, a witness and defendant, reported that he was prosecuted because of his reluctance to testify against the other prisoners. [44] James H. Rollins claimed he was originally summoned to testify against the others, but soon found he was a defendant and not a witness. [45] William Huntington, Sr., went into hiding after hearing rumors that local ruffians intended to throw him in prison to prevent him from testifying for the defense. According to his son, Huntington later reached an "understanding" with these men and did not testify. [46] John Murdock complained that he went to Richmond for the hearing "but was not allowed to testify." [47] Regarding those who did testify for the defense, Ebenezer Robinson wrote that "our witnesses were treated so badly, and intimidated to such an extent it was considered useless to attempt to make an

---

43. *HC* 3:408, 443, Hyrum Smith and Lyman Wight, affidavits, 1 July 1843.
44. "Reminiscences of Columbia Prison," p. 1.
45. "Sketch," p. 8.
46. O. B. Huntington, "History," p. 38.
47. "Journal," p. 106. Murdock stated, incorrectly, that no one was allowed to testify for the defense.

extended defense." [48]

Although the defense witnesses were intimidated and threatened with prosecution, the evidence suggests that many of the other claims regarding the conduct of the hearing are exaggerated. The defendants do not give the names of the forty defense witnesses who were reportedly thrown in jail, nor do any Mormon individuals report receiving such treatment because they were called to testify. [49] Neither Peter H. Burnett nor Erastus Snow, who both attended the hearing, reported this gross obstruction of justice. [50]   There is no evidence corroborating Mormon reports of mass jailings of their witnesses. In addition, Mormon claims that they were not allowed to testify, to bring witnesses, or to have legal counsel are not true. The court record shows that seven witnesses testified for the defense. The court record also states that the defendants themselves declined the opportunity to be examined. [51] And two of the best-known defense lawyers in western Missouri, Alexander W. Doniphan and Amos Rees, handled the case for the defendants. [52]

Two related issues should also be examined. The first deals

48. "Items of Personal History," p. 235.

49. One of the defense witnesses, Thoret Parsons, later said that he suffered "false imprisonment" in Missouri, but he does not supply additional information regarding when, where, or for what reason he was imprisoned ("Affidavit, May 6, 1839." Petitions, LDS Archives). Missouri law stipulated: "While any witness, for or against the prisoner, is under examination, the magistrate may exclude from the place in which such examination is had, all witnesses who have not been examined, and he may cause the witnesses to be kept separate, and prevented from conversing with each other, until they all shall have been examined" (*Revised Statutes of the State of Missouri* [1835], p. 476). Many Missourians feared that Mormon witnesses would testify falsely in order to free their brethren from jail. It is possible that local officials attempted to keep the witnesses away from the courtroom and separated from each other before they testified at the hearing. Although Parsons did not state that his imprisonment was connected with the Richmond hearing, he may have been detained to separate him from other witnesses. This, however, is merely speculation, since neither Parsons nor any other Mormons reported that they were arrested or detained because they were subpoenaed to testify for the defense

50. Snow, "Journal January 1838 to June 1841," pp. 41–42. Photocopy, LDS Archives; and Burnett, *Recollections*, pp. 63–64.

51. *Document,* p. 146.

52. The court record shows that during the hearing the Mormon defendants also hired a third lawyer, John R. Williams, to handle their case (*Document*, pp. 132, 145).

with Judge King's alleged prejudice against the Saints. King's brother-in-law had been killed in a skirmish with the Mormons in Jackson County in 1833. During the 1838 disturbances he wrote to Governor Boggs and charged that the Mormons had become the aggressors in the conflict. The defendants asserted that throughout the hearing the judge made statements revealing his prejudice and determination to throw them in prison. "If the Governor's exterminating order had been directed to me," King reportedly told the defendants, "I would have seen it fulfilled to the very letter ere this time." [53] Should King have disqualified himself and requested another judge to sit in his place?

Judge King's previous involvement in the Mormon disturbances, even when evaluated by the less rigid standards of frontier society, was sufficient to warrant his disqualification from the Richmond hearing. If King made the statements attributed to him by Mormon defendants, then clearly he lacked the impartiality to preside at the hearing. There is no evidence, however, that any other judges were considered for the hearing. Perhaps part of the problem was that no judge in western Missouri was completely free from bias; yet, bringing a new judge a hundred miles across the state to conduct a preliminary hearing would have been unusual for this period. King, as judge of the Fifth Judicial Circuit, was the logical choice to conduct the hearing because his jurisdiction included all the counties where the alleged crimes had been committed.

Regardless of whether King should have sat at the hearing, the evidence suggests that Mormon claims regarding his behavior are exaggerated. Missourians connected with the hearing praised King's handling of the examination. William T. Wood, who served as a lawyer for the Saints in Jackson County and assisted the prosecuting attorney at the Richmond hearing, denied the Mormon claims regarding the Court of Inquiry. "The trial was not a 'mock trial.' Judge King presided in good faith and with fairness . . . ," Wood asserted. [54] General Clark reported: "Every facility was afforded the prisoners in getting their witnesses, &c. that could be, and as far as I could observe the investigation

---

53. *HC* 3:448, Lyman Wight, affidavit, 1 July 1843.
54. "Mormon Memoirs," *Liberty Tribune*, 9 April 1886.

was conducted upon legal grounds."[55] Amos Rees, one of the Mormon lawyers, reported in a private letter that the defendants were tried and committed according to the law:

> . . . Judge King sitting as a court of enquiry, heard all the evidence in a regular way and had it all reduced to writing as required by law, the mormons were then heard by their counsel in defence, &c. and after this the Judge proceeded to commit some of them for treason and murder, to discharge others, and to admit to bail the great majority of them . . . .[56]

Finally, an examination of the court record reveals that Judge King, regardless of any prejudice he may have had, charged and committed the defendants on the evidence against them. In fact, he released nearly half the Mormon prisoners due to insufficient evidence.

The charge of treason represents another controversial issue related to the hearing. Missouri state law stipulates:

> Every person who shall commit treason against the state, by levying war against the same, or by adhering to the enemies thereof, by giving them aid and comfort, shall, upon conviction, suffer death, or be sentenced to imprisonment in the penitentiary for a period not less than ten years.[57]

The Mormons gathered in Missouri to establish a religious community, not to levy war against their neighbors. No evidence exists to indicate treasonous intent in Mormon teachings or activities—but this does not necessarily imply that Judge King was mistaken in his ruling. The testimony at the Richmond hearing provided sufficient evidence *for the purposes of a preliminary hearing* to charge Mormon leaders with treason. Witnesses testified that (1) Mormon leaders publicly declared they would

55. *Document*, p. 93, Report of General Clark, 29 November 1838.

56. Amos Rees to Abiel Leonard, 1 November 1839. Joint Collection: University of Missouri and State Historical Society of Missouri. Although Alexander Doniphan discussed his association with the Mormons in at least two reminiscences, he makes only a brief reference to serving as a lawyer for the Mormons during this period. He provides no information regarding the conduct of this hearing.

57. *Revised Statues of the State of Missouri (1835)*, p. 166, Article 1, Crimes and Punishments.

resist state authority; (2) Mormon soldiers attacked state troops, burned two towns, and drove settlers from their homes; (3) Mormon leaders directed the secret Danite organization, which threatened and forcibly expelled from their homes Saints who would not obey the Prophet; and (4) the Mormons planned to build a temporal kingdom in western Missouri. Judge King's ruling did not represent a judgment of guilt against the defendants, but rather indicated his belief that the evidence warranted further investigation of the charges.

The Mormon defense against the charge of treason—and against all the charges brought against them—rested not on the contention that they had not committed the acts described at the hearing, but on their motives for taking up arms. Why, then, did they not explain their actions and disprove the charges against them? If, as the Mormons' lawyer asserted, the Richmond hearing was conducted according to normal procedures, why did the defendants present such a meager defense?

It was the nature of the Richmond hearing, rather than a deliberate obstruction of justice, that limited the Mormons' defense. The hearing was a preliminary examination to evaluate the state's evidence against the defendants—not a trial to prove their innocence or guilt. Thus, Judge King told Morris Phelps that "we do not want to here [*sic*] any testimony on that side of the question" when Phelps attempted to testify on behalf of the prisoners.[58] Similarly, the prosecuting attorney objected to the testimony of another Mormon witness, arguing that "this was not a court to try the case, but only a court of investigation on the part of the state."[59]

In addition, the overwhelming evidence against the defendants made it inadvisable for them to make an extended defense at that time. A lengthy defense, even if admitted by the court, would have been counterproductive. The Mormons' defense was largely an explanation of why they committed the acts alleged to be crimes: they had acted in self-defense. Mormon soldiers invaded Daviess County and attacked state troops at Crooked River because they were trying to protect themselves from anti-Mormon vigilantes. Mormon leaders condemned Missouri officials and engaged in extralegal activities because lawful

---

58. Phelps, "Reminiscences of Columbia Prison," p. 1.
59. *HC* 3:419, Hyrum Smith, affidavit, 1 July 1843.

methods had failed to protect their people. Their intentions had been defensive rather than aggressive. An assertion of these arguments by the defendants, however, would have required a concurrent admission of involvement in the alleged criminal acts. For the purposes of the preliminary hearing, this would have confirmed the suspicion of guilt already created by the prosecution, but would have availed nothing toward securing the prisoners' release. Explanations regarding why they committed their alleged crimes were appropriately saved for their future trials.

Viewed from this perspective, the reason why Doniphan and Rees advised their clients not to testify becomes clear. While they had little hope of dispelling the suspicion of guilt created by the state's witnesses, their own testimonies might further incriminate themselves or other Mormons not yet charged. Witnesses for the defense carried the same risk. In the process, Mormon lawyers would unnecessarily reveal to the prosecution their intended line of defense at future trials. These strategic considerations, along with a genuine fear for the safety of Mormon witnesses, probably influenced the decision to bring few witnesses to Richmond.

Evaluation of the Richmond Hearing

This reexamination of Mormon claims regarding the Richmond hearing may lead the reader to conclude that justice was served by this judicial inquiry. Just the opposite is true. Although Mormon leaders presented inaccurate and misleading descriptions of the court's proceedings, their basic contention was correct: the Richmond inquiry did not represent a thorough—or, therefore, unbiased—investigation of the disturbances. Missouri officials made no effort to prosecute anti-Mormon vigilantes who drove Mormon settlers from their homes, plundered, and burned. There was no court of inquiry to investigate the killing of William Carey or the slaughter of Mormon settlers at Haun's Mill. Western Missouri officials conducted a one-sided investigation into the causes of the disturbances.

Injustice resulted, however, not because the Missourians sought deliberately or cynically to subvert the law and railroad

Mormon defendants into prison, but because Missourians held a one-sided view of the conflict–a myopic perception common to Mormons as well. Both Mormons and non-Mormons viewed the other as the cause of trouble; each group justified its own activities as "defensive" but viewed the actions of the other as aggressive and threatening; neither understood how its own activities contributed to the disturbances. As in most wars, the hostility and fear generated by the conflict caused the participants to hold rigidly to their biased views. Consequently, after the surrender, Missouri officials prosecuted Mormons only, because their biased view led them to conclude that the Mormons were the guilty party.

The prosecution of the Mormons illustrates how the judicial process, even when properly administered, can be used to enforce majority rule. When extralegal violence is accepted as the norm, participants on both sides engage in illegal acts. Judicial officials, however, cannot put everyone in prison; and yet, it is unlikely that they can objectively determine "who threw the first stone" and is therefore most guilty. Consequently, judicial proceedings following a vigilante war tend to become processes by which the empowered group in the community enforce their will upon the less powerful minority–which is what they were trying to do in the first place. But this enforcement of majority rule comes through the execution of law, not through its subversion.

This is what happened to the Mormons at the preliminary hearing. The hearing was properly held; the evidence against them was basically true; the judge committed them according to the evidence. Nevertheless, the judicial investigation, as a whole, was not fair because local officials did not examine the activities of non-Mormons who committed crimes during the disturbances. Blame for the conflict fell exclusively–and thus unjustly–upon the Mormons.

The absence of any investigation into their enemies' activities led the Mormons to believe that Missouri officials were not really intent upon executing justice. After languishing several months in prison, Parley P. Pratt wrote to Judge King:

. . . when the authorities of the State shall redress all these wrongs [against the Saints], shall punish the guilty according to law, and shall restore my family and friends to all our rights, and shall pay all the damages which we, as a people, have sustained, then I shall believe them sincere in their professed zeal for law and justice; then shall I be convinced that I can have a fair trial in the State.[60]

Pratt requested that he be tried before a federal judge, or that he be released from prison and allowed to leave the state "without further persecution."

60. Letter of 13 May 1839, published in Pratt, *Autobiography*, p. 232.

13
Expulsion

The outcome of the Richmond hearing did not resolve all questions relating to the Mormon War. The Mormons had to decide whether the apparent failure of Joseph Smith's policies—and his subsequent imprisonment as a result of those policies—meant that another leader should direct the Church. In addition, Mormon leaders petitioned Missouri officials to allow them to remain in their homes. The question regarding whether the state should expel the Saints was debated in both the Missouri press and the state legislature, with many non-Mormons arguing that their government had no right to remove an entire group of citizens. The issue was ultimately settled, as were most issues in the conflict, by the popular opinion of citizens in northwestern Missouri. The majority favored the expulsion of the Saints, and state officials showed little inclination to oppose them in the matter.

Questions Regarding Joseph Smith's Leadership

The testimony at the Richmond hearing revealed information that proved disturbing to many of the Saints, for it appeared that Joseph Smith and other Church leaders had espoused highly illegal and unwise policies during the conflict. Many Mormons denounced the crimes committed by their soldiers. David Lewis, when asked by a group of Missourians about the Danites, replied: "What is a Danite . . . those that has taken an oath to kill and rob and steal plunder take bear meat and sweet oil, I am no Danite."[1] Abner Blackburn reported that his parents objected both to the Danite activities and to teachings that the Indians would slay the Saints' enemies. "My parents were disgusted with the Mormons and moved to Illinois and left the

1. Lewis, "Excerpt From The Journal," p. 5.

219

saints," he said.[2]   Isaac Scott also objected to certain Mormon practices and teachings. "The Church cut me off in Missouri for no crime only opposing Daniteism, stealing, swearing, lies, etc.," Scott wrote. "I have seen them there steal thousands of dollars worth of property and heard them afterwards swear in court they did not do it."[3]   Previous revelations issued by Joseph Smith had stated that he held the authority to lead the Church—provided he obeyed the commandments. In 1834 he had ordained David Whitmer to be his successor if "he did not live to God himself."[4]   Although Whitmer no longer adhered to Mormonism, the Lord could appoint another to take Smith's place. Rumors now circulated among the Saints that Joseph was a fallen prophet. "About one half of the church has got to themselves a [golden] calf for they think that Joseph wil[l] be distroyed and there religion is gon[e] . . . ," wrote Allen J. Stout regarding the widespread disillusionment.[5]

The Mormon prophet, seeking to reassure his people, insisted that he was not responsible for the Saints' troubles, nor was he in jail because he had committed any crimes. "Know assuredly, dear brethren," he wrote from Liberty Jail on 16 December, "that it is for the testimony of Jesus that we are in bonds and in prison."[6]   He said that neither he nor Mormon soldiers were guilty of the charges against them: "We stood in our own defense, and we believe that no man of us acted only in a just, a lawful, and a righteous retaliation against such marauders."[7]   Smith further claimed that Sampson Avard and other evil-designing men had propagated the teachings for which he and other Mormon leaders were condemned:

We have learned also since we have been prisoners, that many false

2. Diary, p. 2.

3. Isaac Scott to Dear Brother, 1 March 1845. Quoted in William Mulder and A. Russell Mortensen, *Among the Mormons: Historic Accounts by Contemporary Observers* (New York: Alfred A. Knopf, 1958), p. 155.

4. *Far West Record: Minutes of The Church of Jesus Christ of Latter-day Saints, 1830–1840*, edited by Donald Q. Cannon and Lyndon W. Cook (Salt Lake City: Deseret Book Company, 1983), p. 151. See also *Doctrine and Covenants* 43:2–4, 64:5.

5. Allen J. Stout to Hosea Stout, 27 January 1839. Photocopy, Utah State Historical Society Library.

6. HC 3:226, The Prophet's Letter to the Church, 16 December 1838.

7. Ibid., p. 229.

and pernicious things, which were calculated to lead the Saints far astray and to do great injury, have been taught by Dr. Avard as coming from the Presidency . . . which the Presidency never knew were being taught in the Church by anybody until after they were made prisoners.[8]

Moreover, Smith declared that the treachery of false brethren—such as George Hinkle, who allegedly betrayed the Prophet into the hands of the Missourians—had brought much of the suffering and persecution the Saints were forced to endure:

. . . we have waded through an ocean of tribulation and mean abuse, practiced upon us by the ill bred and the ignorant, such as Hinkle, Corrill, Phelps, Avard, Reed Peck, Cleminson, and various others, who are so very ignorant that they cannot appear respectable in any decent and civilized society, and whose eyes are full of adultery, and cannot cease from sin.[9]

Corrill, Peck, and others had opposed the militant policies of Joseph Smith and other Mormon leaders because they believed those policies would ultimately lead to conflict and ruin. Ironically, the Prophet now blamed these men for bringing that destruction upon the Saints.

By linking Sampson Avard with John Corrill, Reed Peck, and John Cleminson, all of whom had bitterly opposed Avard and the Danite movement, Smith was able to discredit both Avard and these dissenters. In addition, because he never specified which "false and pernicious" teachings originated with Avard, the Mormon prophet skillfully disassociated himself from the Danites without offending his many loyal supporters in that organization. The Mormons who belonged to the Danites and knew of the Prophet's former support did not feel condemned because he

8. Ibid., p. 231. It may be true that Avard taught things of which Joseph Smith was not aware. For example, Smith probably did not know about Avard's plan, proposed late in the conflict, to poison the Missourians' crops. Smith was directing Mormon troops at Diahman when Avard devised this scheme. According to John Corrill, only half a dozen Mormon leaders knew about Avard's proposal; even the majority of Danites knew nothing about it. Corrill reported that when he accused Smith and Rigdon of developing the plan, "they both denied it promptly" (*A Brief History*, p. 32). Thus, Smith's claim in this letter to the Saints is not inconsistent with evidence that he knew and approved of Danite teaching and activities.

9. *HC* 3:232.

had not criticized the Danites, but only certain teachings of Avard; but the Mormons who opposed the Danite teachings and activities—even those teachings previously approved by Smith—came to believe that Avard had been responsible for the group.

Although they had abandoned Mormonism, many of the dissenters did not regard themselves as enemies of the Saints. During the siege of Far West, John Cleminson had refused an invitation by Missouri militia officers to evacuate the town, and instead chose to remain with the Saints throughout the conflict. [10]   After the surrender, John Corrill signed affidavits and presented a petition on behalf of the Mormons to the Missouri legislature. In addition, Corrill and a number of other dissenters joined with loyal Mormons in selling their land for funds "to be given to the most distressed of the sisters and their children" among the impoverished Saints. [11]   The dissenters were therefore quite surprised by the vituperatives leveled at them by Joseph Smith and other Mormons. "No man ever knew me to complain of, or inform on any one . . . ," George Hinkle later told W. W. Phelps. "When the court of inquiry held its session in Richmond, I did not turn state's evidence, but was legally subpoenaed, as you know." [12]   According to his son, George Hinkle "always maintained that the leading men of the church had never given him a chance to explain his actions in Missouri and had condemned him on the spot without judge or jury, and having once condemned him they stuck to it and never gave him a chance." [13]

These men subsequently believed they had been made scapegoats for the Prophet's failings. Reed Peck wrote:

You may here ask in conclusion of the story how Joseph Smith retains the confidence of his followers and even binds them more closely to the cause when the ultimate of all his plans has been total failure He tells them as an excuse for being in the hands of his

10. See *HC* 3:410, Hyrum Smith, affidavit, 1 July 1843; and Rigdon, *Appeal*, p. 34.

11. Book T, p. 156, Caldwell County Recorder's Office, Kingston, Mo. Other so-called dissenters who signed this deed were Oliver Cowdery and Burr Riggs.

12. "Letter to W. W. Phelps, August 14, 1844," p. 452.

13. S. J. Hinkle, "A Biographical Sketch of G. M. Hinkle," p. 447.

enemies after the delivery of so many brave speeches "that he was betrayed" The very men who risked their lives at his request to open a communication with the army are now branded as traitors When no others would venture we stepped forward and were instrumental in saving the lives of hundreds perhaps by bringing about a treaty Propositions were made to us and we faithfully reported the same to the presidency and they understood the whole matter, still Joseph pretends to the church that he was betrayed by us as christ was by Judas.[14]

One of the most persistent myths about the dissenters is that they somehow reaped financial gains at the expense of their fellow Saints. George Hinkle, it was said, accepted a bribe to betray Church leaders. Although the Missourians allowed many of the disaffected Saints to remain, many others left the state in the Mormon exodus. Samuel J. Hinkle reported that his once-wealthy father was destitute when he left Missouri. "I am told [he] had to walk out and carry some of the smaller children in his arms, with the Gentiles persecuting him and the Saints shunning him as they had been warned," wrote Hinkle's son.[15]

The number of Mormon dissenters, however, should not be exaggerated. Although it appeared to the Missourians that many had abandoned Mormonism, in relative terms there were few. Of the nine to ten thousand Mormons in Missouri, perhaps only two or three hundred left the Church. Most Mormons, though shaken by the events, retained their faith.

Shortly after Joseph Smith was placed in prison, Church leaders in Far West met to express their feelings regarding

14. "Manuscript," p. 32.

15. "A Biographical Sketch of G. M. Hinkle," p. 445. In later years, blame for the "betrayal" of the Prophet fell primarily upon Hinkle, and secondarily upon John Corrill and Reed Peck. Arthur Morrison, who never left the Church, and W. W. Phelps, who returned to the Church, received no blame, even though they were present during all the negotiations with the militia officers and Mormon leaders. In response to reports then prevalent among the Saints that he had accepted a bribe to betray Mormon leaders at Far West, Hinkle demanded that Phelps, who resided with the Mormons in Nauvoo, set the record straight. Hinkle wrote: "Now, sir, as you are the man who was engaged in the whole affair with me, I request that you write a letter for publication, and either put [it] in the *Times and Seasons*, or send it to me; and in it exempt me from those charges, and correct the minds of that people and the public on this subject; for you know that they are as base as the blackness of darkness, and as false as Satan himself" ("Letter to W. W. Phelps, August 1, 1844," p. 453).

present conditions. At a High Council meeting on 13 December, Brigham Young declared that his faith "was the same as ever" and sought affirmations from his fellow leaders. [16]   Some of the brethren said the hand of the Lord was in their scourges, purifying and preparing the Church for His return. Samuel Bent said that "his faith is as ever and that he feels to praise God in prisons and in dungeons and in all circumstances whatever he may be found." [17]   Thomas Grover proclaimed that "the time would come when Joseph would stand before kings and speak marvelous words." Simeon Carter said:

. . . as to his faith in the work it was the same as ever, he did not think that Joseph was a fallen Prophet; but he believed in every revelation that had come through him: Still he thought that perhaps Joseph had not acted in all things according to the best wisdom yet how far he had been unwise he could not say; he did not think that Joseph would be removed and another planted in his stead; but he believed he would still perform his work . . . .[18]

Several others present also asserted their belief that Joseph was not a fallen prophet. At a High Council meeting the following week, Harlow Redfield acknowledged that "he did not feel to fellowship all the proceedings of the brethren in Daviess County. He thought they did not act as wisely as they might have done." [19]   Nevertheless, his faith "was as good as it ever was."

The faith of these people contrasted sharply with those who believed the failure of Smith's plans conflicted with his prophetic claims. When asked whether she continued to believe that Joseph Smith was a prophet, Eliza Snow responded, "I have not seen or heard anything which caus'd me to doubt it even for a moment: If *possible*, I have *better* testimony that J. Smith is a prophet, than that Jeremiah was one, altho' he has not been kept in prison quite so long." [20]   The rumors that Smith was a fallen prophet soon subsided. "When Joseph ordains another in his stead I shall be willing to receive him but not till then,"

16. *Far West Record*, p. 221.
17. Ibid., p. 222.
18. Ibid.
19. Ibid., p. 224.
20. "Letter from Missouri, Feb 22, 1839," p. 549.

wrote William Law. [21]

The Mormon War Investigated

During these early weeks following the Mormon surrender, while western Missouri officials sought to affix blame for the disturbances upon the Mormons, eastern Missouri newspapers continued to question the state's action against the Saints. The *Missouri Argus* claimed that the Mormons could not be legally forced to leave the state. "If they [the Mormons] choose to remain, we must be content," argued one of its readers. "The day has gone by when masses of men can be outlawed, and driven from society to the wilderness . . . ." [22] The newspapers reprinted articles from out-of-state newspapers, which universally condemned Missouri's handling of the disturbances. One article lampooned the Missouri militia:

It is said, that a company of 20 Missourians espied a big Mormon near the North East corner of Caldwell county on Tuesday last. They retreated for the time being, but intended, as soon as reinforced by 30 or 40 of their companions, to hazzard an attack upon him. [23]

The enormous expenditures by the state to resolve the crisis, and the growing evidence that wrongdoing existed on both sides, prompted a call for an impartial investigation by the state legislature. "An *exparte* examination, in which the witnesses may be taken altogether from one side, is not such an investigation as the people of the State demand," declared the *Missouri Republican*. "The whole truth should be told." [24]

Jefferson City, where the Missouri legislature began its sessions shortly after the Mormon War ended, buzzed with excitement regarding the disturbances. David H. Redfield, who carried Mormon petitions to the capital in mid-December, said the city was filled with rumors that the Mormons were keep-

21. William Law to Dear Brother, 27 March 1839. Quoted in " 'Brother Joseph Is Truly A Wonderful Man, He Is All We Could Wish a Prophet to Be': Pre-1844 Letters of William Law," *BYU Studies* 20 (Winter 1980): 215.
22. 20 December 1838.
23. Reprinted from the *Louisville Journal* in the *Missouri Republican*, 19 November 1838.
24. 10 November 1838.

ing up their Danite system and planning to spill more blood
before they left the state.[25]   Missouri congressmen debated
the fairness and legality of the state's action against the Saints.
Gen. David Atchison, representing Clay County, denounced
the governor's extermination order. The *Missouri Republican*
reported concerning his speech, "This order he looked upon
as unconstitutional, and he wished to have an expression of
the Legislature upon it. If the Governor of the state, or any
other power, had the authority to issue such orders, he wished
to know it, for, if so, he would not live in any state where
such authority was given."[26]   John Corrill, the Mormons' representative from Caldwell County, also asked the legislature to
rule on the constitutionality of Boggs's order, for he wanted
to know whether it was legal for Missouri officials to force the
Mormons to deed over their property and leave the state.

Corrill presented to the legislature a "Memorial" signed by
Brigham Young, Heber C. Kimball, and other leading Mormons
at Far West describing the injustices and abuse suffered by the
Mormons in western Missouri and requesting that the Mormons
be allowed to stay.[27]   This petition, which mentioned little of
the Mormon crimes and outrages, instigated vicious charges
and countercharges regarding who were the aggressors in the
conflict. "There is not a word of truth in it, so far as I have heard
. . . ," said James Chiles, the Jackson County representative,
regarding the Mormons' petition. "We got rid of a great evil
when we drove them from Jackson County, and we have had
peace there ever since; and the state will always be in difficulty
so long as they suffer them to live in the state; and the quicker
they get that petition from before this body, the better."[28]
Other representatives concurred, claiming that the Mormon
petition "grossly misrepresented" and "slandered" settlers in the
western counties. Corrill, somewhat surprised and intimidated
by the vehement opposition, tried to defend the Memorial,
but he finally admitted that some of the Mormon claims were

25. "Book, Far West, January 13, 1839," p. 1. LDS Archives.
26. 27 December 1838.
27. For debate on the petition, see ibid., 24 December 1838.
28. Johnston and McClumphy, *History of Clinton and Caldwell Counties*,
p. 250.

exaggerated and withdrew the petition. [29]

This did not end the matter. In December the legislature appropriated two thousand dollars for the relief of Mormons and non-Mormons rendered homeless by the disturbances. In addition, Atchison, Corrill, and a number of other legislators fought to have a joint investigation by the House and Senate of the disturbances. Atchison proposed that the governor be required to act upon the report of the investigating committee. Sen. William M. Campbell supported this proposal, declaring that "this investigation should not be confined to the charges against a few guilty Mormons, but should go into the whole history of the matter—how far others have acted, who took the first steps in these disturbances, and how they were prosecuted." [30] Campbell also argued that the legislature, not the executive branch, should conduct the investigation. "To leave the whole matter to the Governor looked . . . like submitting the lamb to the keeping of the wolf," he said.

Citizens in the western counties supported these measures, but for a different reason: they wanted an investigation in order to refute Mormon charges regarding their conduct. The citizens of Daviess County passed a resolution recommending a "thorough investigation of the Mormon insurrection . . . before so many anathemas are hurled against the much injured citizens of this county." [31] Similar resolutions were adopted by neighboring counties. Neil Gilliam, a state senator representing Platte and Clay counties, demanded that the legislature take action:

I urge an investigation. I, sir, have nothing to fear from it. I want my conduct to be open to the world. I know there has been much said about smothering this matter—about concealing facts; but, Sir, I deny it. I insist upon this investigation—I want it to be full, fair, and open. I repeat that I insist upon it—it is of right due to the people I have the honor to represent and the citizens of upper Missouri

29. *Missouri Republican*, 24 December 1838; Redfield, "Book, Far West," pp. 5–8; and *HC* 3:217–24, Memorial of a Committee to the State Legislature of Missouri in Behalf of the Citizens of Caldwell County, 10 December 1838.

30. *Missouri Republican*, 9 January 1839.

31. *Missouri Argus*, 31 January 1839; and *Missouri Republican*, 20 February 1839.

generally.[32]

Gilliam and his constituents confidently believed that an investigation would demonstrate the Mormons' culpability in the conflict. Most of his Senate colleagues agreed, and they voted in January 1839 to create a joint Senate-House committee to investigate the disturbances.

The Senate bill met with firm opposition in the House. Some representatives said it would be too costly. Others argued that, because a number of Mormons had been cited to appear at future trials, a legislative investigation would usurp the authority of the local court system and perhaps prejudice the trials against the Mormon defendants.[33]   Those representing the counties where the disturbances had occurred insisted that their constituents had nothing to hide; yet, a majority of them opposed an immediate investigation. In early February the Missouri House voted to table until 4 July the Senate resolution to investigate the disturbances.

Their action brought charges of a cover-up. David Atchison claimed that his western colleagues were attempting to protect their constituents, who "were more deeply implicated than mine in those unfortunate disturbances." Atchison protested that "for myself and my constituents, we desired an investigation that the guilty might be dragged to the light, and that they might be held up to the scorn and curse of the world."[34] A. B. Chambers, editor of the *Missouri Republican*, also viewed the House action as an attempt to "smother and prevent investigation":

They talked about wanting an investigation—their constituents had nothing to fear, they desired an investigation, and all that; and yet, they were opposed to the bill. They offered no amendment to it, they did not attempt to change any of its provisions, but whilst they urged the necessity of killing it, they professed that they wanted an investigation. Such running one way and looking another, never

32. *Missouri Argus*, 15 February 1839.

33. Senate and House members were apparently sincere in their desire to protect Mormon rights: they prevented the pretrial publication of the testimony given at the Richmond hearing, which contained much damaging information regarding Mormon military operations.

34. *Missouri Republican*, 20 February 1839, David Atchison, letter to the editor, 10 February 1839.

was witnessed before in any deliberative body.[35]

Both Atchison and Chambers believed the majority of citizens in the western counties still desired an investigation. The House action, they asserted, disgraced Missouri and its people.

It is interesting to note that all senators from the western counties voted for the investigation. Two of the most active participants in the conflict, Neil Gilliam and Daniel Ashby (Ashby participated in the attack on Haun's Mill), voted in favor of the bill. If there was an attempt by Missouri legislators to protect their constituents, the Senate apparently was not involved. Nevertheless, members of the House undoubtedly realized that their action doomed the Mormon cause, because it prevented the legislature from evaluating or repealing the governor's expulsion order before the Mormons left the state—and this, rather than a cover-up of alleged crimes, was probably their chief goal. In July, when the House again considered the Senate resolution, few Mormons remained in Missouri. By then interest in the conflict had waned, and the proposal was defeated. No investigation was ever undertaken by the Missouri legislature.

Governor Boggs, for the most part, stayed out of the public debate. Although heavily criticized by Mormons, by several Missouri and out-of-state newspapers, and by a number of legislators for his handling of the crisis, Boggs showed little inclination to respond publicly to his critics. The little information available on Boggs's actions and attitudes following the Mormon surrender indicates that, in many respects, he tried to act legally and justly in bringing the crisis to a resolution: he instructed his generals to deliver Mormon prisoners to the civil authorities for trial; he instructed General Clark to gather information regarding the disturbances so he could make a proper report to the Missouri legislature; he responded to reports of depredations and violence against the Mormons by sending a company of soldiers to protect them; and he advised Judge King to prosecute non-Mormons who abused the Saints.[36] But the evidence also

35. Ibid., 8 February 1839.
36. *Document*, pp. 70, 81–82, 95, the Governor to Gen. Clark, 6 November 1838, the Governor to Gen. Clark, 19 November 1838, and Hon. A. A. King to the Governor, 23 December 1838; and Redfield, "Book, Far West," pp. 2–3.

shows that Governor Boggs did not regret his harsh order, nor did he doubt that the Mormons had instigated the conflict.

Governor Boggs issued his extermination order in an atmosphere of fear and panic, when desperate communications from western settlers demanded an immediate and forceful response to the alleged Mormon rebellion. Nearly a week later, after the governor presumably had time to dispassionately reflect on his order, he sent another letter to General Clark repeating his instructions to *exterminate* the Mormons or drive them from the state. In an 1840 address to the Missouri legislature, Boggs defended his action against what he called an "infatuated and deluded sect":

These people had violated the laws of the land by open and avowed resistance to them—they had undertaken without the aid of the civil authority to redress their real or fancied greivances— they had instituted among themselves a government of their own, independent of and in opposition to the government of this State— they had, at an inclement season of the year, driven the inhabitants of an entire county from their homes, ravaged their crops and destroyed their dwellings. Under these circumstances it became the imperious duty of the Executive to interpose and exercise the powers with which he was invested, to protect the lives and property of our citizens, to restore order and tranquility to the country and maintain the supremacy of our laws.[37]

The governor admitted that non-Mormons too may have committed excesses during the conflict, "but they must be attributed to the excited nature of the contest of the parties and not to any desire on the part of our constituted authorities to wilfully or cruelly oppress them."[38] Although Governor Boggs played no direct role in supervising the expulsion of the Saints after their surrender, their removal was carried out with his approval.

The citizens of northwestern Missouri overwhelmingly supported the governor's actions to quell the disturbances. Following the Mormon surrender, the citizens of Daviess, Ray, Chariton, Livingston, and Lafayette counties passed resolutions praising the governor's expulsion order and "devoutly pray[ing]

37. *Document*, pp. 9–10, Extract from Gov. Boggs' Message of 1840.
38. Ibid., p. 9.

that the same be promptly carried into effect."[39] These meetings were prompted more by the desire of local settlers to defend themselves against claims that they had persecuted the Mormons than by a desire to defend Boggs's actions; but as Missouri newspapers and legislators raised questions regarding their conduct, non-Mormon settlers linked their own actions with Boggs's, claiming that both were just and necessary to preserve the peace in northwestern Missouri. "I can assure you that Gov. Boggs stands higher in upper Missouri than he ever did," a Jackson County settler wrote in the *Jeffersonian Republican*.[40]

The citizens in the upper counties also continued their efforts to round up suspected Mormon offenders. Even after the Richmond hearing, Captain Bogart's company of soldiers continued "hunting the Danites" who had participated in the attack at Crooked River.[41] Nancy Tracy reports that Bogart and his men searched her home, looking for her husband, Moses Tracy, who had gone into hiding following the surrender. Not finding Moses at home, Bogart placed a double guard at the door and window to capture him upon his return.[42] Another participant at the Crooked River battle, Joseph Holbrook, was wounded and unable to flee Far West, so he hid in Levi Hancock's hayloft. On one occasion he escaped detection by pretending to be a sick, bedridden woman.[43] On another occasion, when Bogart and a couple of soldiers appeared with a search warrant at the Hancock home, both Levi and his wife, Clarissa, grabbed axes and a gun to defend the injured man. According to Holbrook, Bogart's men swore "they would take me to the battle grounds on Crooked River and there shoot me . . . ."[44] The Hancocks placed their axes behind the door and Clarissa stood to the side with a loaded rifle while Levi conversed with the soldiers in the doorway. Fortunately, the

39. *Missouri Argus*, 31 January 1839. Other newspapers reporting public meetings supporting the governor's actions include the *Jeffersonian Republican*, 19 January 1839, and the *Missouri Republican*, 16 February 1839.

40. 26 January 1839.

41. Drusilla Hendricks, "Historical Sketch," p. 21.

42. "Life History of Nancy Naomi Alexander Tracy Written By Herself," p. 21. Typescript, BYU Special Collections.

43. Ibid.

44. "Life," p. 25.

Missourians decided not to search the premises. [45]   Bogart's relentless efforts to track down and capture Mormon soldiers appeared to be a personal vendetta against the men who had attacked him at Crooked River. All of those sought by Bogart, however, successfully eluded capture and eventually fled the state.

The Mormons were not as successful in reclaiming their homes and property. Although Mormons living in Caldwell County were allowed to return to their farms to gather their crops and property, they often found their crops and property destroyed or stolen. Outside Caldwell, the settlers generally prevented the Mormons from returning to their homes. In Daviess County, for example, the Missourians allowed only a committee of twelve men to gather the Saints' crops and settle their affairs. When Anson Call, who was not a member of this committee, attempted to secure his property on Grand River, he was brutally beaten by a man who had taken possession of his farm. [46]   Given only one month to accomplish their task, the Mormon committeemen collected but a portion of their property and crops in Daviess County.

Although Captain Bogart's troops were stationed in Caldwell to protect the Saints—which, in fact, they did on a number of occasions—the Mormons still suffered from random acts of violence. In late November, Michael Arthur, a wealthy Liberty resident, informed the Clay representatives of the mob outrages:

Those demons are now constantly strolling up and down Caldwell county, in small companies armed, insulting the women in any and every way, and plundering the poor devils of all the means of subsistence (scanty as it was) left them, and driving off their horses, cattle, hogs, &c., and rifling their houses and farms of every thing therein, taking beds, bedding, wardrobe and all such things as they see they want, leaving the poor Mormons in a starving and naked condition. [47]

Arthur's letter soon became public. Governor Boggs, who was

45. Mosiah Hancock, "The Life Story of Mosiah Lyman Hancock," p. 11. Typescript, BYU Special Collections.

46. "The Life Record of Anson Call," pp. 14–15. Typescript, LDS Archives.

47. *Document*, p. 94, M. Arthur, Esq. to the Representatives from Clay County, 29 November 1838.

also informed of the Mormons' condition by David Redfield, dispatched Col. Sterling Price with a company of men to Caldwell County to protect the Saints. Boggs advised Judge King to use his power to prosecute the non-Mormon ruffians.

The accusations made by Arthur angered Judge King, for they called into question King's ability to maintain the peace and protect citizens in the upper counties. After Price's arrival, King wrote to Boggs and acknowledged that the claims made by Arthur and others were, to a certain extent, true; but, King argued:

If, instead of writing those inflammatory letters to members of the Legislature, these same men would come before me, and give such information as the law requires against these lawless characters, I should bring them to an immediate account . . . . I have heard frequent complaints, and have uniformly invited them to institute a legal investigation, but no person has thought proper to do so.[48]

The Mormons, of course, feared retaliation if they initiated complaints against non-Mormon citizens, but King did not address that issue in his letter. Of greatest concern to the judge was his fear that the Mormons would attempt to stay, which would lead to a renewal of hostilities. "The Mormons appear lately to have taken new courage, and to be determined not to move," King wrote. "The citizens are equally determined they shall; for nothing but expulsion or the other alternative will satisfy this community, that is, if the Mormons hold out under their former principles and practices."[49]

Judge King said that he did not encourage these attitudes among the settlers, but on 26 December he chaired a public meeting in Richmond at which local citizens passed resolutions refuting Arthur's charges and defending their conduct in the recent disturbances. Perhaps at King's request, their carefully worded resolutions refrained from passing judgment on the guilt or innocence of the Mormon defendants. Nevertheless, King was roundly condemned for participating in the general excitement because he was scheduled to sit at the grand jury

48. Ibid., p. 95, Hon. A. A. King to the Governor, 23 December 1838.
49. Ibid., p. 96.

examination of Mormons in Daviess County. After hearing that
King had chaired the Ray County meeting, Sen. Charles R. Scott
of Randolph County declared that King "is the most unfit man
I know of" to preside at future Mormon trials.[50]

Judge King's attitude toward the Mormons had been relatively
neutral when the disturbances began in the summer of 1838.
Some Mormons praised him for his quick and effective response
when he called out the militia to quell the September disturbances. But Mormon military operations during the conflict,
along with the evidence presented at the Richmond hearing,
convinced King that the Mormons had instigated the war. He
also believed that persecution against the Saints, to a large degree, resulted from their practice of gathering. "If the Mormons
would disperse, and not gather into exclusive communities of
their own . . . the people might be reconciled to them . . . ,"
King asserted. "Suggest the matter to them as I have done, for
the sake of their peace and safety, and they will give you many
scriptural reasons why they should not do so."[51]   His leading
role at the Richmond public meeting in late December, and
his insensitivity to the outrages against the Mormons following
their surrender, suggest that King was no longer qualified to
preside at Mormon trials. A change in circuit court boundaries
later removed the Mormon hearings from his jurisdiction.

Exodus from Missouri

Although some Mormons began leaving the state soon after
the surrender, most remained in Far West or on their Caldwell
County farms, hoping they would not be expelled from the state.
By late January, however, Mormon leaders realized that the
Missouri legislature would not act on their behalf. In addition,
the longer they remained, the greater was the animosity of
local citizens, who watched jealously for any indications that
the Mormons might break their treaty agreement. Local officials
showed little inclination to protect the Saints from mobs that
continually harassed them. Many Mormons also came to believe
that Joseph Smith and the other Mormon prisoners were being

50. *Missouri Republican*, 9 January 1839.
51. *Document*, pp. 95–96, Hon. A. A. King to the Governor, 23 December
1838.

held simply to insure that the Mormons left the state: the prisoners' release would not occur until the expulsion was completed. Eventually the Mormons decided they must leave Missouri.

In late January the Mormons began organizing to remove from the state. The large number of poor in Far West prompted a proposal that the Saints pool their resources and assist each other in the exodus. On 29 January the Mormons adopted a proposal by Brigham Young:

. . . we this day enter into a covenant to stand by and assist each other to the utmost of our abilities in removing from this state . . . we will never desert the poor who are worthy, till they shall be out of the reach of the exterminating order of General Clark, acting for and in the name of the state.[52]

After appointing a committee of seven to superintend their removal, nearly four hundred Latter-day Saint men and women signed a covenant placing their property at the disposal of the committee. All Mormons desiring to leave the state would be assisted; none would be left behind.[53]

A large number of the destitute among the Mormons were the families of men who were imprisoned or had fled the state. The wives of these men struggled to provide for their families and find the means to remove from Missouri. Sarah Rich, although pregnant with her first child, took into her home seven families, including John Page, a recently ordained apostle, and his critically ill wife, Lorain. Lorain died shortly after, but "the mob was troubling us so severely at this time," Sarah wrote, "[that] it was impossible to have Sister Page buried for three days."[54] Missouri troops, seeking to arrest Sarah's husband, Charles, for his participation in the Crooked River battle, searched her home twice while Lorain "lay in the house a corpse." Phoebe Patten, whose husband had led the attack at Crooked River, lived in constant fear that the Missourians would capture and torture her, so great was their hatred for the slain apostle. Following the surrender she prepared for the

52. *HC* 3:250.
53. *HC* 3:249–54.
54. "Autobiography of Sarah D. Rich," p. 22. Typescript, LDS Archives. Two Page children also died shortly after the surrender.

worst. "I can never forget her fearless and determined look," wrote Helen Mar Whitney about her visit to Phoebe Patten's home. Phoebe greeted her guests wearing a large bowie-knife. On her stove was a large iron kettle full of boiling water to throw upon any "demons" who tried to molest her. "She did not seem in the least excited, her countenance was perfectly calm . . . ," Whitney said, "she only thought of avenging the blood of her husband." [55]

Drusilla Hendricks's husband, James, had also fought in the Crooked River battle. Shortly after the battle Drusilla had received word that James had been wounded and brought to a nearby cabin. She found James lying near David Patten and some of the other wounded, shot in the neck "where it cut off all feeling of the body." She immediately tried to revive his muscles. "I went to work to try and get my husband warm but could not," Drusilla wrote. "I rubbed and steamed him but could get no circulation. He was dead from his neck down." [56] During the next several months Drusilla continued to rub her husband with vinegar, salt, and liniments. Joseph Smith, Sr., and some of the brethren anointed James and administered to him, which brought some movement back to his shoulders, but he still could not move his legs and arms. Drusilla consequently took responsibility for gathering their possessions—their home had been plundered of everything but their beds—and selling their land to buy a wagon, cattle, and provisions for their exodus from Missouri. James remained a cripple for life.

Under these trying conditions a number of women also bore children. Eliza Ann Snow, having traveled from Kirtland to Far West during her pregnancy, bore her first child, a daughter, less than a month after her arrival. The child was born on 30 October in "an old log house that we could poke a cat out between the logs." Snow relates that, because the Mormons were preparing for battle with the militia, "I could not keep the midwife long enough to dress my child. . . . The mob was blowing horns and firing guns all night long." [57]   Harriet

55. "Early Reminiscences," *Woman's Exponent* 8 (15 May 1880): 188; and Martha P. J. Thomas, "Family Genealogy," p. 22.

56. "Historical Sketch," p. 20.

57. Eliza Ann Carter Snow's account is contained in Dominicus Carter, "Life History of Dominicus Carter," n.p. Typescript, BYU Special Collections. Eliza Ann's daughter, Sarah, later married Joseph Young, who, on the very

Wight, a mother of five children, had given birth to her fourth child in December 1833, shortly after she fled Jackson County. Her child was born in a tent made of two poles and a quilt while the family camped along the bank of the Big Blue River. Harriet's husband, Lyman, left less than a month later to join Zion's Camp, the Mormon army marching to Jackson County to restore the Saints to their homes. In 1836 Harriet gave birth to another child while Lyman was away on church business in the east. In early November 1838, shortly after Lyman was taken prisoner and sentenced to be shot, Harriet bore their sixth child in a small cabin at Diahman. "The house was surrounded by the mob indulging in much loud and incencious talk, including their boasts of what they had done with Joseph Smith and Lyman Wight," recalled her oldest son, Orange, regarding the circumstances of this birth. [58]   Mary Fielding Smith, whose husband, Hyrum, was imprisoned with Wight and other Mormon leaders, also bore a child while her home was surrounded by hostile troops. Their son, Joseph F. Smith, would become the sixth president of the Mormon church.

Like James and Drusilla Hendricks, most Mormons sold their land and improvements to pay their expenses out of the state. The deed of trust signed by the Mormon men after the surrender was so patently unlawful that it was not carried into effect, and so the Mormons retained ownership of their land—where they had made public purchases. But the Mormons did not own all of the land where they had settled. The land at Diahman, for example, was not owned by the Mormons because it did not come up for sale until 12 November, about two weeks after their surrender. The Rev. Sashel Woods, John Cravens, and Thomas Callaway jointly purchased the town shortly after the land became available. A letter to the editor of the *Missouri Republican* reported that Diahman was not the only Mormon land purchased by Missourians:

. . . at the recent land sales the lands of Caldwell and Daviess were brought into market, and . . . some of the citizens who have been

---

day she was born, barely escaped with his life during the attack on Haun's Mill.

58. "Recollections of Orange L. Wight, Son of Lyman Wight," p. 3. Typescript, LDS Archives.

the most active in the excitement against the Mormons, purchased a number of the Mormon tracts of land. Where the Mormons had made settlements and improvements, it is said, these citizens have purchased them for speculation. It is said, that the town of "Adamon Diamond," a Mormon town in Daviess, in which there are several houses—a very valuable site for a town—was purchased at these sales for a dollar and a quarter an acre.[59]

The *Republican* remarked concerning this development:

Much as we censure the course of the Mormons, there is no act, of which we have any knowledge, which will at all compare with the unrighteousness of those who, it seems, got up this crusade in order to obtain possession of the houses and lands of their victims.[60]

Exodus of the Saints from Missouri. C. C. A. Christensen painting, ca. 1878. Courtesy Permanent Collection of Brigham Young University.

59. 13 December 1838. In addition to the Mormon town of Diahman, Sashel Woods and John Cravens copurchased over one dozen tracks of land in Daviess County immediately following the Mormon surrender. Leland Gentry and Charles Allen have pointed out to me the possibility that the other lands purchased by Woods and Cravens were also Mormon farms and settlements. It is perhaps these men to whom the *Missouri Republican* referred. For additional information, see Leland H. Gentry, "The Land Question at Adam-ondi-Ahman" (unpublished paper presented to the Mormon History Association, May 1982).

60. Ibid.

Mormons with land to sell found they could get but a fraction of its worth. Most Mormons consequently traded their land in Missouri for land in Illinois, where they moved after the expulsion. But those who needed cash and equipment accepted the low offers, and many Mormons reported trading their farms for a wagon and team of cattle. The expulsion of the Saints, Reed Peck wrote after their departure, opened "a field for speculators who now reap the advantages of labor done by the *banished* Mormons." [61]

The exodus from Missouri proved physically exhausting and often strained the Mormons' resources to their limits. Some of the men earned extra cash at Fort Leavenworth to pay the expenses of the trip. Others worked while they traveled, stopping to break prairie, put up fences, and perform various jobs for farmers along the way. Daniel McArthur reported that, when the Saints purchased provisions for their journey, some Missourians charged them as much as seventy-five cents for a bushel of corn that they had earlier purchased for five cents a bushel from Mormons desperately in need of cash.[62] Lucy Mack Smith, the Prophet's mother, said Missourians often refused to give them lodging for the night or offered them only the use of a filthy outhouse for shelter from the rain. [63] Nancy Carey, whose husband was beaten and killed by a Missouri soldier, made two trips to Illinois, traveling over one hundred miles each way with a four-horse team in the winter snow, to move her family out of the state. [64] Nancy Hammer, whose husband was killed at Haun's Mill, relied on a blind horse and a small wagon to move her family of six children. Her son, John, wrote:

Into this small wagon we placed our clothes, bedding, some corn meal and what scanty provisions we could muster, and started out into the cold and frost to travel on foot, to eat and sleep by the wayside with the canopy of heaven for a covering. . . . When night approached we would hunt for a log or fallen tree and if lucky enough to find one we would build fires by the sides of it. Those

61. "Manuscript," p. 31.
62. "Journal," p. 30.
63. *Biographical Sketches of Joseph Smith the Prophet*, p. 322.
64. Nathan Tanner, "Reminiscences," published in George S. Tanner, *John Tanner and His Family* (Salt Lake City: Publishers Press, 1974), p. 389.

who had blankets or bedding camped down near enough to enjoy the warmth of the fire, which was kept burning through the entire night. Our family, as well as many others, were almost barefooted, and some had to wrap their feet in cloths in order to keep them from freezing and protect them from the sharp points of the frozen ground. This, at best, was very imperfect protection, and often the blood from our feet marked the frozen earth. My mother and sister were the only members of our family who had shoes, and these became worn out and almost useless before we reached the then hospitable shores of Illinois. All of our family except the two youngest—Austin and Julian—had to walk every step of the entire distance, as our one horse was not able to haul a greater load . . . . There was scarcely a day while we were on the road that it did not either snow or rain. The nights and mornings were very cold.[65]

Not all Mormons suffered as much as the Hammer or Smith families. John D. Lee reported that "we were kindly treated by most of the people; many of them requested us to stop and settle down by them."[66]   Despite the invitations to remain, Lee and the other Mormons left the state as required by the expulsion order and gathered just across the border in Quincy, Illinois, where compassionate citizens welcomed and assisted the weary exiles.

Sarah Rich and Samantha Stout, who had covenanted not to separate until they reunited with their husbands, left Far West in January with Sarah's cousin and her father, who had come from Illinois to assist her in the journey. When they arrived at the Mississippi River, just across from Quincy, the exhausted travelers found that half the river was running with huge ice floes. They would be unable to cross in their wagons. Their husbands, upon hearing that Sarah and Samantha had reached the opposite shore, immediately obtained a small boat and braved the dangerous floes to cross the river. True to the covenant made three months earlier when Charles and Hosea had fled Far West, both couples had remained together until their reunion on the frozen river bank. Less than two months later Sarah gave birth to the Rich's first child, Sarah Jane. Samantha Stout, having suffered from exposure during the

---

65. Quoted in Lyman O. Littlefield, *Reminiscences of Latter-Day Saints* (Logan, Utah: The Utah Journal Co., Printers, 1888), pp. 72–73.

66. *Mormonism Unveiled*, p. 96.

arduous journey to Illinois, lay bedridden for several months and finally died in November 1839 as a consequence of her hardships.

During the exodus the Mormon prisoners continued to seek release. Their efforts included an appeal to the state legislature for a change of venue, an appeal to be released on writs of habeas corpus, and an attempted escape from jail. Joseph Smith and the others charged with treason were held in Liberty Jail, a small but sturdy prison divided into an upper room and a dungeon. The prisoners often spent the day in the upper room, but at night were locked in the dungeon, where the two small windows provided little ventilation or light for the six men crowded in the fourteen-foot-square cell. Alexander McRae could not stand upright under the jail's six-foot ceilings. The Mormon prisoners claimed they were badly mistreated by their jailers, who fed them poisoned food and even human flesh. These charges were denied by Clay County citizens, who believed that they were uniquely benevolent in their treatment of the Mormons.[67] A local judge granted Sidney Rigdon's release on a writ of habeas corpus, but the other prisoners remained locked up until their grand jury examination in Daviess County.

The Mormon prisoners, accompanied by a fifteen-man guard, arrived in Gallatin on 8 April for their grand jury hearing. "The people of the county collected in crowds, and were so incensed that we anticipated violence toward the prisoners," wrote Peter H. Burnett, who, with Amos Rees, served as legal counsel for the defendants.[68] One of the prisoners, Alexander McRae, reported that the people gathered menacingly around their wagon. Hoping to calm the crowd, Joseph Smith stood and said, "We are in your hands; if we are guilty, we refuse not to be punished by law."[69] Following Smith's short speech, William Peniston and another man mounted a bench and advised the settlers to keep the peace. "We do not want the disgrace of

---

67. See, e.g., William T. Wood, "Mormon Memoirs," *Liberty Tribune*, 9 April 1886.

68. *Recollections*, p. 65.

69. Alexander McRae to the Editor [*Deseret News*], 1 November 1854, published in Joseph and Eunice McRae, *Historical Facts Regarding the Liberty and Carthage Jails* (Salt Lake City: Utah Printing Company, 1954), p. 31.

taking the law into our own hands," they said. The irony of Peniston's speech must have been apparent to the Mormons— Peniston had instigated the 6 August election battle in Gallatin— yet they were grateful for its effect. The two speeches mollified the crowd, and no harm came to the prisoners.

The Mormon prisoners and their lawyers stayed in a rough log schoolhouse, about twenty-five-feet square. According to both Mormon and non-Mormon accounts, the Daviess guards treated the Mormons well. The guards and prisoners sat up during the night, drinking whiskey and exchanging stories about their recent conflict. "Wight would laughingly say, 'At such a place' (mentioning it) 'you rather whipped us, but at such a place we licked you,'" Burnett reported.[70]   The prisoners were visited by a number of local citizens, including two preachers who argued theology with the Mormon prophet. Burnett viewed Smith as the superior in intelligence and ability. "He invariably silenced them sooner or later," said Burnett.[71]   Prior to the hearing the citizens also persuaded Smith, who was reputedly a skilled wrestler, to wrestle their county champion. The Mormon prophet threw the man several times in succession, much to the delight of the spectators.

The Missourians' friendliness, however, was not carried into the grand jury hearing, and the defendants were indicted for all crimes previously charged against them. Among those impaneled on the jury were Robert Peniston, whose Millport home had been burned by the Mormons, and Jacob Rogers, who had killed Thomas McBride at the Haun's Mill massacre. Sampson Avard again appeared as a chief witness against the defendants. Following their indictment, the Mormons received a change of venue to Boone County because the new judge of the circuit court, Thomas Burch, had served as prosecuting attorney at the Richmond hearing. The Mormon prisoners, escorted by Sheriff William Morgan and four deputies, left on 15 April for Boone County.

The Mormons escaped the next night as their guards slept. According to Hyrum Smith and Lyman Wight, the guards said they were instructed to let the Mormons go.[72] Hyrum and Joseph

70. *Recollections*, p. 66.

71. Ibid.

72. *HC* 3:423, 449, Hyrum Smith and Lyman Wight, affidavits, 1 July 1843; and *HC* 3:372, Joseph Smith, "A Bill of Damages," 4 June 1839.

also reported that the guards were intoxicated when they went to sleep. Taking the guards' horses, the five Mormon prisoners traveled along out-of-the-way roads and under assumed names, informing people they met that they were land seekers from the East. At one farm where the Mormons stayed, four of them took an early morning stroll while Alexander McRae conversed with the owner. The farmer asked McRae his name, which the farmer had forgotten from the night before. Unfortunately, McRae had also forgotten his fictitious name. McRae immediately developed a terrible stomach cramp, which threw him into spasms and rendered him unable to speak. The alarmed farmer ran outside and brought in the others, who asked, "Mr. Brown, what is the matter with you, what have you been eating?" The relieved Mr. Brown began to recover right away; but in the meantime the farmer brought in a jug of whiskey, which he recommended for Mr. Brown's illness. The others also took a drink, just in case the disease was contagious. Orange Wight reported that after the former prisoners arrived in Quincy, when offered beer or any other stimulants, they would always recommend to "give Brother McRay some first—he has the cramp and can't tell his name."[73]

The Mormons' escape proved less amusing to Daviess County citizens. Rumors quickly spread that the guards had been bribed. Although the prisoners did not mention a bribe, they reported that the guards had assisted in the escape. Both Joseph H. McGee and Ebenezer Robinson claimed that one of the guards later visited Nauvoo and received pay for his horses and trouble.[74] It is not clear how many guards were involved, but the evidence suggests that at least one of them assisted in the prisoners'

73. "Recollections," p. 4.

74. McGee, "The Mormons in Missouri," an 1898 newspaper clipping in the Library of the State Historical Society of Missouri, Columbia, Missouri; and Robinson, "Items of Personal History," *The Return* 2 (April 1890): 243. McGee and Robinson disagree regarding which of the guards came to Nauvoo. Gentry states the evidence also argues strongly that Judge Austin A. King engineered the prisoners' escape ("History of the Latter-Day Saints in Northern Missouri," pp. 590–91, 596–97). Gentry cites a reminiscence of Gen. John B. Clark, in which Clark wrote: "I had an understanding with King that they [the Mormon prisoners] were to be put in prison, but were not to be guarded too closely, and if they got away and left the state, they would be allowed to go" (quoted in Stevens, *Centennial History of Missouri*, 2:119). A number of inconsistencies in Clark's reminiscence have caused me to reject

escape. In response to these charges, William Morgan signed an affidavit asserting that the prisoners "made the escape without the connivance consent or negligence of myself or said guard."[75] Daviess citizens, however, were not convinced. Enraged settlers rode Sheriff Morgan through the town on an iron bar, and they dragged William Bowman by his hair across the town square. Joseph McGee reported that Morgan died shortly after as a result of his violent ride.[76]

---

his assertions here. First, Clark claimed that he effected the surrender at Far West. In fact, he did not arrive at Far West until 4 November, four days after the Mormon surrender. In addition, the Mormon prisoners were kept only a short time under Clark's supervision. Joseph Smith and the other prisoners spent the bulk of their time in Liberty Jail, long after the general had returned to Howard County. Finally, the contemporary letters of Judge King and General Clark reveal no disposition on their part to engineer their prisoners' escape.

75. Statement, 6 July 1839. Joint Collection, University of Missouri and State Historical Society of Missouri.

76. McGee, "Some of the Waste Places of Zion," *Deseret News*, 10 September 1904, p. 23; and *History of Daviess County* (1882), p. 206.

14

Conclusion

Both the Mormons and Missourians believed the Mormon War had resulted from an unlawful conspiracy by the other to seize property and power. Missourians viewed the Mormons' theocratic rule in Caldwell County, the secret teachings and oaths of the Danite band, the unwillingness of Mormon leaders to submit to local authorities, and the military operations of their soldiers as evidence of Mormon intentions to overthrow the government in western Missouri and supplant it with one of their own. Consequently, following the surrender, Missouri officials arrested Mormon leaders on charges of treason.

Conversely, the Mormons believed the disturbances represented a conspiracy by Missourians to drive them from the state and steal their land. As evidence they advanced the unsubstantiated claim that Daviess settlers had burned their own homes and then blamed the Mormons to inflame prejudice against them. Others contended that the vigilantes had purposely goaded the Mormons into violence as a pretext for seizing their farms and property. The swiftness with which some Missourians moved onto Mormon land following the surrender made it appear as if this had been their plan all along. Even General Atchison, the staunchest opponent of the vigilantes, was denounced by Mormon leaders as being party to a conspiracy "concocted by the governor down to the lowest judge" to expel them from the state.[1]

Conspiratorial designs, however, played little part in the conflict. The causes of the Mormon War—and the resulting expulsion of the Saints—are best understood when viewed

1. *HC* 3:421, Hyrum Smith, affidavit, 1 July 1843. For other statements by Mormons describing a conspiracy to drive them from the state, see, *HC* 3:368, Joseph Smith, "A Bill of Damages," 4 June 1839; Owen, "Memorial," pp. 3–4; Pratt, *History of the Late Persecution*, pp. 30, 37; Rigdon, *Appeal*, p. 36; and William Smith, "Infatuated and Deluded Sect," *Times and Seasons* 2 (15 February 1841): 314–16.

as several related problems. At one level, the disturbances represented a conflict between the Mormons and their non-Mormon neighbors. Misunderstandings, escalating hostilities, and irreconcilable differences, exacerbated by the rapid influx of Mormon emigrants, eventually led to bloodshed and destruction. At another level, the conflict represented a struggle by civil authorities to maintain law and order. Prejudice, poor judgment, and an inefficient state militia prevented state and local officials from effectively or fairly resolving the crisis. Finally, the conflict typified conditions and attitudes that have contributed to extralegal violence throughout American history. Both the Mormons and Missourians accepted the principles of democracy and majority rule that allowed them to adopt extralegal methods to resolve disputes, defend their interests, and expel unwanted persons from their communities. The Missouri government gave legal sanction to these principles—and thus endorsed the notion that the will of the majority is the law—by expelling the Saints from the state.

The initial source of trouble was the Missourians' fear of the "gathering" Saints. Both General Clark and Judge King later identified the Mormon practice of establishing exclusive communities as a chief cause of their trouble, for it tended to "excite the jealousies of the people."[2]   Many Missourians believed that any county where the Mormons settled would soon be dominated by them. A Mormon-dominated county, they believed, would not reflect their own interests or values. They especially feared a loss of control—economic, political, and spiritual—resulting from takeover by a group whose leaders controlled the temporal affairs of their people. "The Mormons must leave the country, and if we do not make them do so now . . . they will be so strong in a few years that they will rule the country as they please," the older settlers declared.[3]   The Mormons, believing that God commanded them to gather in Zion and that this activity was fully protected by the Constitution, refused to abandon their homes.

Religious prejudice played an important role in shaping the participants' perceptions and actions during the disturbances. The Mormons' belief in new prophets, new scriptures, and

2. See pp. 190 and 234 above.
3. Lee, *Mormonism Unveiled*, p. 67.

new miracles—beliefs, ironically, not inconsistent with biblical teachings—stamped them as fanatics and dupes. Neil Gilliam's daughter described the influence of religion upon her father's view of the Mormons:

Father believed the Bible, particularly where it said smite the Philistines, and he figured the Philistines was a misprint for the Mormons and he believed it was his religious duty to smite them. He believed they should be exterminated root and branch. He was a great hand to practice what he preached so he helped exterminate quite a considerable few of them.[4]

One might argue, as did Gilliam and other anti-Mormon vigilantes, that it was not the Mormons' religious beliefs they opposed, but the lawless and aggressive actions that resulted from those beliefs. Thus, the vigilantes generally pointed to alleged crimes and violations of the law by the Mormons, and rarely to the Mormons' religious beliefs, as the reasons for their opposition. It is interesting to note, however, that Missourians who were acquainted with individual Mormons generally believed they were honest and industrious citizens. Many Mormons reported that, after the surrender, their neighbors invited them to remain in Missouri—if they renounced Mormonism. Missourians' preconceived notions about Mormon beliefs and practices caused them to regard Mormons, as a group, with suspicion and fear, even though they found individual Mormons to be acceptable neighbors. Their perception of Mormonism as an alien, un-Christian religion prejudiced their perceptions of Mormon activities and intentions. It is not surprising that three ministers, Neil Gilliam, Samuel Bogart, and Sashel Woods, led much of the opposition to the Saints.[5]

The Mormons carried religious prejudices of their own into the conflict. Their confidence in the spiritual and moral superiority of Mormonism, and their belief that all other Christians "without one exception, [will] receive their portion

4. Lockley, "Reminiscences of Martha Elizabeth Gilliam," pp. 359–60.

5. Although competition for converts occasionally stimulated animosity between competing ministers and congregations in frontier America, there is no evidence that fear of "sheepstealing" contributed to these ministers' opposition to Mormonism.

with the devil and his angels," distorted their perceptions of
non-Mormon activities and intentions.[6]   Mormon leaders did
not realize, for example, that Missourians were genuinely
alarmed by reports of Danite teachings and activities. Those
leaders interpreted all opposition as persecution of God's
chosen people. Their confidence in the righteousness of their
cause led them to disregard warnings by dissenters and non-
Mormons that their activities would bring the entire state
against them. The Saints adopted an aggressive rather than a
conciliatory stance because they believed God would protect
His people. Ebenezer Robinson, a member of the Mormon
militia, commented regarding the outcome of their policies:

> Thus, within the short space of four months from the time the church
> made that threatning boast that if a mob should come upon us again,
> "we would carry the war to their own houses, and one party or the
> other should be utterly destroyed," we found ourselves prisoners of
> war, our property confiscated, our leaders in close confinement, and
> the entire church required to leave the state or be exterminated.
>
> We admonish all christian people to let this be a solemn warning
> to never suffer themselves to make a threatening boast of what
> they would do under certain circumstances, as we are not our own
> keepers, and we feel certain the Lord will not help us fight any
> such battles.[7]

Just as the religious prejudices of many Missourians distorted
their view of Mormon activities and beliefs, the Mormons' own
religious biases contributed to the conflict with their neighbors.

The question of religious prejudice leads to questions regarding the make-up of the Missouri vigilante committees. Who
joined the vigilantes? In Carroll and Daviess counties, where the
disturbances began, the older citizens were most opposed to
Mormon settlements in their counties. These people believed
that they had first claim to the land, and that they had the
right to exclude the Mormons. In addition, as discussed above,
the only ministers who are known to have participated actively in the conflict sided with the vigilantes. The anti-Mormon
vigilantes in both counties also included local officials; consequently, they used the legal system to help expel the Mormons.

6. *Elders' Journal* 1 (August 1838): 60.
7. "Items of Personal History," *The Return* 2 (February 1890): 210.

Writs were issued against alleged Mormon criminals during the disturbances, and in Carroll non-Mormon sympathizers were jailed, but few vigilantes were brought to trial.[8] Generalizations about the Missourians, however, do not strictly apply. In Daviess County, for example, men such as Josiah Morin, a respected member of the community, befriended the Saints and spoke out on their behalf. Some people who were religious opposed the vigilantes; others not particularly religious joined them.

Similarly, it is difficult to state with any certainty the percentage of people who were pro-Mormon, anti-Mormon, or neutral in the conflict. The answer to that question depends, to a large degree, on the time and location of the disturbances. The settlers living closest to the Mormon settlements were generally the least sympathetic to their presence. Carroll and perhaps Daviess were the only counties where a majority of the citizens initially supported the vigilantes. Many of the surrounding counties, such as Chariton, Howard, Ray, and Clay, sent either representatives to investigate the disturbances or troops to quell the violence. Very few sent support during the early months of conflict. Consequently, through September 1838, the state militia successfully prevented a clash between the vigilantes and the Mormons.

As the conflict continued, however, support for the vigilantes increased, partly because Missourians perceived the Mormons as irrational fanatics, and partly because Mormon activities seemed to validate those perceptions. Even if non-Mormons objected to the vigilante activities, they had little incentive to take up arms against them: after all, the vigilantes directed their violence against the Saints; their activities posed no threat to most Missourians. But Mormon military operations frightened Missourians. They believed the Mormons would direct their activities against not only the vigilantes, but all Missourians—as apparently evidenced by Mormon depredations in Daviess and Ray counties—and so they eventually took up arms against the Saints. Even Generals Atchison and Doniphan, who vehemently opposed the vigilantes, regarded the Mormons as fanatics capable of directing their vengeance against innocent

8. Not surprisingly, in Caldwell County only non-Mormons were brought to trial for offenses committed during the disturbances. Mormons who sympathized with Missourians were threatened by their leaders.

citizens. Both men eventually joined the military operations against the Saints.

The dilemma faced by Atchison and Doniphan points out the dilemma presented to all settlers—Mormons and non-Mormons— concerning how to end the violence. In examining the attitudes and activities of the participants in the conflict, this history has presented evidence and conclusions that differ significantly from previous research on the subject:

(1) The Missourians were not so completely prejudiced against the Mormons as previous histories contended. Not all approved of vigilantism, and many vacillated between a regard for the law and a belief that they must resort to extralegal action for their own protection. The civil authorities made sincere, legitimate attempts to halt the violence. Many citizens intervened—often saving Mormon lives and property—and attempted to quell the anti-Mormon spirit among their neighbors. The evidence also shows that, prior to the surrender, the vigilantes and militia were not as violent as claimed by the Mormons. Bands of ruffians disarmed Mormon settlers and ordered them from their homes, but they destroyed relatively little property at that time. Following the Mormon surrender, however, non-Mormon soldiers and vigilantes gave vent to an intense hostility and fear—exacerbated by several months of conflict—that resulted in the widespread plunder and abuse of the Mormon people.

(2) The militant spirit and lawless activities of the Saints can be traced directly to Joseph Smith. Some Mormons later asserted that Sidney Rigdon was responsible for the excesses emanating from the Mormon leadership. Although Rigdon, who was known to have a violent temperament, played an important role in these events, nearly all Mormon accounts—both contemporary journals and reminiscences—place Joseph Smith at the head of Mormon activities. He knew and approved of the Danites. He directed the plundering and burning of non-Mormon homes in Daviess County. In addition, the Mormons destroyed a considerable amount of property in Daviess—much more than was destroyed by the anti-Mormon vigilantes. And the evidence shows that the Mormons were not acting on orders from state militia officers, as they later claimed, but on their own initiative. The military operations of the Saints undercut a large portion

of their support among the non-Mormon settlers.

(3) The Mormon dissenters, John Corrill, Thomas Marsh, George Hinkle, and others, were not cowards, nor were they simply bitter apostates trying to incite violence against the Saints. Their disaffection from the Church stemmed from a sincere opposition to the militant and criminal acts of the Mormon people. These men foresaw the disastrous consequences of the Mormon policies, but their warnings brought only condemnation from their leaders. Most important, their statements and claims regarding the militant and unlawful nature of the Mormons' activities are generally supported by evidence from both Mormon and Missouri sources.

(4) The Richmond Court of Inquiry was not a "mock hearing." The prosecution's witnesses, whatever their motives for testifying, generally gave accurate descriptions of Mormon activities and policies. In addition, Missouri officials conducted the hearing according to accepted procedures for preliminary hearings. The prisoners were assigned counsel, had the opportunity to cross-examine witnesses and present their own defense, and were charged according to the evidence against them. The hostile atmosphere in Richmond intimidated Mormon witnesses, but this was not the primary reason why the Mormons presented a meager defense. The nature of preliminary hearings, rather than prejudice against the defendants, served to limit their defense. An understanding of the purpose of preliminary hearings is essential to understand the Richmond Court of Inquiry.[9]

Mormon historians have been reluctant to acknowledge the extent to which Mormon militancy and aggression contributed to the conflict, lest that recognition be construed as an admission

9. The failure to understand the nature and purpose of preliminary hearings has led some historians to draw erroneous conclusions about certain aspects of these events. Donna Hill, for example, writes, "The state legislature, embarrassed over the [Richmond] hearing's violation of legal procedure, debated whether to publish the transcript. It was published eventually with apology . . ." (*Joseph Smith*, p. 250). Although some of the legislators believed that Judge King, in actions subsequent to the hearing, manifested a prejudice against the Saints, there is nothing in their statements to indicate that they believed the hearing violated legal procedure. Neither is there an apology in their publication of the Richmond court record. Missouri legislators stated that "they consider the evidence adduced in the examination there held, in a great degree *ex parte* [on one-side only], and not of the character which should be desired for the basis of a fair and

that the Mormons instigated the disturbances and, therefore, deserved expulsion. These issues require comment.

This history has presented considerable evidence that the Mormons adopted an aggressive and militant posture before the disturbances began. Nevertheless, the conflict began in Carroll County not as an immediate result of Mormon militancy, but because Mormons moved into the county without permission from local settlers. Non-Mormons took the first illegal steps in the conflict. The Mormons did not desire conflict and would have been satisfied to practice their religious and social programs in peace. Their military operations were a response to the threats against their communities outside Caldwell County.

Simply asserting that non-Mormons in Carroll initiated the disturbances, however, does not explain why the conflict developed as it did. Many Missourians also opposed the anti-Mormon vigilantes, and yet, by the end of the conflict, nearly all the citizens in northern Missouri opposed the Saints. To understand this development the historian must examine the attitudes and conduct of all participants, Mormon and non-Mormon. Missourians feared Mormon control of their communities. Mormons, having suffered years of persecution, were determined not to be driven from their homes. Participants on both sides broke laws, overreacted to rumors of violence, and demonstrated little understanding of or sympathy for the other's position. Both groups justified their own activities by pointing to the provocative and illegal activities of their alleged enemies. Both excused their own excesses as the unfortunate consequences of war, while they pointed to the excesses of the other as evidence of aggressive intentions. Non-Mormons in Carroll County initiated the disturbances, but militancy and intolerance on both sides aggravated hostilities and contributed

---

candid investigation" (*Document*, p. 2, Report of the Joint Committee on the Mormon Investigation, 18 December 1838). Missouri legislators recognized that the Richmond hearing did not represent an impartial investigation of the disturbances, but they did not state that the hearing was improperly conducted. Preliminary hearings focus mainly on the prosecution's case against the defendants. A properly conducted preliminary hearing is, by its nature, a one-sided examination. Thus, the state legislators, who were debating whether to conduct their own investigation of the Mormon War, concluded that the Richmond Court of Inquiry could not serve as the basis for an objective investigation into the causes of the disturbances.

to the general conflict in northwestern Missouri.

But this understanding of the disturbances does not lead to the conclusion that the Mormons received fair or just treatment. Mormon soldiers committed many crimes—which led, eventually, to the governor's expulsion order—but anti-Mormon vigilantes committed many crimes as well. Missouri officials, however, did not prosecute non-Mormons who drove Mormon settlers from their homes, plundered, and burned. There was no court of inquiry to investigate unlawful acts committed by non-Mormons. Joseph Smith exaggerated little when he complained that the law "is always administered against us and never in our favor."[10] Despite the efforts of many citizens to enforce the law and impose an impartial settlement, the application of the law by Missouri officials generally worked against the Saints' interests. The eventual outcome of the conflict, the enforced exodus of the Saints, violated the Mormons' right to settle where they chose.

When viewed from this perspective, the disturbances can be. seen as the working out of dominant forces in American social and political development. In this respect, the Mormon War represented a Jacksonian expression of democracy and majority rule. The Mormons found themselves in the same position as Indians, blacks, abolitionists, and other groups whose activities, values, or physical appearance conflicted with community norms. The particular circumstances for each group were different: the moral and legal justifications for excluding free blacks were different from those used to expel the Mormons; the events that led to the removal of Indians from their lands were not the same as those leading to the Mormons' removal. In some cases popular will was expressed through extralegal violence; in other cases the legal power of the state enforced majority will. But the outcome was always the same. In Missouri, regardless of who was at fault or who broke the law, it was Mormon leaders who were jailed, and Mormons who were forced to abandon their homes. The state government ratified the notion of majority will by carrying out the vigilantes' demand to expel the Saints from their communities.

The importance of viewing the Mormon War as several related

10. Peck, "Manuscript," p. 18.

problems now becomes clear. A focus upon the concrete details and sequence of events reveals the participants' motivations, and helps to shed light on the causes of conflict. But an examination of the disturbances at a more abstract level illuminates the larger forces within American society that influenced the participants' actions and responses. The decentralized structure of frontier society concentrated power in the local populace, and an unreliable peace-keeping force, often the state militia, provided little check to local majorities that sought to enforce their will through extralegal methods. Moreover, a large portion of American citizens—including many of the nation's leaders—accepted vigilantism as a legitimate means to protect community values. "Lynch law," wrote Jacksonian publicist Francis Grund, "is not, properly speaking, an opposition to the established laws of the country . . . , but rather . . . a supplement to them—a species of *common* law." [11]   The eventual outcome of the Mormon War was shaped by a powerful American tradition of adherence to the principles of democracy and majority rule, which often superseded principles of fairness and the rule of law.

This perspective on the conflict suggests that the Mormons' chances for building their Zion in northern Missouri were indeed slim at that time. For nearly two years the Missourians allowed the Mormons to settle and build in Caldwell County; but when the Saints began settling in large numbers outside of Caldwell, the Missourians immediately invoked their "right" to remove the Mormons from their communities. Had the Mormons responded passively to the vigilante demands, they most likely would have been expelled from their homes, since non-Mormon opposition to the vigilantes was not strong enough to halt the anti-Mormon proceedings. But the aggressive response adopted by the Mormons proved just as ineffective, because it ignited fears of Mormon fanaticism and eventually brought out the entire non-Mormon community against them. The belief of many Missourians that they had the right to prevent unwanted persons from settling among them, and their perception of the Mormons as undesirable neighbors, stood as a barrier to

11. *The Americans, In Their Moral, Social, And Political Relations* (Boston: Marsh, Capen and Lyon, 1837), p. 180. See also David Grimsted, "Rioting in Its Jacksonian Setting," pp. 364–65.

the expansion of the Mormon kingdom outside of Caldwell County.

One final point merits attention. The conflict between the Mormons and their neighbors had many aspects of a classic frontier confrontation over land, a confrontation with both temporal and spiritual dimensions. For the Mormons, Zion represented both the physical location where the Saints would dwell and the religious community where all would live according to the order of God. The Mormons had retained possession of their land in Jackson County, even after being expelled, because they considered it an abandonment of their religious principles to sell their land in Zion. Zion represented the physical embodiment of their faith.[12] Missourians sought control of the land in order to obtain its economic resources, but they also recognized that whoever controlled the land determined the type of society that developed. Control of the land meant control of community values. In this sense, the Missourians' attachment to the land was, like the Mormons', both temporal and spiritual. Neither group saw its actions as being motivated by greed, by the struggle to control and exploit land—though each accused the other of such motives. For the Mormons, the conflict was over religious principles; for the non-Mormon vigilantes, it was over community values.

Epilogue

When Joseph Smith escaped his guards in April 1839, few Mormons remained in Missouri. Shortly after midnight on 26 April, six apostles and about twenty Latter-day Saints met secretly at the Far West temple site to solemnize the apostles' mission to Great Britain. Although the apostles were in great danger, they returned from Illinois to fulfill Smith's revelation, given the previous July, that commanded them to depart on their mission on that very day and from that exact spot. The Mormon apostles left Far West soon after their meeting, and by May nearly all Mormons had left Missouri. At this time, four Mormons remained in jail at Columbia in Boone County, where they had been transferred on a change of venue. Parley

12. Mormon leaders finally decided to sell their land in Jackson County in March 1839 to raise money to move from the state.

P. Pratt and Morris Phelps escaped from jail on 4 July; Luman Gibbs had his case dismissed; and King Follett was acquitted by a jury. No Mormons were convicted for crimes committed during the Mormon War.

Following their departure from Missouri, the Mormons sought redress through appeals to the federal government. In 1839 and 1840 Mormon delegations brought over seven hundred petitions to Congress describing their sufferings in western Missouri and requesting compensation for their losses. The congressional delegation from Illinois, where the Mormons resettled, presented their petitions and pleaded their cause in the nation's capital. Joseph Smith and Elias Higbee also argued the Mormons' case in a personal interview with Pres. Martin Van Buren. Although most politicians expressed sympathy with the Mormons' plight, they also insisted that the troubles in Missouri were a state matter and that the federal government had no legal right to intervene. A strong tradition of states' rights, and a number of Supreme Court decisions restricting the Bill of Rights' guarantees to the national government, inhibited a response by the federal government. [13]   "What can I do? I can do nothing for you," President Van Buren informed the Mormon delegation. "If I do anything, I shall come in contact with the whole state of Missouri." [14]   The exasperated Mormon prophet later referred to the doctrine of states' rights as a "stink offering in the nose of the Almighty." [15]   The Mormons' failure to secure redress from the federal government reinforced their desire to create a separate, self-sufficient theocracy, for they were convinced they would receive little justice or protection from worldly political institutions.

The eventual costs of the Mormon War, for both Mormons and Missourians, amounted to over a million dollars. Immediately following the conflict, the Missouri legislature appropriated about two hundred thousand dollars to pay the expenses of the conflict;

13. For a discussion of the legal and political forces that limited action by the federal government on the Saints' behalf, see Lynn D. Stewart, "Constitutional Rights and the Mormon Appeals for National Redress of Missouri Grievances" (Master's thesis, Brigham Young University, 1967).

14. *HC* 4:40, Letter of Joseph Smith, Jr., and Elias Higbee to Hyrum Smith, 5 December 1839.

15. *HC* 6:95. These remarks, made in November 1843, were prompted by Mormon plans for another appeal to the federal government.

but for nearly a decade the state continued making additional payments to citizens for militia duty, for providing provisions to soldiers, for guarding Mormon prisoners, and for damages to crops and livestock caused by Missouri troops during the disturbances. In addition, Daviess County settlers lost a large amount of property and crops. The Mormons calculated their losses, in both property and suffering, as amounting to several million dollars. In land alone they claimed losses of three hundred thousand dollars. Although some Mormons claimed exorbitant damages for their expulsion—Edmund Nelson assessed Missouri five hundred thousand dollars for "loss of liberty"[16] —their property losses were considerable. In addition, the Mormons suffered twenty killed and about the same number wounded in military engagements; one Mormon was killed and perhaps another ten were injured in beatings by the Missourians. A number of Saints also died as a result of the suffering and exposure brought on by their expulsion. The Missourians suffered one killed and about a dozen wounded in the conflict.

After the Saints' departure, many of the Missourians who played significant roles in the Mormon War continued to pursue distinguished public careers. Alexander W. Doniphan rose to prominence as western Missouri's foremost criminal lawyer, and also gained distinction serving as a colonel in the Mexican War. Peter H. Burnett, who also served as a lawyer for the Mormons, migrated to California and became that state's first governor in 1849. Although Doniphan, Burnett, and other lawyers successfully defended numerous Mormon defendants, Mormon leaders denounced them as cowardly and incompetent. [17] David R. Atchison, criticized by both the Mormons and some of his own troops for his failure to quell the disturbances, was appointed to the United States Senate in 1843 (at age 36) and was elected to the position in 1844 and 1849. Ironically, the peaceably inclined Atchison became the leader of Missouri vigilantes who raided Kansas during the

16. "Statement," n.d. Petitions, LDS Archives.
17. For criticism of the Mormon lawyers, see *HC* 3:288–89; *HC* 3:292–93, Joseph Smith, The Prophet's Epistle to the Church, 23 March 1839; *HC* 3:327; and *HC* 3:372, Joseph Smith, "A Bill of Damages," 4 June 1839.

border wars of the 1850s.[18] Judge Austin A. King of Ray County continued his successful career in politics, serving as governor of Missouri from 1848 to 1852 and as representative to the United States Congress during the Civil War.[19] Sterling Price, who, as a representative from Chariton County, investigated the disturbances and publicly defended Joseph Smith and other Mormons, succeeded King as governor, serving from 1852 to 1856.[20]

One of the Mormons' chief antagonists in the conflict, Col. Neil Gilliam, continued his controversial yet colorful career. After serving three terms in the Missouri Senate, in 1844 he led a wagon train of over five hundred people to Oregon, where he subsequently held a number of responsible positions in local government. He died in 1848 after leading a successful campaign against Cayuse Indians involved in the massacre at the Marcus Whitman mission. Gilliam was pulling a tangled rope from a supply wagon when a loaded rifle accidentally discharged and sent the cleaning rod through his skull, killing him instantly. Gilliam County, Oregon, was later named in his honor.[21]

Lilburn W. Boggs's political career plummeted after his term as governor. The settlers in western Missouri generally supported his actions in the disturbances, but many citizens from counties not directly involved in the conflict believed that he mismanaged the crisis. In addition, people throughout the nation condemned the Mormon expulsion as singularly harsh and inhumane. Boggs suffered a number of other setbacks during his administration that, added to the controversy surrounding the Mormon War, rendered him politically impotent by the end of his term. Joseph Gordon states that

18. Biographical information on Atchison is from Parrish, *Atchison*, pp. 35–37, 48–50, 70–72, 209–10.

19. Shoemaker, *Missouri Day by Day*, 2:191–92.

20. Ibid., 2:168–69. When Price ran for the United States Congress in 1844, some western Missouri settlers opposed him because of his pro-Mormon stance during the 1838 disturbances; ironically, Mormon leaders claimed Price was one of their chief persecutors in Missouri. See *Western Pioneer* (Liberty, Mo.), 21 June 1844, "Letter from Grand River"; and *HC* 3:327.

21. Bancroft, *History of Oregon*, 1:448–58, 700–725; and *History of the Pacific Northwest: Oregon and Washington*, 2 vols. (Portland, Ore.: North Pacific History Company, 1889), 2:335–42.

when Governor Boggs left office "he was a man without a party and, as far as the state as a whole was concerned, without friends or support." [22] Boggs returned to his home in Independence, resumed his business as a merchant, and served two terms in the state legislature. During the night of 6 May 1842, an assassin shot Boggs in the head while the ex-governor sat reading a newspaper in his home. Suspicion quickly fell upon a Mormon named Porter Rockwell, who was arrested shortly after, and rumors spread that Joseph Smith had ordered the crime. Although a Jackson County grand jury refused to indict Rockwell, the incident revived old animosities and instigated renewed attempts by Missouri officials to extradite Joseph Smith and other Mormons indicted for crimes during the Mormon War. Boggs recovered and later migrated to California, where he was appointed alcalde of the northern California district after the Mexican War. He lived comfortably until his death in Napa Valley in 1860.

Mormon dissenters followed different paths. Some remained in Missouri after the Mormons left (those who renounced their faith were allowed to stay), others moved back to their home states, and some, expressing regret for their actions, rejoined the Saints in Illinois. Although dissenters were viewed as a chief cause of persecution and suffering, the Mormons welcomed back these penitent sinners as would a father his prodigal son. Shortly after the expulsion, Apostle Orson Hyde and W. W. Phelps returned to the Church, and each resumed activities of responsibility and trust. Apostle Thomas B. Marsh, whose disaffection from Mormonism arose from personal problems as well as from objections to the Saints' militancy, returned to the Church in 1857, after an absence of almost twenty years. By the time he joined the Saints, the fifty-seven-year-old Marsh had suffered a paralyzing stroke and appeared a decrepit,

22. "Lilburn W. Boggs," p. 68. Other information on Boggs from ibid., pp. 106–9; William Boggs, "Biographical Sketch of Lilburn W. Boggs," p. 106; Marriott, "Lilburn W. Boggs," pp. 77–78; and Shoemaker, *Missouri Day by Day*, 2:432. For information on the attempted assassination of Boggs see Monte B. McLaws, "The Attempted Assassination of Missouri's Ex-Governor Lilburn W. Boggs," *Missouri Historical Review* 60 (October 1965): 50–62; and Harold Schindler, *Orrin Porter Rockwell: Man of God, Son of Thunder* (Salt Lake City: University of Utah Press, 1963), pp. 67–102.

broken-down old man. "If there are any among this people who should ever apostatize and do as I have done, prepare your backs for a good whipping," he warned the Saints upon his return; ". . . if you will take my advice, you will stand by the authorities; but if you go away and the Lord loves you as much as he did me, he will whip you back again." [23]   Marsh died in Ogden, Utah, in 1866.

John Corrill never returned to Mormonism. As a Missouri state legislator he introduced a bill to prevent religious swindling and crimes by prohibiting anyone from prophesying or speaking in the name of the Lord. He told fellow legislators that the bill was necessary "to prevent the recurrence of the evils heretofore experienced with the Mormons."[24] The Missouri legislature defeated the measure by a vote of 44 to 41. Corrill also wrote a brief history of the Church and of his own involvement in Mormon affairs, with emphasis upon the recent conflict in Missouri. He still believed in God, the Bible, and the Savior, but not in Mormonism. "I can see nothing that convinces me that God has been our leader; calculation after calculation has failed, and plan after plan has been overthrown, and our prophet seemed not to know the event till too late," he wrote.[25] Corrill advised the Mormons to rely on common sense rather than on their leaders' pretended visions and revelations, which only served to rob them of their freedom and bind them under an intolerable yoke. "I had rather enjoy liberty in hell than suffer bondage in heaven," he concluded. [26]

As for the Mormon Danite organization, the evidence indicates that the group effectively disbanded after the Mormon expulsion, though Mormon military organizations continued to prac-

23. "Return of Thomas B. Marsh To The Church," *Journal of Discourses*, 5:206. See also Lyndon W. Cook, " 'I Have Sinned Against Heaven and Am Unworthy of Your Confidence, But I Cannot Live Without A Reconciliation': Thomas B. Marsh Returns to the Church," *BYU Studies* 20 (Spring 1980): 389–400. It was reported to members of the Reorganized Latter Day Saints (headquartered in Independence) that Marsh accepted the Reorganization prior to his death. See *History of the Reorganized Church of Jesus Christ of Latter Day Saints*, 3:427–28.

24. *Missouri Republican*, 25 January 1839.

25. *A Brief History*, p. 48.

26. From a handwritten copy of Corrill's *A Brief History*. Joint Collection: University of Missouri and State Historical Society of Missouri. This quote concludes the fourth paragraph on page 48 of *A Brief History*, but was not included in the published account. Corrill expressed similar sentiments during a debate in the Missouri legislature, stating that "He himself had

tice Danite drills and formations in both Illinois and Utah. [27] The Mormons later came to believe—and it is the official view of the Church today—that the Danites were solely the creation of Sampson Avard and that the group consisted of renegade and apostate Mormons who had little influence in the Church. In fact, just the opposite is true. The Danites consisted primarily of the most loyal and influential Mormons, such as Lyman Wight, David W. Patten, Elias Higbee, Dimick Huntington, Albert P. Rockwood, and other staunch men. Joseph Smith subsequently awarded many of these men with responsible positions in the Church hierarchy. Elias Higbee, captain-general of the Danites, served in the Mormon delegation seeking redress in Washington, D. C.; Lyman Wight, leader of the secret organization at Diahman, was chosen to replace the slain David W. Patten as a Mormon apostle. It is interesting to note that both Mormon dissenters and Missourians regarded the Danite general Sampson Avard as a scoundrel—and that Joseph Smith was informed of their views. But it was not until after Avard turned state's evidence and testified against the Saints that Mormon leaders also adopted this view. The fact that, following the expulsion, other Danite leaders continued to serve in positions of responsibility and trust suggests that Avard's greater crime was the betrayal of his brethren, rather than his promulgation of teachings that Mormon leaders found distasteful. Sampson Avard was excommunicated from the Church in March 1839.

After Joseph Smith escaped from prison he immediately reassumed leadership of the Church at its new location in Nauvoo, Illinois. Few Mormons shared John Corrill's interpretation of the events. Despite the persecution, suffering, and failure of their plans, the Saints never lost faith in their prophet. They believed that their troubles had been caused by dissenters and other enemies of God, and they accepted their plight as a scourge from the Lord to purify the Church and perfect the Saints.

---

been a Mormon, but had now quit them, he belonged to no religion, and professed none, but good will to all men and the performance of his duty; and if this religion would not take him to Heaven, Heaven must do without him" (*Missouri Republican*, 24 December 1838).

27. On Danite drill formations in Illinois and Utah, see Hosea Stout, *On the Mormon Frontier*, 1:141, 197.

During the next several years Mormonism prospered and grew. Under Smith's leadership, Nauvoo became one of the largest and most influential cities in Illinois. The Mormons elected Smith mayor of Nauvoo and general of the Nauvoo militia, and in 1844 they nominated him for president of the United States. But the Mormons encountered the same opposition to their activities in Illinois as they had in Missouri, and hostilities resumed. On 27 June 1844, an anti-Mormon mob broke into the jail at Carthage, Illinois, and shot and killed Joseph Smith while he awaited trial on charges of treason and riot—the same charges from which he had fled in Missouri.

The conflict in Illinois continued until the Mormons abandoned Nauvoo in 1846. The next year Brigham Young, the new Mormon prophet, led his people across the prairies to Utah, where there were no white settlers and too few Indians to oppose their settlements. In Salt Lake City and the surrounding region the Mormons finally established their Kingdom of God.

*   *   *

On 25 June 1976, Governor Christopher S. Bond of Missouri issued the following *Executive Order*:

WHEREAS, on October 27, 1838, the Governor of the State of Missouri, Lilburn W. Boggs, issued an order calling for the extermination or expulsion of Mormons from the State of Missouri; and

WHEREAS, Governor Boggs' order clearly contravened the rights to life, liberty, property and religious freedom as guaranteed by the Constitution of the United States, as well as the Constitution of the State of Missouri; and

WHEREAS, in this Bicentennial year as we reflect on our nation's heritage, the exercise of religious freedom is without question one of the basic tenets of our free democratic republic;

NOW, THEREFORE, I, CHRISTOPHER S. BOND, Governor of the State of Missouri, by virtue of the authority vested in me by the Constitution and the laws of the State of Missouri, do hereby order as follows:

Expressing on behalf of all Missourians our deep regret for the injustice and undue suffering which was caused by this 1838 order, I hereby rescind Executive Order Number 44 dated October 27, 1838, issued by Governor Lilburn W. Boggs.

Appendix: Chronology of Events in Missouri, 1838–1839

14 March 1838	Joseph Smith arrives in Far West.
June	Danites organize in Far West.
17 June	Sidney Rigdon delivers "Salt Sermon" condemning Mormon dissenters.
19 June	After receiving warning, dissenters flee from Caldwell County.
28 June	Mormons lay out town and organize a Stake of Zion at Adam-ondi-Ahman in Daviess County.
July	Mormons open settlements at DeWitt and throughout northwestern Missouri.
4 July	Fourth of July celebration at Far West. Rigdon declares Mormons will wage a "war of extermination" against mobs.
14 July	Carroll citizens meet to oppose Mormon settlement at DeWitt. Meetings and threats against Mormons at DeWitt continue throughout the summer.
6 August	Gallatin election battle. Daviess settlers talk of organizing against the Mormons.
7 August	Joseph Smith leads one hundred fifty Danites to Diahman to protect the Saints. Mormons threaten Judge Adam Black and others suspected of anti-Mormon activities. Reports of Mormon "invasion" spread through upper counties.
13 August	Daviess County judges issue writs for the arrest of Joseph Smith and Lyman Wight.
13 August	Committee of Carroll citizens orders the Saints to leave the county.
20 August	One hundred armed men ride into DeWitt and threaten Mormons.
20–30 August	Citizen groups and vigilantes meet in upper counties and resolve to assist Daviess and Carroll counties in bringing alleged Mormon criminals to justice.

30 August	Governor Lilburn W. Boggs, responding to reports of civil and Indian disturbances in western counties, orders twenty-eight hundred state troops to stand ready to march.
3 September	David R. Atchison and Alexander W. Doniphan are hired as lawyers for Smith and Wight.
7 September	Smith and Wight are tried at a preliminary hearing in Daviess County. Judge Austin A. King orders the defendants to post bail and appear at the next hearing of the grand jury in Daviess.
9 September	Excitement in upper counties continues as Mormons capture three men attempting to transport guns to vigilantes in Daviess County. Mormons and Missourians petition Judge King to quell the disturbances.
10 September	Judge King orders General Atchison to raise four hundred troops and disperse the Mormons and non-Mormon vigilantes.
13 September	Carroll vigilantes postpone assault on DeWitt and march to Daviess to assist settlers against the Mormons.
18 September	After receiving reports of disturbances, Governor Boggs orders out two thousand troops and prepares to lead march to western Missouri.
20 September	Atchison disperses vigilantes in Daviess County and leaves one hundred troops under General Parks to maintain peace.
21 September	Carroll County vigilantes, returning from Daviess, resolve to expel the Saints from DeWitt.
24 September	Governor Boggs receives letter from Atchison stating that vigilantes in Daviess have dispersed. Boggs dismisses troops and returns to Jefferson City.
1 October	Vigilantes attack DeWitt, burn the home and stables of Smith Humphrey. During the next several days Mormons appeal to Governor Boggs and other civil authorities

for protection.

6 October — General Parks arrives in DeWitt with one hundred troops to quell disturbances. Anti-Mormon spirit among troops forces Parks to return to Ray County a few days later.

9 October — Messenger reports to Mormons that the governor said they must rely on local authorities for protection. He will not intervene.

11 October — Mormons at DeWitt surrender and move to Caldwell and Daviess counties. Carroll vigilantes resolve to help settlers expel Mormons from Daviess.

14–15 October — Joseph Smith and Sidney Rigdon call upon Mormon troops to ride to Diahman to protect the Saints, threatening those who will not join the Mormon army. Four hundred soldiers march to Daviess County.

16–17 October — Generals Doniphan and Parks prepare to march with troops to Daviess, but inclement weather and anti-Mormon sentiment in militia causes generals to abandon expedition. Parks continues to Daviess alone.

18 October — Mormon soldiers attack Gallatin, Millport, and other settlements in Daviess, driving non-Mormon settlers from their homes, plundering, and burning. Missourians retaliate.

18 October — General Parks visits Mormons and Missourians in Daviess. Parks discovers that civil war has broken out and declares that Mormons are now the aggressors.

22 October — Mormon troops return to Far West after driving nearly all non-Mormons from Daviess.

24 October — Apostles Thomas B. Marsh and Orson Hyde sign affidavits in Ray County describing Mormon activities. Ray committee returns from Daviess with similar reports of depredations. Capt. Samuel Bogart calls out Ray troops to prevent invasion by Mormons.

24 October	Bogart and his troops harass Mormon settlers in Ray and Caldwell counties. They capture two Mormon spies and threaten to execute them.
25 October	Capt. David W. Patten leads Mormon troops to rescue spies. Troops clash at Crooked River, with three Mormons and one Missourian killed. Exaggerated reports of Crooked River battle spread throughout the state. Fearing the Mormons intend to continue attacks, Generals Atchison, Doniphan, and Parks call out state militia to quell alleged Mormon rebellion.
27 October	Governor Boggs, responding to reports of Mormon depredations in Daviess County and their attack on state troops at Crooked River, orders that the Mormons must be "exterminated or driven from the state."
30 October	Missouri troops, under command of Gen. Samuel D. Lucas of Jackson County, arrive outside Far West. Mormon leaders send messengers to learn intentions of troops.
30 October	Two hundred soldiers from Livingston and nearby counties overrun Mormon village of Haun's Mill, killing eighteen and wounding fifteen.
31 October	Col. George Hinkle, John Corrill, and other Mormon representatives attempt to negotiate with General Lucas, but receive demands for surrender. Joseph Smith, Sidney Rigdon, Lyman Wight, and other Mormon leaders give themselves up as hostages. About seventy-five Mormon soldiers, advised of the surrender plans, flee from Far West during the night.
1 November	Joseph Smith advises Mormon troops at Far West and Diahman to surrender. Mormon War ends.
1 November	General Lucas holds a court-martial of seven Mormon leaders. Opposition of General Doniphan and others prevents the execution of Mormon prisoners.

2 November	Mormons forced to deed over their property to pay expenses for the war. This part of the surrender agreement is later declared illegal.
4 November	General Clark arrives with troops and announces his intention to carry out the surrender terms exacted by General Lucas.
12–29 November	Judge Austin A. King presides at Court of Inquiry held in Richmond, Ray County. Joseph Smith, Sidney Rigdon, and a number of other Mormons are committed to prison on the basis of testimony against them.
December-February 1839	Missouri legislature debates whether to investigate the disturbances and allow the Mormons to remain. Legislation to investigate is tabled until July, after the Mormons have already left the state.
February	Mormons pool resources and organize to leave Missouri.
11 April	Joseph Smith and four other Mormons are indicted for crimes in Daviess County, and are granted a change of venue to Boone County.
16 April	Smith and other prisoners escape from their guards and return to Saints, who are gathering at Quincy, Illinois.
May	Nearly all the Saints have left Missouri.

Bibliographical Essay

An abundance of primary-source materials exists pertaining to the Mormon experience in Missouri in 1838. Most of these materials are located in the archival collection of the Church of Jesus Christ of Latter-day Saints, in the Church Office Building in Salt Lake City (hereafter: LDS Archives); and in the Joint Collection: University of Missouri Western Historical Manuscript Collection, Columbia, and State Historical Society of Missouri Manuscripts (hereafter: Joint Collection: University of Missouri and State Historical Society of Missouri). Manuscript and documentary materials can also be found in the library-archives of the Reorganized Church of Jesus Christ of Latter Day Saints, in the World Headquarters, Independence, Missouri (hereafter: RLDS Archives); in the Manuscript and Special Collections, Brigham Young University Library, Provo, Utah; in the Manuscript and Special Collections, University of Utah Library, Salt Lake City; and in the Library of the Utah State Historical Society, Salt Lake City. In addition, much valuable material is located in Missouri libraries, courthouses, and historical societies.

There are over two hundred journals, diaries, sketches, and reminiscences written by Mormons who lived in Missouri during the period of this study. Although most of these writings are listed as journals or diaries, only a dozen were actually written contemporaneously with the events in Missouri. Almost all are reminiscences written ten to fifty years after the expulsion of the Mormons. These reminiscences, though colored by the passage of time and by the collective memory of the Saints, are still an important source of information on the disturbances in Missouri. Among the most detailed accounts of this period are William Moore Allred, "Biography and Journal," LDS Archives; Anson Call, "The Life Record Of Anson Call," LDS Archives; William Draper, "A Biographical Sketch Of The Life And Travels And Birth And Parentage Of William Draper," LDS Archives; Drusilla Dorris Hendricks, "Historical Sketch of James Hendricks and Drusilla Dorris Hendricks," LDS Archives; Joseph Holbrook, "The Life of Joseph Holbrook," LDS Archives; Oliver B. Huntington, "History of the Life of Oliver B. Huntington," Library of the Utah State Historical Society; Benjamin F. Johnson, *My Life's Review* (Independence, Missouri: Zion's Printing & Publishing Company, 1947); John D. Lee, *Mormonism Unveiled; or The Life and Confessions of the Late Mormon Bishop, John D. Lee* (St. Louis: Bryan, Brand, & Co., 1877); David Lewis, "Excerpt From The Journal of David Lewis," LDS

Archives; Daniel D. McArthur, "Journal," Brigham Young University Special Collections; John Murdock, "Journal," LDS Archives; Morris Phelps, "Reminiscences," LDS Archives; Ebenezer Robinson, "Items of Personal History," *The Return*, vols. 1–2; Luman A. Shurtliff, "History of Luman Andros Shurtliff," LDS Archives; George A. Smith, "History of George A. Smith," LDS Archives; and Nathan Tanner, "Journal of Nathan Tanner," LDS Archives.

Of the contemporary accounts, four were especially valuable for this study. George W. Robinson, "The Scriptory Book of Joseph Smith Jr. President of the Church of Jesus Christ of Latterday Saints in All the World" (LDS Archives), covers the period from April to September 1838. Robinson served as the Church recorder and was an intimate associate of the Prophet. His account represents almost an official church record of these events. Albert P. Rockwood, "Journal October 6, 1838 to January 30, 1839" (LDS Archives; original in the Yale University Library, New Haven, Connecticut), is a kind of journal-letter that he mailed to members of his family. John Smith, Diary (LDS Archives), is sketchy, but also contains important details. Warren Foote, "Autobiography of Warren Foote" (LDS Archives), though written after Foote left Missouri, was taken from a diary or notes he kept while he lived in the state. These contemporary sources provide important information about the Danites and the military operations of the Mormons—information that other Mormon sources discreetly omitted.

Mormon men and women also wrote numerous letters and statements describing their experiences in Missouri. Among the most detailed and informative are Josiah Butterfield to Mr. John Elden, 17 June 1839 (LDS Archives); Vinson Knight to William Cooper, 3 February 1839 (LDS Archives); David H. Redfield, "Book, Far West, January 13, 1839" (LDS Archives); Franklin D. Richards and Phineas Richards, Letters, 1839 (Brigham Young University Manuscript Collections); Hyrum Smith, Letters to Mary Smith, March 1839 (LDS Archives); Joseph Smith and Sidney Rigdon to Stephen Post, 17 September 1838 (LDS Archives); Joseph Smith, Letters to Emma Smith, 4 and 12 November 1838 (RLDS Archives); Parley P. Pratt, Letters, 1838–1839 (LDS Archives); John Murdock to Sister Crocker & all the faithful Saints, 21 July 1839 (LDS Archives); Jamon Aldrich to Mr. Daniel Aldrich, 30 September 1838 (LDS Archives); and Eliza R. Snow, "Eliza R. Snow Letter from Missouri: Caldwell Co, Feb 22, 1839," *BYU Studies* 13 (Summer 1973): 544–52.

The Mormons published one periodical during this period, *The Elders' Journal*, which supplied useful information for this study.

Following their expulsion from Missouri, Mormon leaders wrote lengthy treatises describing their persecution in Missouri. Among the most prominent of the published accounts are Sidney Rigdon, *An Appeal To The American People: Being An Account Of The Persecutions Of The Latter Day Saints; And Of The Barbarities Inflicted On Them By The Inhabitants Of The State Of Missouri* (Cincinnati, Ohio: Glezen and Shepard, 1840); John P. Greene, *Facts Relative To The Expulsion Of The Mormons Or Latter Day Saints From The State Of Missouri, Under The "Exterminating Order"* (Cincinnati: Printed by R. P. Brooks, 1839); Parley P. Pratt, *History Of The Late Persecution Inflicted By The State Of Missouri Upon The Mormons* (Detroit: Dawson & Bates, Printers, 1839); John Taylor, *A Short Account of the Murders, Roberies, Burnings, Thefts, and Other Outrages Committed by the Mob and Militia of the State of Missouri, Upon the Latter Day Saints* (pamphlet, Springfield, Ill., 1839; rpt. Provo, Utah: Martin Mormon Pamphlet Reprints, 1975). In addition, Mormon leaders wrote numerous petitions and affidavits, which were published in the above-mentioned works and also in the *History of the Church*, volumes 3 and 4 (see below). These petitions and treatises generally set forth the official Mormon view of the disturbances in Missouri.

Hundreds of Mormon individuals also wrote petitions and affidavits describing their experiences and detailing their losses in Missouri. Mormon representatives brought these statements to Washington, D.C., hoping that the federal government would intervene and restore the Saints to their Missouri homes. Over two hundred of these petitions are located in the United States Archives in Washington, D.C. (they have also been photocopied and can be examined in the Special Collections of the Brigham Young University Library). Over five hundred additional petitions are located in the LDS Archives in Salt Lake City. Approximately seven hundred Mormons wrote individual petitions. Their petitions, though generally short, are in some respects more valuable than the lengthier reminiscences of the Saints because the petitions were written only a year or two after the expulsion, and thus are more accurate and specific in their details.

Special mention should be made of Joseph Smith, *History of the Church of Jesus Christ of Latter-Day Saints*, 7 vols. (Salt Lake City: Deseret Book Company, 1978), compiled under the editorship of B. H. Roberts. The first six volumes were purportedly written by Joseph Smith, or rather, extracted from his private journals and diaries. The *History of the Church* also contains numerous documents, letters, newspaper articles, and other source materials relating to Mormonism. Volume 3 covers the period of this study. Joseph Smith, however, did not write the *History of the Church* commentary for this period of Mormon history. A comparison of sources shows that the commentary for volume 3 was taken from other sources and then edited and written as if Smith were the author. Additionally, the commentary for this period was not written until after the Prophet's death. Among the most prominent sources incorporated into Smith's commentary in volume 3 of the *History of the Church* are George W. Robinson, "Scriptory Book"; Albert P. Rockwood, "Journal"; Morris Phelps, "Reminiscences"; Parley P. Pratt, *History Of The Late Persecution*; and Sidney Rigdon, *An Appeal To The American People*. The *History of the Church* serves as a vital source for primary documents and materials on the Mormon experience in Missouri, but I have been careful in using its commentary as a source of information because the original sources are sometimes unreliable or altered in the commentary. I have instead attempted to identify and cite the original sources.

Another source consisting of a variety of documentary materials is the Journal History of the Church of Jesus Christ of Latter-day Saints. The Journal History is a day-by-day record of events containing letters, newspaper clippings, journal entries, and other miscellaneous documents relating to Mormon history. Unlike the *History of the Church*, however, the Journal History usually identifies the original source.

A number of Mormon dissenters (who opposed the militant activities of their fellow Saints) also wrote accounts of their experiences in Missouri. Most valuable to this study were John Corrill, *A Brief History Of The Church Of Christ Of Latter Day Saints* (St. Louis: For the Author, 1839; Salt Lake City: Modern Microfilm, n.d.); Reed Peck, "The Reed Peck Manuscript" (Typescript, Salt Lake City: Modern Microfilm, n.d.); William Swartzell, *Mormonism Exposed, Being A Journal Of A Residence In Missouri from the 28th of May to the 20th of August, 1838* (Pekin, Ohio: Published by the Author, 1840; Salt Lake City: Modern Microfilm, n.d.); and John Whitmer, "The Book of John Whitmer" (Typescript, Salt Lake City: Modern Microfilm, n.d.). Letters by dissenters include Thomas B. Marsh and Orson Hyde to Brother and Sister Lewis Abbot, 25 October 1838 (Brigham Young University Special Collections); Oliver Cowdery, "Letters 1833–1846" (on microfilm at LDS Archives); George M. Hinkle, "Letter to W. W. Phelps, August 14, 1844," *Journal of History* 13 (October 1920): 448–53; and David Whitmer to Joseph Smith III, 9 December 1886, published in "Letters from David and John C. Whitmer," *Saints' Herald* 34 (5 February 1887): 89–93. A number of affidavits and statements written by Mormon dissenters are also found in the *Document Containing The Correspondence, Orders, &C. In Relation To The Disturbances With The Mormons* (see below). The statements and claims of the dissenters provide a balance to the accounts of loyal Church members, illuminating the causes of and the events leading to the Mormon War.

Regarding materials from Missouri sources, a large number of letters, affidavits, and documents pertaining to the Mormon War are contained in *Document Containing The Correspondence, Orders, &C. In Relation To The Disturbances With The Mormons; And The Evidence Given Before The Hon. Austin A. King* (Fayette, Mo.: Office of the Boon's Lick Democrat, 1841). The *Document* contains materials from both Mormon and non-Mormon sources, but the majority of information presents the non-Mormon view of the disturbances. The *Document* includes much of the correspondence of Governor Boggs and the militia generals responsible for resolving the conflict. It also contains the evidence from the Richmond Court of Inquiry, held in November 1839, at which some fifty Mormons, including Joseph Smith, were tried for crimes allegedly committed during the Mormon War. Most of those who testified at the trial were Mormon dissenters or Missourians. Since this was a preliminary hearing, most of the testimony presented only the prosecution's side of the matter. The *Document* is an indispensable collection of primary materials relating to the Mormon-Missourian conflict.

Some of the Missouri participants later published recollections and autobiographies that included reminiscences of this period, among which are Peter H. Burnett, *Recollections and Opinions of an Old Pioneer* (New York: D. Appleton and Company, 1880); Joseph H. McGee, *Story of the Grand River Country, 1821–1905: Memoirs of Major Joseph H. McGee* (Gallatin, Mo.: North Missourian Press, 1909); and Joseph Thorp, *Early Days in the West: Along the Missouri One Hundred Years Ago* (Liberty, Mo.: Liberty Tribune, 1924). William T. Wood wrote a memoir that was printed in the *Liberty Tribune* (Liberty, Mo.), 9 April 1886; Alexander W. Doniphan was interviewed concerning his role in the disturbances by the *Kansas City Journal*, 12 June 1881, and by the *Saints' Herald* 31 (2 August 1884): 490. And a brief statement by Gen. John B. Clark is found in Walter B. Stevens, *Centennial History of Missouri*, 4 vols. (St. Louis & Chicago: S. J. Clarke Publishing Company, 1924), 2:119–20. Unfortunately, none of the other leading Missouri participants, such as Gov. Lilburn W. Boggs, David R. Atchison, or Judge Austin A. King, left accounts of these events.

The LDS Archives, the RLDS Archives, and the Joint Collection: University of Missouri and State Historical Society of Missouri also house a vast number of documents from non-Mormon sources that pertain to the Mormon War. Among the most valuable are I. H. Arnold to Isaac Arnold, 12 August 1838 (RLDS Archives); Thomas G. Bradford, Correspondence (LDS Archives), which includes letters written from Carroll County during the disturbances; David R. Atchison to Joseph Smith, 1 September 1838 (LDS Archives); David R. Atchison and

Alexander W. Doniphan to Lt.-Col. R. B. Mason, 27 October 1838 (LDS Archives); George Franhouser, Letter to Andrew Franhouser, 26 October 1838 (McQuown Papers, University of Utah Manuscript Collections); John Hunt to David Hunt, 22 January 1839 (Brigham Young University Manuscript Collections); Amos Rees, Letter to Abiel Leonard, 1 November 1839 (Joint Collection: University of Missouri and State Historical Society of Missouri); "Pay Accounts of the Missouri Militia for the Mormon War—1838 in Missouri" (Joint Collection: University of Missouri and State Historical Society of Missouri); and the records for various trials of alleged Mormon criminals, held in Caldwell, Daviess, and Boone counties (Joint Collection: University of Missouri and State Historical Society of Missouri). In addition, the Joint Collection contains about a dozen letters (from Judge King, Alexander Doniphan, and other Missourians) with information relating to the Mormon War.

An abundance of valuable information is also contained in the Missouri newspaper accounts of the disturbances. Although these accounts were often based on rumor and unsubstantiated reports, they still reveal the general attitudes of Missouri citizens toward the conflict. There were surprisingly many pro-Mormon accounts. Many newspapers printed letters from participants and observers of the events. The newspapers also published the minutes and resolutions from some of the anti-Mormon vigilante meetings. The newspaper collection at the State Historical Society of Missouri houses the most comprehensive collection of Missouri newspapers. Brigham Young University and the LDS Archives also have large microfilm collections of newspaper articles pertaining to Mormonism. The Snider Collection (Brigham Young University Library) and the Max Parkin Collection (LDS Archives) were useful supplements to the newspaper collection at the State Historical Society of Missouri. The newspapers that published the most extensive reports of the disturbances were the *Jeffersonian Republican* (Jefferson City, Mo.); the *Missouri Argus* (St. Louis, Mo.); the *Missouri Republican* (St. Louis, Mo.); and the *Southern Advocate* (Jackson, Mo.).

Each of the counties in northwestern Missouri has at least one published history of its county. Most of the county histories were published in the 1880s. Because local biases often crept into these histories, I used them with caution. Several, however, provided important details about the disturbances. *The History of Caldwell and Livingston Counties, Missouri* (St. Louis: National Historical Company, 1886), was based on evidence gathered from non-Mormon participants and presents a relatively objective account of the Mormon War. The "History of Carroll County, Missouri," *An Illustrated Historical Atlas of Carroll County, Missouri* (n.p.: Brink, McDonough, & Co., 1876), includes information on the disturbances obtained from Judge A. C. Blackwell, a leading member of the Carroll vigilante committee. Other histories, such as James H. Hunt, *Mormonism, Embracing the Origin, Rise and Progress of the Sect, With an Examination of the Book of Mormon; Also Their Troubles in Missouri, and Final Expulsion From the State* (St. Louis: Printed by Ustick & Davies, 1844), also draw on local sources, but their extreme anti-Mormon bias limited their usefulness.

The study of land records (located at the Bureau of Land Management, Alexandria, Virginia) and census records (located at the Bureau of the Census Library, Suitland, Maryland) gave a better understanding of land problems, settlement patterns, and the relative strength of the Mormon and non-Mormon populations in northwestern Missouri.

The general works on Mormon history and Mormonism that proved most useful for the purposes of this study were James B. Allen and Glen M. Leonard, *The Story of the Latter-day Saints* (Salt Lake City: Deseret Company, 1976); Leonard J. Arrington and Davis Bitton, *The Mormon Experience: A History of the Latter-day Saints* (New York: Alfred A. Knopf, 1979); Thomas F. O'Dea, *The Mormons* (Chicago: University of Chicago Press, 1957); B. H. Roberts, *A Comprehensive History of the Church of Jesus Christ of Latter-day Saints*, 6 vols. (Salt Lake City: Deseret News Press, 1930); and Richard L. Bushman, *Joseph Smith and the Beginnings of Mormonism* (Urbana and Chicago: University of Illinois Press, 1984).

For general histories of Missouri, I found that Edwin C. McReynolds, *Missouri: A History of the Crossroads State* (Norman: University of Oklahoma Press, 1962); and Paul C. Nagel, *Missouri: A Bicentennial History* (New York: W. W. Norton & Company, 1977), presented balanced and impartial accounts of the Mormon experience in Missouri. General reference on various topics relating to Missouri and its early history was provided by Howard L. Conard, ed., *Encyclopedia Of The History Of Missouri, A Compendium Of History And Biography For Ready Reference*, 6 vols. (New York, Louisville, St. Louis: The Southern History Company, 1901); and Floyd C. Shoemaker, *Missouri Day by Day*, 2 vols. (Jefferson City: Mid-State Printing Co., 1943).

The many county histories and articles from the *Missouri Historical Review* provided background information on Missouri and its people. Among the more informative articles from the *Missouri Historical Review* were Hattie M. Anderson, "The Evolution of a Frontier Society in Missouri, 1815–1828," *Missouri Historical Review* 32 (April 1938): 298–326; 32 (July 1938): 458–83; 33 (October 1838): 23–44; Hattie M. Anderson, "Missouri, 1804–1828: Peopling a Frontier State," *Missouri Historical Review* 31 (January 1937): 150–

80; Lewis E. Atherton, "Missouri's Society And Economy in 1821," *Missouri Historical Review* 65 (July 1971): 450–77; Jerena East Giffen, "Missouri Women in the 1820's," *Missouri Historical Review* 65 (July 1971): 478–504; Howard I. McKee, "The Platte Purchase," *Missouri Historical Review* 32 (January 1938): 129–47; and Marie George Windell, "The Background of Reform on the Missouri Frontier," *Missouri Historical Review* 39 (January 1945): 155–83. John G. Westover, "The Evolution of the Missouri Militia, 1804–1919" (Ph.D. diss., University of Missouri, 1948), and Leslie G. Hill, "The Pioneer Preacher In Missouri" (Master's thesis, University of Missouri, 1948), provided information on specialized topics in Missouri history.

Studies on extralegal violence and the role of the militia in combatting this violence gave insights into the Mormon experience in Missouri: Richard M. Brown, *Strain of Violence: Historical Studies of American Violence and Vigilantism* (New York: Oxford University Press, 1975); Hugh Davis Graham, "The Paradox of American Violence: A Historical Appraisal," in *Collective Violence*, ed. James F. Short, Jr., and Marvin E. Wolfgang (Chicago and New York: Aldine Atherton, 1972); David Grimsted, "Rioting in Its Jacksonian Setting," *American Historical Review* 77 (April 1972): 361–97; Theodore M. Hammett, "Two Mobs of Jacksonian Boston: Ideology and Interest," *Journal of American History* 2 (March 1976): 845–68; Richard Hofstadter and Michael Wallace, eds., *American Violence* (New York: Alfred A. Knopf, 1970); Lawrence F. Kohl, "The Concept of Social Control and the History of Jacksonian America," *Journal of the Early Republic* 5 (Spring 1985): 21–34; Craig B. Little and Christopher P. Sheffield, "Frontiers and Criminal Justice: English Private Prosecution Societies and American Vigilantism in the Eighteenth and Nineteenth Centuries," *American Sociological Review* 48 (December 1983): 796–808; Carl E. Prince, "The Great 'Riot Year': Jacksonian Democracy and Patterns of Violence in 1834," *Journal of the Early Republic* 5 (Spring 1985): 1–19; and Robert Reinders, "Militia and Public Order in Nineteenth-Century America," *Journal of American Studies* 11 (April 1977): 81–101.

Studies on United States land policy and the colonizing of the west also contributed to the understanding of the events in this study: Paul W. Gates and Robert W. Swenson, *History of Public Land Law Development* (Washington, D.C.: U.S. Government Printing Office, 1968); Paul W. Gates, *Landlords and Tenants on the Prairie Frontier* (Ithaca, N.Y.: Cornell University Press, 1973); and David M. Ellis, ed., *The Frontier in American Development* (Ithaca, N.Y.: Cornell University Press, 1969).

Among the many theses and dissertations treating the Mormon experience in Missouri, Leland H. Gentry, "A History of the Latter-Day

Saints in Northern Missouri from 1836 to 1839" (Ph.D. diss., Brigham Young University, 1965), discusses most of the major problems relating to the disturbances and was an indispensable source of information and insight. Also helpful were Warren A. Jennings, "Zion Is Fled: The Expulsion of the Mormons from Jackson County, Missouri" (Ph.D. diss., University of Florida, 1962); Max H. Parkin, "A History of the Latter-Day Saints in Clay County, Missouri, from 1833 to 1837" (Ph.D. diss., Brigham Young University, 1976); Lynn D. Stewart, "Constitutional Rights and the Mormon Appeals for National Redress of the Missouri Grievances" (Master's thesis, Brigham Young University, 1967); and Patricia A. Zahniser, "Violence in Missouri, 1831–1839: The Case of the Mormon Persecution" (Master's thesis, Florida Atlantic University, 1973).

The two best biographies of Joseph Smith are Donna Hill, *Joseph Smith: The First Mormon* (Garden City, N.Y.: Doubleday and Company, 1977); and Fawn M. Brodie, *No Man Knows My History: The Life of Joseph Smith, the Mormon Prophet* (1945; rpt. New York: Alfred A. Knopf, 1971). Hill writes as a believer in Mormonism, Brodie a non-believer. Together they provide a balanced treatment of the Mormon prophet. Linda King Newell and Valeen Tippetts Avery, *Mormon Enigma: Emma Hale Smith* (Garden City, N.Y.: Doubleday and Company, 1984) provides additional information on Smith and his family.

Helpful biographies of other prominent Mormons and Missourians include Andre Paul Duchateau, "Missouri Colossus: Alexander W. Doniphan, 1808–1887" (Ph.D. diss., Oklahoma State University, 1973); Joseph F. Gordon, "The Public Career of Lilburn W. Boggs" (Master's thesis, University of Missouri, 1949); David W. Magnusson, "George M. Hinkle: A Biography and Analysis of the Betrayal at Far West" (unpublished paper, Brigham Young University, 1977); F. Mark McKiernan, *The Voice of One Crying in the Wilderness: Sidney Rigdon, Religious Reformer, 1793–1876* (Lawrence, Kans.: Coronado Press, 1971); and William E. Parrish, *David Rice Atchison of Missouri: Border Politician* (Columbia: University of Missouri Press, 1961). Andrew Jenson, *Latter-Day Saint Biographical Encyclopedia*, 4 vols. (Salt Lake City: Deseret News, 1901), contains sketches and short biographies of hundreds of Mormons.

Countless scholarly articles and essays on Mormonism have been published in recent years. Much of the background information on Mormon history and culture that contributed to this study was provided by articles from the *Journal of Mormon History* (annually, 1974–); *Brigham Young University Studies* (quarterly, 1959–); *Dialogue: A Journal of Mormon Thought* (quarterly, 1966–); *John Whitmer Historical Association Journal* (annually, 1981–); *Courage* (quarterly, 1970–1973); and *Restoration* (quarterly, 1982–), though such information was by no means limited to articles from these journals.

Articles dealing specifically with the Mormon experience in Missouri included Leonard J. Arrington, "Church Leaders in Liberty Jail," *BYU Studies* 13 (Autumn 1972): 20–26; Alma R. Blair, "The Haun's Mill Massacre," *BYU Studies* 13 (Autumn 1972): 62–76; Rollin J. Britton, "Early Days on Grand River and the Mormon War," *Missouri Historical Review* 13 (January 1919): 112–34; (April 1919): 287–310; (July 1919): 388–98; 14 (October 1919): 89–110; (January 1920): 233–45; and (April-July 1920): 459–73; Richard L. Bushman, "Mormon Persecutions in Missouri, 1833," *BYU Studies* 3 (Autumn 1960): 11–20; Reed C. Durham, "The Election Day Battle at Gallatin," *BYU Studies* 13 (Autumn 1972): 36–61; Leland H. Gentry, "The Danite Band of 1838," *BYU Studies* 14 (Summer 1974): 421–50; Clark V. Johnson, "Missouri Persecutions: The Petition of Isaac Leany," *BYU Studies* 23 (Winter 1983): 94–103; Clark V. Johnson, "The Missouri Redress Petitions: New Evidence of the Mormon Side of the Missouri Conflict in 1834 and 1838" (unpublished paper, n.d.); F. Mark McKiernan, "Mormonism on the Defensive: Far West, 1838–1839," in *The Restoration Movement: Essays in Mormon History*, ed. F. Mark McKiernan, Alma Blair, and Paul M. Edwards (Lawrence, Kans.: Coronado Press, 1973); Paul C. Richards, "Missouri Persecutions: Petitions for Redress," *BYU Studies* 13 (Summer 1973): 520–43; R. J. Robertson, "The Mormon Experience in Missouri, 1830–1839," *Missouri Historical Review* 68 (April 1974): 280–98; (July 1974): 393–415; W. J. Rounds, "Colonel George M. Hinkle (Was he a hero or a villian?)," *Restoration Trail Forum* 9 (August 1983): 3–4; John E. Thompson, "A Chronology of Danite Meetings in Adam-ondi-Ahman, Missouri, July to September 1838," *Restoration* 4 (January 1985): 11–14; and John E. Thompson, "The Far West Dissenters and the Gamblers at Vicksburg: An Examination of the Documentary Evidence and Historical Context of Sidney Rigdon's Salt Sermon," *Restoration* 5 (January 1986): 21–27.

Index

Adam-ondi-Ahman. *See* Diahman
Army of Israel: Joseph Smith leads, 112; actions defended, 115–16, 123, 207–8, 220–21; Missourians fear, 119, 126, 128, 143–45, 156; depredations of, 117–20; and Danites, 125n35
Arnold, I. H., 58
Arthur, Michael, 232–33
Ashby, Charles, 163–64
Ashby, Daniel, 229
Atchison, David R., 5, 18–19, 78, 84, 249–50; early career, 78; lawyer for Saints, 79–81; commands militia, 88–89, 91–95, 129–30, 145, 146; reports on Mormons, 100–101, 145, 153; criticizes governor, 111, 227; criticized by militia officers, 130; criticized by Mormons, 245; relieved of command, 157–58; favors investigation, 227–29; subsequent career, 257–58
Austin, W. W.: leads vigilantes, 55, 88, 92–93, 97, 103
Avard, Sampson, 119n20, 261; leader of Danites, 40–44, 45n51, 64, 73, 125n35; teachings to Danites, 42, 114–15, 120; threatens Adam Black, 65–66; Black condemns, 79; poisoning crops, 124, 221n8; captured by militia, 189; testifies against Mormons, 189, 199–201, 242; condemned by Mormons 208, 220–22
Averett, Elijah, 174

Baldwin, Caleb, 205
Bent, Samuel, 224
Black, Adam, 194; Mormons intimidate, 65–66, 79; affidavit against Mormons, 67–68; testifies against Mormons, 82–83, 93; conducts preliminary examination, 192–93
Blackburn, Abner, 19, 219–20

Blackwell, A. C., 55, 144
Bogart, Samuel, 247; criticizes generals, 130; leads Ray militia, 132–34, 137; at Crooked River battle, 139–41; fires at Charles C. Rich, 162; guards Mormon prisoners, 198, 206; testifies at Richmond hearing, 138n26, 203; seeks to arrest Mormons, 231–32
Boggs, Lilburn W., 95–96; generals request assistance, 5, 94–95, 106, 111, 150; leads militia, 96–97; and DeWitt, 101, 105, 107–8; receives reports on disturbances, 130, 131–32, 137; issues extermination order, 150–53; relieves Atchison of command, 157–58; on court martial, 183n14; after Mormon War, 229–31, 232–33; subsequent career, 258–59; extermination order rescinded, 262
Bond, Christopher S., 262
Book of Mormon, 9, 10
Bowman, William, 67–68, 244
Bradford, Arthur, 146
Brunson, Seymour, 118, 125, 178
Burch, Thomas, 131, 242
Burnett, Peter H., 132; on Sampson Avard, 42; on Daviess settlers, 59; opposes execution of Mormon prisoners, 182–83; at Richmond hearing, 200, 212; lawyer for Mormons, 241–42; subsequent career, 257
Butler, John L., 46, 174; and Gallatin election battle, 62–63, 64, 68
Butterfield, Josiah, 180

Cahoon, Reynolds, 46, 67
Caldwell, A. C., 105, 107–8
Caldwell County: early settlement, 23–27; Mormons agree to settle exclusively in, 25–26, 56. *See also* Far West
Call, Anson, 46, 125n35, 232

278